The European Union and e-Voting

The European Union and e-Voting investigates one of the latest potential changes in the 'technology of democracy' – electronic voting. The book explores how e-voting may impact on traditional mechanisms of democratic participation, raising issues that go to the very core of contemporary governance.

Among the many questions tackled are the implications of introducing e-voting for European Parliamentary elections and its possible impact, not just on the quantity aspects of electoral turnout but also on the quality dimension of democratic participation. The contributors assess e-voting's compatibility with existing legal and constitutional principles and how to best design new online voting systems in order to ensure both security and convenience of use. Furthermore, the prospects for institutional innovation stemming from the introduction of e-voting and other e-democracy techniques are also addressed. Besides enriching the literature with new ideas at a time in which the European integration process is entering a distinctly more overt political phase, this volume also provides fruitful insights for the development of e-voting and e-democracy across the world.

This book deals with the political, social, legal and technological issues related to the possible introduction of electronic voting for future European Parliamentary elections. It will be of interest to all students and researchers of elections and the European Union.

Alexander H. Trechsel is Director of the e-Democracy Centre at the University of Geneva, Switzerland. He was recently Professor of Political Science and the first holder of the Swiss Chair in Federalist Studies at the European University Institute, Florence, Italy.

Fernando Mendez is a researcher at the Department of Political Science, European University Institute in Florence, Italy. He is currently a research fellow of the e-Democracy Centre at the University of Geneva.

Routledge Advances in European Politics

The European Union and e-Voting

Addressing the European Parliament's internet voting challenge

Edited by Alexander H. Trechsel and Fernando Mendez

Routledge
Taylor & Francis Group

LONDON AND NEW YORK

To Maxime and Manon
– future e-voters?

First published 2005
by Routledge
2 Park Square, Milton Park, Abingdon, Oxon OX14 4RN

Simultaneously published in the USA and Canada
by Routledge
270 Madison Ave, New York, NY 10016

Routledge is an imprint of the Taylor & Francis Group

Typeset in Baskerville by
Florence Production Ltd, Stoodleigh, Devon
Printed and bound in Great Britain by
MPG Books Ltd, Bodmin

British Library Cataloguing in Publication Data
A catalogue record for this book is available from
the British Library

Library of Congress Cataloging in Publication Data
The European Union and e-voting: addressing the European
    Parliament's internet voting challenge/edited by
    Alexander H. Trechsel and Fernando Mendez.
        p. cm.
    Includes bibliographical references and index.
    1. Internet voting – European Union countries.
    I. Trechsel, Alexandre H.   II. Mendez, Fernando, 1972–
    JN45.E974 2004   324.6'5'02854678—dc22
    2004007496

ISBN 0–415–32879–9

Contents

PART III
Designing e-voting
145

PART IV
Institutional visions
185

Figures

Tables

Contributors

Andreas Auer is Professor of Constitutional Law at the University of Geneva. Also, since 1993, he has been the Director of the Research and Documentation Centre on Direct Democracy (c2d) at the University of Geneva. He earned his Ph.D. at the University of Neuchâtel, Switzerland. His current research interests include comparative constitutional law, civil liberties, e-voting, direct democracy and European integration. He has published widely in German, French, English and Italian and is the co-author (together with Giorgio Malinverni and Michel Hottelier) of a recent two-volume textbook on Swiss constitutional law.

Stephen Coleman is Professor of e-Democracy at the Oxford Internet Institute, University of Oxford. Until recently, he was the Director of the e-Democracy program at the Hansard Society for Parliamentary Government in the UK. He was formerly Lecturer in Media & Communication at the London School of Economics and has also been the chair of the Independent Commission on Alternative Voting Methods. He is the author of several recent works on e-democracy.

N. Ben Fairweather has been Research Fellow in the Centre for Computing and Social Responsibility since 1996. His previous academic background included computing, politics and philosophy. He has written numerous responses to consultations on issues related to electronic voting and identity cards. Currently, Ben is a consultant advising the UK government on the use of ICT to address social inclusion. He has published papers on Privacy, Codes of Ethics, Globalism, Ethics of Computer Games, RSI Prevention Policies, Electronic Patient Records, Telework and Disability as well as Electronic Voting. He is editor of the *Journal of Information, Communication and Ethics in Society* and associate editor of *Telematics and Informatics*: an interdisciplinary journal on the social impacts of new technology.

Pierre Garrone is Head of the Division of Elections and Referendums at the Secretariat of the European Commission for Democracy through Law (or Venice Commission) (Council of Europe). He was educated at the University of Geneva where he earned his Ph.D. in Law with a thesis on elections and election systems. He earned his Master of Advanced European Studies at the College of Europe (Bruges) in 1992 and has been lecturer in European law at the University of Geneva from 1993 to 1997. His latest book was published in 1996 (*La libre circulation des marchandises*). His current research interests include electoral law and electronic democracy, constitutional law and European Union law.

Rachel K. Gibson is a fellow and Deputy Director of the ACSPRI Centre for Social Research in the Research School of Social Sciences at the Australian National University. She has been interested in the topic of e-democracy since 1997 and is the author of a number of books and articles on the subject of internet campaigning by political parties and candidates.

Raphaël Kies is a researcher at the Department of Political Science of the European University Institute in Florence, Italy. He currently is a research fellow at the newly established e-Democracy Centre (e-DC) and a visiting Research Fellow at the Political Science Department of the University of Antwerp. His research focuses on the political and social impact of the internet. He has published various articles on the possibilities for introducing internet voting.

Hanspeter Kriesi is Professor of Political Science at the University of Zurich. From 1988 to 2002, he was Professor of Political Science at the University of Geneva where he taught Comparative Politics and Swiss Politics. He earned his Ph.D. in Sociology at the University of Zurich, Switzerland. His recent research interests include direct democracy, political behaviour, e-democracy and new social movements. He has published extensively in Dutch, German, French and English. He is currently writing, together with Alexander H. Trechsel, a textbook on the Politics of Switzerland (Cambridge University Press forthcoming 2005).

Karl-Heinz Ladeur is currently Dean of the Law Faculty at the University of Hamburg. He has previously been Professor of Legal Theory and Media Law at the European University Institute in Florence, Italy. He has widely published on the network society, standards, European Community law, multimedia law and e-voting.

Fernando Mendez is a researcher at the Department of Political Science of the European University Institute in Florence, Italy. He is currently working for the Research and Documentation Centre on Direct Democracy (c2d) at the University of Geneva and is a research fellow at the newly established e-Democracy Centre (e-DC). His current research focuses on internet governance from a comparative policy perspective and he has published articles on cybercrime, federalism and e-voting.

Mario Mendez is a researcher at the Law Department of the European University Institute in Florence, Italy. He holds an LLM from the College of William and Mary, a BCL in European and Comparative Law from the University of Oxford and an M.Res. from the European University Institute. His current research focuses on the nature of the relationship between the Community legal order and the WTO.

Pippa Norris is the McGuire Lecturer in Comparative Politics at the John F. Kennedy School of Government, Harvard University. Her research compares political communications, gender politics, public opinion and elections. She has published almost three dozen books including a quintet for Cambridge University Press: *Sacred and Secular: Religion and Politics Worldwide* (co-authored with Ronald Inglehart, 2004), *Electoral Engineering: Electoral Rules and Voting Choices* (2004), *Rising Tide: Gender Equality Around the World* (co-authored with Ronald Inglehart, Spring 2003), *Democratic Phoenix: Political Activism Worldwide* (2002), *Digital Divide* (2001) and *A Virtuous Circle* (2000). She co-founded the *Harvard International Journal of Press/Politics*, and serves on ten journal boards. She holds a Doctoral degree in politics from the London School of Economics.

Lawrence Pratchett is a reader in Local Democracy and Director of the Local Governance Research Unit in the Leicester Business School, De Montfort University. His work concentrates upon two aspects of local democracy: public participation and electronic democracy. Among a number of projects he was Director of the UK Government spon-sored research into the Implementation of e-voting in the UK (2002) and is Academic Advisor to the Office of the Deputy Prime Minister's National Project on Local e-Democracy. He has edited several books on local democracy and democratic renewal and is currently writing a book on Local Democracy in Britain (Palgrave, forthcoming).

Simon Rogerson is Director of the Centre for Computing and Social Responsibility at De Montfort University and the UK's first Professor in Computer Ethics. Following a successful industrial career he now combines research, lecturing and consultancy in the management, organisational and ethical aspects of information and communication technologies. Simon was the winner of the 1999 IFIP Namur Award for outstanding contribution to the creation of awareness of the social implications of information technology. In 2003 he was a finalist for the World Technology Award in ethics. He is a member of the Parlia-mentary IT Committee and Vice-President of the Institute for the Management of Information Systems.

Hermann Schmitt is a senior research fellow of the Mannheimer Zentrum für Europäische Sozialforschung and the Director of its research area on Parties and Political Linkage. He received his Ph.D.

from the University of Duisburg and his *venia legendi* for Political Science from the Free University of Berlin. During the 1990s, he was the Director of the ZEUS institute at Mannheim University. Firmly rooted in the empirical-analytical tradition, he has written extensively on political parties, general elections, political representation and European unification. His current research interests focus on the perspectives of democratic governance in the European Union.

Philippe C. Schmitter is Professor of Political Science at the European University Institute in Florence, Italy. He took his doctorate at the University of California at Berkeley. He has published books and articles on comparative politics, on regional integration in Western Europe and Latin America, on the transition from authoritarian rule in Southern Europe and Latin America, and on the intermediation of class, sectoral and professional interests. His current work is on the political characteristics of the emerging Euro-polity, on the consolidation of democracy in Southern and Eastern countries, on the possibility of post-liberal democracy in Western Europe and North America as well as on e-democracy in Europe.

Alexander H. Trechsel has recently been Professor of Political Science and the first holder of the Swiss Chair in Federalist Studies at the European University Institute in Florence, Italy. He is currently Vice-Director of the Research and Documentation Centre on Direct Democracy (c2d) at the University of Geneva. He is also currently directing the e-Democracy Centre (e-DC) at the University of Geneva, a joint initiative with the European University Institute and the Oxford Internet Institute. He earned his Ph.D. in political science at the University of Geneva. His research interests are e-democracy, direct democracy, federalism, European integration and political behaviour. He is currently writing, together with Hanspeter Kriesi, a textbook on the Politics of Switzerland (Cambridge University Press, forthcoming 2005).

Melvin Wingfield is a research fellow in the Local Governance Research Unit at De Montfort University. An interest in local governance and new democratic initiatives is matched by his teaching responsibilities. Prior to his involvement in academia he had an eclectic career in a number of industrial professions. Allied to that was a close interest in the work of trade unions. Away from the heady heights of intellectual rigour he has a passion for the beautiful game, which is embodied in the spirit of an institution that was there at the birth, once was great, but now this is probably the closest they will get to Europe.

Acknowledgements

This book is drawn from the conference 'e-Voting and the European Parliamentary Elections' held in May 2002 at the European University Institute (EUI) in Florence. It was organised by the Robert Schuman Centre for Advanced Studies (RSCAS) in Florence, and the Research and Documentation Centre on Direct Democracy (c2d), at the University of Geneva (Switzerland). The editors are above all grateful to Yves Mény who believed in this project from the beginning and whose help and input were invaluable. We would like to thank the European Commission and, in particular, DG Research, for its generous support in sponsoring the conference. This project would not have been possible without the close collaboration and friendship of Raphaël Kies. We gratefully thank him for all his hard work and support throughout the preparation of the conference and this book. We would like to especially single out the individuals that made the conference possible, Helen Wallace, Aris Apollonatos and Angela Liberatore. This book would not, however, have been possible without the intellectual inspiration and constructive feedback provided by the conference participants: Antonio Alabau, Giuliano Amato, José Benedito, Franck Biancheri, Stefano Bartolini, Sara Birch, Rory Domm, James Fishkin, Navraj Ghaleigh, Maria Gratschew, Volker Hartmann, Agnès Hubert, Norbert Kersting, Pierre Lévy, Neil Mitchison, Rene Peralta, Dieter Richter, Stefano Rodotà, Zsolt Szolnoki, Peter Wagner, Michel Warynski, Bob Watt and Jacques Ziller. Earlier versions of some of the chapters in this book were presented at the conference and we would like to record our thanks to our contributors for amending or completely rewriting their papers. The helpful feedback of the two anonymous reviewers at Routledge helped to shape the eventual framework that was adopted in this book and we gratefully acknowledge their contribution.

The administrative support of the EUI and RSCAS staff is especially noted and we thank Sandra Brière, Monique Cavallari, David Crowley, Filipa De Sousa, Catherine Divry, Kathinka Espana, Mei Lan Goei, Alexandra Howarth, Inaki Lopez Martin, Roberto Nocentini and Gabriella Unger-Gentile.

Numerous friends and colleagues have helped in various fashions to ensure the completion of this book and we especially thank Caroline Chaix, Vicky Triga and Valérie Vulliez for their great help. Also, the editors would like to warmly thank Richard E. Warren for his invaluable assistance during the stressful final stages and, in particular, our patient editors at Routledge, Heidi Bagtazo and Grace McInnes, who supported this book right from the outset. Finally, Katia Trechsel cannot be thanked enough for her unwavering support.

1 The European Union and e-voting

Upgrading Euro-elections

Fernando Mendez and Alexander H. Trechsel

Introduction

To the reader it may appear somewhat precipitate to raise the issue of e-voting[1] for European Parliamentary elections much less to compile an edited book on the subject. Perhaps it would be more prudent to make progress at the national level before even considering any moves towards offering online voting facilities at the supranational level. The sheer scale of the enterprise – the European Union (EU) is the only supranational democracy that exists today – as well as the logistical complexity, the substantial financial and administrative resource implications, not to mention the considerable technical and security hurdles that would need to be overcome, all suggest that this is, for the time being, an unviable proposition. And let us not forget the problem of the European digital divide that some have argued[2] could, if e-voting were to be implemented, skew political participation towards the more affluent socio-economic groups (both within and among EU member states) given that internet penetration rates vary substantially from Finland in the north to Portugal in the south and from Ireland in the west to Slovakia in the east. So why bother 'upgrading' elections that have been described by one prominent observer as decentralised and apathetic affairs in which a small number of voters participate and where barely any transnational deliberation on European issues takes place.[3] There are, as we shall argue, some very good reasons why the e-voting/EU nexus may acquire an increasing significance and this introductory chapter is, in part, a justification for addressing the question of e-voting from an EU perspective.

A first sign as to why e-voting and the European Parliament may become increasingly connected has recently come to the fore. In May 2002 a motion for a resolution on e-democracy and e-citizenship was tabled at the European Parliament by MEPs from eight different transnational political groups. It called on member states 'to promote electronic voting and, in particular, voting arrangements using e-voting monitored polling stations for the 2004 European elections'.[4] A year later, in September 2003, the UK's Secretary of State for Constitutional Affairs directed the Electoral Commission, an independent body that reports on electoral issues, to recommend electoral regions that would be suitable for e-voting pilots for European Parliamentary elections. Both these events, and the continuing discussions on the issue in the institutions of the EU and its member states, suggest that e-voting could become an item of considerable political discussion. As the UK example illustrates, it is possible that e-voting could slowly creep on to the political agenda of the member states. And to the extent that it does, it is likely that local elections and European Parliamentary elections, which are characteristically low salience elections, will become the focal point for experimentation with e-voting pilots. Thus, it is probable that e-voting for European Parliamentary elections will, for the majority of EU member states, and especially the larger member states, precede e-enabled national elections. This is, of course, unless a remarkable popular demand emerges and a consensus among politicians is achieved on the need to introduce e-voting before the next European Parliamentary elections in 2009, enabling member states to hold full-scale national elections online. Without trying to anticipate trends in e-voting technologies, popular demand among the electorate and the willingness of political elites to introduce new voting modalities, this is unlikely to be the case. Instead, e-voting is likely to be the subject of experimentation with low salience elections (especially local elections, but also European Parliamentary elections) before tackling the riskier enterprise of first-order national elections.

What is also revealing about the two aforementioned examples are the different perspectives adopted. In contrast to the enthusiasm of the promoters of the European Parliament resolution, the report by the UK Electoral Commission states that '[t]he Commission does not recommend that an e-enabled element be included in any pilot scheme, as we believe that no region is ready for such innovation at this stage in the development of the electoral modernisation programme'.[5] This contrast serves to highlight the tension that exists among analysts, pundits and policymakers. Some observers like to focus on the transformative potential of the ICTs and give primacy to the long-term dynamics of e-voting and potential interaction effects with other e-democratic techniques. For others the focus is more pragmatic and short term, such as the significant technical and security hurdles or the logistical and financial costs. These perspectives, however, are not necessarily mutually exclusive and it is possible to be pragmatic about the short term obstacles while acknowledging the transformative potential over the longer term. Incidentally, the main reason for the Electoral Commission's negative verdict on e-voting for the European Parliamentary elections of 2004 was that there was insufficient time given the higher level of complexity of organising regional pilots as opposed to the e-voting pilots that had been previously organised for the May 2003 local elections. Nonetheless, it is helpful to note this distinction between the short-term implementation issues and the potential longer-term institutional implications.

Most chapters in this book focus on the short-term horizon although, in the final section, and in line with the distinction identified above, the authors have addressed longer-term dynamics. In many respects the contributors to this book, all of whom are acknowledged specialists in their respective fields, have approached the subject matter from a variety of different yet enriching perspectives. The following disclaimer should, however, be noted at this point: this is a book that has been largely written by social scientists and, as such, it reflects a social science bias in its overarching approach. This does not mean the contributors have necessarily agreed in their prognoses for e-voting, especially where claims with regard to potential increases in participation rates are concerned.

The rest of this chapter will proceed along the following lines: we begin by first mapping out certain conceptual and theoretical issues which we maintain is a necessary precursor to any discussion of e-voting. We then proceed to evaluate in greater detail the e-voting and EU nexus with particular attention directed to the EU's so-called democratic deficit. In the penultimate section we identify four broad issue areas that we contend will have a substantial impact in determining e-voting trajectories within the EU context. The main threads of the argument are then tied together and some further reflections are offered in the concluding section.

Conceptual frames

The issue of e-voting has increasingly become a controversial topic among political commentators, in some cases arousing great passions. But why are we thinking about it? Is it because we believe that by offering citizens new voting tools it is possible to slow down the perceived erosion of participation rates or, more optimistically, turn around the apathy that is said to afflict modern democracies? Or is there an even more ambitious agenda behind the proliferation of 'e' initiatives? In this section we will attempt to place the issue of e-voting within its wider theoretical context by linking it to the concept of e-democracy.[6] To illustrate our line of argumentation, and the theoretical questions that are raised, we will return to the aforementioned motion for a European Parliamentary resolution. The initiative is interesting because it links e-voting with e-democracy and in doing so raises some pertinent theoretical questions. The promoter of the initiative, the MEP Marco Cappatto, declared at the time that democracy was the number one problem for the EU and that on 'the specific issue of "e-voting", the 2004 European elections are the best occasion to implement a project at the European level'.[7] Although his ambitious goals have conspicuously not been realised, the objective of the proposed resolution is straightforward: to harness the democratising potential of information and communication technologies (ICT) to bring decision-making closer to the EU citizen. At first glance this is a desirable and relatively unproblematic objective. It argues that European citizenship ought to imply the 'right of access' to any public document and meeting via the internet and calls for the Treaties to be amended so that all EU public meetings can be broadcast live and archived on the internet. The aim is to increase executive accountability by employing the *transparency* enhancing properties of the internet to bring the EU closer to its citizens. Furthermore, the proposed resolution stated that citizens should be able to enjoy their rights of European citizenship (e.g. complaints to the Ombudsman, access to the European Court of Justice or petitions to the European Parliament) also through the internet. These and similar proposals are interesting from a theoretical perspective because they raise questions as to whether *Information Rights* could become an increasingly important component of citizenship. More speculatively, could this signal a trend towards an ICT-induced extension of T.H. Marshall's famous trilogy of civil, political and social rights?[8]

Although the proposed resolution is mainly concerned with *transparency* enhancing measures, in calling for e-voting to be implemented for European Parliamentary elections it is raising a conceptually distinct dimension – namely *participation* in the democratic process. Voting in elections is one of the principal mechanisms through which citizens exercise their right to participate in the political process. This is, however, not the only channel available for citizens to express their political preferences. To take an example: since the end of the Cold War, Eastern and Central Europe have witnessed a proliferation of direct democratic mechanisms within the national constitutions of the new democracies. Also over the past two decades, in both the old and the new European democracies, referendums have been frequently held. The debate on whether direct democracy should be promoted is not in any way new. It centres most prominently on the question of *civic competence* and splits political philosophers and theorists. For thinkers such as Bobbio there is simply not enough time in the day for voters to consider all the elements involved in each and every issue put to the vote.[9] It follows that more frequent participation does not mean better informed decision-making. Bobbio echoes thinkers such as Burke,[10] Dahl,[11] Schumpeter[12] and Sartori,[13] in arguing that democracy is best served by strengthening the competitive or representative model of democracy whereby different parties compete for the citizens' vote. For scholars such as Barber,[14] Budge[15] or Kriesi,[16] however, it is difficult to see how citizens could be competent enough to elect their representatives but not competent enough to decide about important policy issues at stake. Also, according to the participatory conception of democracy, it is through exposure to direct democratic decision-making processes that voters will increase their interest in politics and, therefore, their civic competence. Over the last couple of decades normative political theory has further developed the 'quality' dimension of democracy by emphasising the deliberative aspect of democracy. Proponents such as Elster,[17] Fishkin[18] and Habermas[19] argue that deliberation among the electorate has to be maximised in order to reach 'good' outcomes. The act of voting should not be seen as an end in itself but, rather, as a mechanism through which preferences that crystallise from the process of deliberation are transmitted.

With this admittedly cursory review of some of the major debates in democratic theory we have outlined three (overlapping) visions of democracy, which emphasise distinct representative, participatory or deliberative elements of democracy. This brings us to the question of how ICT and its possible introduction into the political realm could alter current practices of democratic decision-making. An expanding literature on 'e-democracy' has blossomed recently to take up this very issue.[20] To examine these issues further we will offer a definition of e-democracy that will provide the conceptual basis for identifying a series of e-democratic techniques (including e-voting) that aim to promote some of the particular elements of democracy discussed above. This section, which draws heavily on a recent study commissioned by the European Parliament,[21] is highly relevant for our present discussions on e-voting, for the latter cannot, and should not, be discussed in a theoretical vacuum.

We consider e-democracy to consist of all electronic means of communication that enable/empower citizens in their efforts to hold rulers/ politicians accountable for their actions in the public realm. Depending on the aspect of democracy being promoted, e-democracy can employ different techniques: (1) for increasing the *transparency* of the political process; (2) for enhancing the direct involvement and *participation* of citizens; and (3) for improving the quality of opinion formation by opening new spaces of information and *deliberation*.[22] We can now build on our working definition of e-democracy and identify some real case examples of the techniques of e-democracy. The matrix shown in Table 1.1 conceptually organises five e-techniques according to the particular aspects of democracy they are intending to promote.

Table 1.1 e-Democracy matrix

e-Techniques	*Aspects of democracy promoted*		
	Increasing transparency	*Increasing participation*	*Increasing deliberation*
e-Access	×		
e-Consultation		×	
e-Petition		×	
e-Voting		×	
e-Forums			×

Source: Trechsel, A., Kies, R., Mendez, F. and Schmitter, P. (2003) *Evaluation of the Use of New Technologies in Order to Facilitate Democracy in Europe: e-Democratizing the Parliaments and Parties in Europe*, European Parliament, STOA (Scientific and Technological Option Assessment) Report, Directorate-General for Research.

Below we offer some concrete examples of e-techniques that have been recently proposed or implemented with an explicit EU dimension. The European Commission's much cited White Paper on Governance, for instance, aims to promote openness and transparency by providing more online information about all stages of EU level decision-making.[23] In a similar vein, the motion for a European Parliamentary resolution discussed above was chiefly concerned with implementing e-access techniques for promoting a 'right of access'. Both aim to promote, via ICT, the first dimension of the matrix, i.e. transparency. The motion for a European Parliamentary resolution also mentioned participatory enhancing techniques such as e-voting and e-petitions. But there are other participatory enhancing techniques that have been the subject of discussion. During the EU Convention on the Future of Europe e-consultation techniques were adopted to 'involve citizens' as called for by the December 2001 Laeken Declaration.[24] Interestingly, in relation to the third dimension of the matrix, the Laeken Declaration also called for *deliberative* initiatives in order to help foster a European public area. The internet was also mentioned as a possible means for achieving such a goal. Nonetheless, the e-forum element (the Futurum website)[25] that was developed did not emerge as a convincing hub of discussion, while the EU Convention President's web-chat was a rare example of interactivity.[26]

In sum, unlike e-access or e-forums, which aim to increase transparency or deliberation, the technique of e-voting is, from a normative perspective, principally conceived as a tool for enhancing participation. But this would be a rather limited and unimaginative conceptualisation. One of the central arguments of this section is that e-voting should be part and parcel of a wider move towards harnessing the democratic potential of ICT.[27] As such, and certainly over the longer term, it is possible to envisage interacting and mutually enhancing combinations of e-techniques that aim to promote, for instance, participation and deliberation. The Kies and Kriesi contribution (Chapter 7) is precisely one such attempt to link the two via the innovative concept of a virtual pre-voting sphere.

The democratic deficit and e-voting

Following the previous section's mainly abstract and normative level discussion of democratic ideal types, we will now move down the ladder of abstraction to focus on the concrete and contentious example of EU level democracy. It would be somewhat untenable not to take up, in a volume that seeks to address e-voting for Euro-elections, the topic of the much touted 'democratic deficit' that is said to characterise the EU polity. The term, first coined in 1979 by David Marquand,[28] has acquired a pre-eminent status in the standard lexicon of EU political affairs. Journalists, politicians, academics and other political pundits use the term indiscriminately, as do Europhiles and Eurosceptics in support of particular viewpoints as to the future trajectory of European integration.

To summarise the vast literature on the democratic deficit two sources to the so-called problem can be identified: first, the European Parliament as the sole directly elected body among the four major institutional players (the others being the Commission, the Council and the European Court of Justice) has a weak popular input. Moreover, its elections are second order events where the relatively small number of citizens that bother to vote select among national parties on the basis of national issues and little discussion of European issues takes place. It is the European executive (principally the Council of Ministers and the Commission) rather than the European Parliament that is responsible for legislation. This is supposed to contrast with other political systems where the parliament is the legislator, leading to a situation in the EU where the executive is both legislator and executive all in one. Second, because of the supremacy of EU law over national law the high-ranking national officials who meet in the Council of Ministers and deliberate behind closed doors over European issues have had their powers increased. Put simply, the structure of the European polity strengthens state executives to the detriment of their respective parliaments.

Why has the label 'democratic deficit' become so popular, especially in the scholarly literature? Of late there have been a number of influential responses to this question. Mény, for instance, argues that the term has become a powerful catchword that can be manipulated by both Euroscepetics and Europhiles alike.[29] There is certainly some truth to this observation. Curiously, both Europhiles and Eurosceptics share a similar diagnosis, in terms of the existence of a purported democratic dysfunctionality, although they, of course, differ with regard to the normative prescription they offer. For the former the solution lies in addressing the first source of the problem identified above and replicating the rules and practices of national democracies so that the EU polity comes to resemble this well-understood political species. For the Eurosceptics the focus is on the second source of the problem and the solution lies in strengthening – and limiting any further erosion of – the role of the national state.

Crucially, when analysing the democratic deficit the benchmark that is used acquires a considerable significance. It is invariably the case that the benchmarks used when comparing the EU are those of national democracies. Is it surprising, therefore, that when comparing the EU to well-established national democracies it will tend to fare badly? Zweifel argues to the contrary, indeed, that when comparing the EU with 'model' democracies such as the US and Switzerland along seven established scales of democracy, the EU performs admirably.[30] Zweifel's conclusion is clear: although there is obviously much room for improvement, the EU does not suffer from a democratic deficit any more so than do the most advanced national democracies. This is echoed by Mény for whom the European system does not suffer from a democratic deficit, but rather from a 'democratic' overload: majority rule applies only partially and when it is formally used it is, usually, where a consensus has previously been reached. Veto points are everywhere ... checks and balances are too many rather than too few.[31]

Moravscik goes one step further in arguing that part of the problem is that the EU tends to be judged, not so much in comparison to other democracies, but against *ideal types*.[32] Therefore, it is not surprising the EU fares badly when using such criteria and that it may appear remote to European citizens. What, then, is the relevance of e-voting to this discussion? Is there a link between the democratic deficit and e-voting? In other words, could the introduction of e-voting help to combat the so-called democratic deficit? Having suggested that the democratic deficit is a slippery term we would be very cautious in postulating any connection between the two – at least in the short term. According to the empirical analyses offered by both Norris and Schmitt (see Chapters 3 and 4), introducing e-voting for the European Parliamentary elections is unlikely to have a significant effect on turnout rates let alone tackle the democratic deficit. To be sure, if e-voting is accompanied by what Schmitter[33] refers to as e-politicking then it is possible that the EU could be brought closer to European citizens – but for the moment that remains a much longer-term agenda. Although e-voting is frequently discussed and promoted as the solution to the problem of low voter turnout, it is more likely that falling turnout is a symptom of dissatisfaction with what is on offer rather than the costs of participation. Focusing on technology as the solution could obscure the argument. e-Voting for European Parliamentary election will not, as Norris has argued elsewhere,[34] provide a digital panacea to what is, in essence, a structural problem. We will return to these issues that are raised by calls for further democratisation of the EU polity and how to go about it using ICT when we address future institutional visions for the EU below.

The European Union and e-voting: some of the major issues considered

e-Voting is a complex and multifaceted issue that will, at a first stage, certainly raise more questions than answers. How such questions are addressed will be crucial in shaping the prospects for introducing e-voting for European Parliamentary elections. To aid us in tackling these thorny issues we will introduce a distinction, drawing on economic theory, between two types of effects. Economic theory has distinguished between two types of trade impacts that result from the introduction of preferential trading arrangements: (1) short run or static effects and (2) long run or dynamic effects. We can use a similar conceptualisation and apply this heuristic understanding for distinguishing between the possible effects of introducing e-voting arrangements. To continue with the trade analogy, the static or short run effects could include the immediate political impact, the necessary legal adaptations, the potential administrative efficiency gains, etc. as suppliers and consumers adjust their behaviour and benefit from the new voting technologies. Over the long run, institutional impacts could also be expected as a result of the dynamic gains and interaction effects of introducing e-voting and other e-democratic techniques as conceptualised above.

In the remainder of this chapter we identify three largely short run issues that spring up including: (1) the possible *political outcomes* (especially in terms of effects on participation rates); (2) the major *legal considerations* e-voting raises; and (3) how to best go about *designing e-voting* systems. These three issues tend to have an *ex ante* dimension but there is also a fourth issue which centres on the potential dynamic effects of introducing e-voting as part of a wider strategy to exploit the democratic enhancing potential of ICT. We refer to this as (4) *institutional visions*. One of the added benefits of approaching the subject matter in this fashion is that we will adopt the same structure as the book and in each section introduce the reader to the major and overlapping themes that are subsequently explored by the contributors to this volume.

Political outcomes

A first and very obvious starting point, if one wishes to discuss political outcomes, is whether a noticeable political will actually exists among European and member state policymakers to offer the electorate new voting mechanisms such as e-voting. Absent the political will, the result can only be failure. Unlike other e-democratic initiatives, such as e-forums, which have a bottom-up element and can develop in the absence of public authorities, the implementation of e-voting requires a top-down element – financial, logistic, and changes in electoral law to name but a few. However, there is a more fundamental question regarding the role of public authorities. By introducing an ICT element into the electoral process there is a danger that the state may become uncomfortably dependent on the skills and resources of private organisations. It would be difficult to envisage the implementation of e-voting systems without some degree of involvement from the private sector. This begs the question of whether the organisation of democratic elections has to be the exclusive obligation of the state and whether underlying parts of the electoral process can be outsourced to private organisations. For some member states the involvement of private intermediaries in the electoral process could be problematic, for others it may be less so. Opponents of e-voting have pointed out that the state should keep its monopoly position with regard to the organisation of elections and any type of public–private partnership should be avoided. Our position, however, is that the potential involvement of the private sector is not the real issue. The private sector's involvement in politically sensitive areas is already a common feature of the contemporary political and economic environment. The array of physical assets and services deemed essential to the functioning of modern societies is overwhelmingly run and owned by the private sector. For instance, certain aspects of defence are subcontracted to private organisations and so, too, is the provision of water or energy (electricity and nuclear). If aspects of the provision of defence and security can be outsourced to private organisations and the entire telecommunications and energy sectors, which were once publicly owned, can be left in private hands, it is not so inconceivable to imagine a private input in the organisation of elections. The authority of the state can always be imposed by regulating private industries (e.g. through a liability regime) as it already does for the telecommunications sector and all the above mentioned examples. We would argue that disagreements over the potential involvement of the private sector in the organisation of elections tend to skirt or obscure the real issue which is one of confidence and trust in the electoral system. Without confidence in the electoral system the legitimacy of election results would be thrown into doubt. The question ultimately becomes one of trust in the state[35] and whether the majority of citizens have confidence in the state to organise, count and validate the vote. As our examples demonstrate, citizens have, on the whole, accepted the delegation of certain tasks to the private sector in areas such as the provision of defence and security or nuclear energy that are potentially as sensitive as the organisation of elections.

Assuming the political will can be generated and a minimum degree of confidence can be ensured, the most likely scenario is that the individual member states will take the lead in the implementation of e-voting for Euro-elections, as demonstrated by the UK initiative discussed above. This is not surprising; indeed, it would be surprising if the EU were to take a prominent role in the implementation of e-voting – at least during the initial stages. The role of the EU as a facilitator is, however, a much more realistic possibility and one that would be consistent with the increasingly discussed new policy instrument, the EU's open method of coordination (OMC). To date, the interest of EU policymakers has been mixed – apart from the proposed European Parliament resolution sponsored by the Radicals and financial support via the 5th and 6th Framework Programmes for R&D efforts – very little has been achieved in the area of e-voting and e-democracy.[36] For the moment, the EU's flagship information society policy, the eEurope Action Plans,[37] are overwhelmingly concerned with e-government issues. But the EU's institutions are not the only supranational organisations with a potential interest in e-voting. Recently, the Council of Europe has begun a formal consultation procedure with its member states with a view to developing European standards for e-voting. A multidisciplinary ad hoc group of specialists was established in February

2003 and the Council of Europe is expected to adopt a Recommendation in mid-2004.[38] In sum, the issue of e-voting is slowly but surely moving onto the political agenda even though progress, to date, has been rather piecemeal.

In Part I, *Political Outcomes*, the authors have focused primarily on the short-term considerations that introducing e-voting could have in the context of European Parliamentary elections. That is not to say that conclusions about the longer term are not proffered (e.g. the need for structural reform of the EU to make elections more decisive) but, rather, that the main focus has been on the short-term considerations (e.g. financial, logistic and security concerns and possible effects on turnout). Gibson's chapter profiles the main variants of e-voting that are currently available to policymakers and assesses the case for their use for the next European Parliamentary elections. Based on the evidence to date, Gibson argues that while the technology would almost certainly deliver a boost to turnout, principally by making voting more convenient, the logistical, financial and legal implications make any immediate move to e-voting unrealistic. In charting the e-voting landscape, Gibson provides us with some taxonomic clarity when differentiating between different e-voting systems. The crucial point stressed is the greater security problems that exist with the more open (and convenient) remote internet voting systems.

In her chapter, Norris takes on the claim that e-voting will enhance convenience with the possibility to strengthen electoral turnout and enhance citizen engagement – especially for the younger generation. Norris draws on evidence from the results of the UK's pioneering e-voting experiments for the May 2003 local elections. The elections, as with those for the European Parliament, are characteristically low salience and turnout is usually low. The evidence Norris presents suggests that compared to postal voting, remote e-voting proved to be far less effective in increasing participation rates. e-Voting, according to Norris, is unlikely to prove a 'magic ballot' and if introduced would only probably have a modest impact upon the younger generation. Until elections for the European Parliament are perceived to matter and citizens believe they can make a difference to policy outcomes, Norris concludes, participation rates will tend to remain low.

The conclusion Norris draws about the need to make European elections more decisive is a theme explored in greater depth by Schmitt. He echoes Norris in questioning the claim that e-voting will increase turnout for European Parliamentary elections. There are certain structural issues – the subject of Schmitt's empirical analysis – that cannot be resolved by the mere introduction of e-voting. Schmitt asks a straightforward question: do people abstain from European Parliamentary elections because of Euro-hostile attitudes, e.g. they disagree with the EU and European integration? If the answer is yes then it logically follows that the introduction of e-voting will not have an impact on the attitudes of this portion of the European electorate. The answer he provides is that nowhere do Euro-hostile attitudes play a role in the decision to participate in Euro-elections. Instead, he points to the lack of excitement and the shortage of any dramatic consequences that explain the 'second-order' logic of European Parliamentary elections. So could e-voting alter the picture? Schmitt is sceptical as e-voting cannot provide a cure against electoral boredom and the lack of visible consequences that characterise Euro-elections. However, on a more upbeat note, Schmitt's second route of empirical analysis explores the current use of the internet as a source of pre-electoral information for both European Parliamentary elections and first-order national elections. Surprisingly the internet is, on average, almost as 'popular' as public meetings, the latter having constituted the most typical forms of electoral campaigning for European political parties.

Legal issues

It should come as no surprise that any attempt to expand existing voting modalities, would raise various legal complications. Chief among these are the tensions that are capable of being provoked with internationally enshrined fundamental rights. Indeed, in a recent contribution, Birch and Watt have come down against the introduction of e-voting precisely because they find it to be inconsistent with a secret ballot.[39] But such a stance is problematic for it implies that the law, whether it be international or otherwise, is completely rigid and unable to adapt to changing circumstances. It is a logic that if followed through to its conclusion renders innovations such as postal voting equally vulnerable. The danger from remote voting, including postal voting, appears to be that the voter could be susceptible to undue pressures, e.g. in the home or at the workplace, to vote for a particular candidate. There is certainly a possibility that instances of undue external pressure could occur. Yet, it is equally possible to imagine solutions such as reversible voting, an option that is available to Swedish voters and that allows them to alter their votes within a specified time period, which would reduce the perceived dangers. We believe there is a problem in framing the issue in such binary terms and, furthermore, that this has tended to be a largely UK-centric debate. Indeed, in a report published by the UK Department of Constitutional Affairs on the implementation of e-voting, a number of international declarations and protocols are highlighted that

> call into doubt whether any form of remote voting, by electronic or other means, would be legal in an international context . . . until this position is clarified, the issue of secrecy and the UK's obligations under international protocols remains a significant barrier to the implementation of RVEM [remote voting by electronic means].[40]

This argument, if taken to its logical conclusion, implies that European countries such as Finland, Switzerland and others, all of which offer postal voting, are in danger of violating international human rights norms. Surely, however, there is a middle ground whereby legal problems can be taken on board without precluding e-voting (or postal voting) experimentation. It is in this vein that the contributors to the legal section of this volume have taken up aspects of this debate.

In his chapter, Garrone underscores the need to ascertain the compatibility of any electoral innovations with the five cardinal principles of Europe's electoral heritage. The principles he enumerates are: (1) universal suffrage; (2) equal suffrage; (3) free suffrage; (4) secrecy of the ballot; and (5) direct suffrage. All of these principles are enshrined, explicitly or implicitly, in international treaties such as the European Convention on Human Rights (ECHR) and the International Covenant on Civil and Political Rights. Garrone considers the various ways in which the introduction of e-voting could clash with these principles that lie at the heart of the European electoral tradition. The conclusion he draws is that if e-voting is introduced as a supplementary voting mechanism these core principles would not be undermined.

Garrone's analysis, which is mainly concerned with the identification of the principles that underpin Europe's electoral heritage and the extent to which the introduction of e-voting would pose significant or new legal problems, paves the way for the legal analysis conducted by Auer and Mendez in the chapter that follows. They explore two particular legal problems that an e-voting agenda would need to tackle. The first is the need for an appropriate legal basis. Essentially, they argue that if the political will exists, then the legal basis for e-voting will ultimately not be an obstacle. However, Auer and Mendez show themselves sensitive to political practicalities and recognise that generating the political will for action at the Community level is an ambitious goal which does not seem attainable any time soon. The possibility of a domestic response, well within the remit of the member states powers and an avenue that is being contemplated to varying degrees by several member states, is considered rather more realistic. They suggest that a pioneering agenda at the domestic level for the European Parliamentary elections is likely to heighten the political salience of e-voting, and it is then that we might expect this matter to gain a foothold on the European agenda. In short, the position advanced is that e-voting can be expected to be state-driven at the domestic level and it is here that the catalyst for action at the Community level will be found.

The second legal problem explored in the Auer and Mendez chapter is e-voting's relationship with fundamental rights. While this issue had also been explored in Garrone's chapter, Auer and Mendez opt for a different approach that focuses on three specific aspects of the fundamental rights problematique and brings forth the complicated relationship between rights enshrined in the ECHR and the Community legal order. The main problem they foresee is a potential clash with the principle of a secret ballot enshrined in the ECHR. While there appears to be a scarcity of legal doctrine on this matter, they nonetheless suggest that it is not very plausible to expect fundamental rights objections, as yet unsubstantiated, to stand in the way of a project that hopes to go some way towards tackling the extant climate of political disinterest.

Design issues

As countless reports maintain,[41] one of the major concerns for the design of e-voting systems is the security dimension. At the risk of extreme over-simplification, security issues can be approached from two perspectives: from a technology or a social perspective. On the one hand, technologists are evidently the best placed to evaluate the systemic security risks of e-voting systems. On the other hand, social scientists have some understanding of electoral systems and voting behaviour but are prone, much to the consternation of technologists, to downplay or simply assume away the sizeable security risks. This seems to generate one of the major fault lines that typify current debates on the feasibility of e-voting. By merging two hitherto separate spheres, technology and crime in the context of elections, imagery of hackers and cyber criminals exploiting insecure networks to the detriment of an unsuspecting electorate is conjured up. To the perplexed observer caught up in the cross-winds of this passionate dispute the effect must be most mystifying. If one is able to conduct sophisticated online financial transactions, such as e-banking or online trading, then why not so for online voting? Technologists are certainly right in arguing that the security standards for internet voting must not be conflated with those that apply to e-commerce or financial transactions. They tend to make two points, first such arguments fail to acknowledge the risks of online financial transactions and, second, the security standards for online voting need to be of a much higher level than for financial and commercial transactions. As one recent report argued 'e-commerce grade security is not good enough for public elections'.[42] While not precluding the eventual deployment of secure online voting systems, the technologist prefers to argue that there is still a very long way to go before the necessary security standards are developed.

For the technologist, the internet is an inherently insecure network and a potential vector for distributed denial of service attacks, viruses, Trojan horses, worms and so forth. On the other hand, those that emphasise the social dimension do not necessarily dispute this conception, but argue that risk – as in other social spheres – must be managed. There is a danger that in framing the issue of risk, some technologists have tended to resort to an idealised or romanticised vision of democracy. Along the course of its long history democracy has fundamentally changed in scope and in scale. As underlined by Dahl, one of the foremost democratic theorists of our times, the very term 'democracy' can be devoid of meaning if its variations over time and space are not considered.[43] Those specific 'technologies of democracy' that have been used for transmitting, collecting, counting and communicating the will of the people have undergone a transformation over time and the notion that an ancient Athenian would comprehend, let alone regard as democratic, current electoral practices is debatable. The practices that determine how political representatives campaign for votes, how they are elected and the method by which those votes are collected, authenticated, tallied up and the results announced to the general public would be anathema to ancient practices of democracy. Current electoral practices are not sacrosanct and neither do they represent a failsafe expression of the peoples' will, mistakes and abuses do occur. Thus, the question becomes whether the benefits heralded by proponents of e-voting outweigh the security risks. Social and political choices, rather than technological ones, will determine what is deemed by a society to be an acceptable and tolerable degree of risk for a given activity. The implication of living in what has been referred to by Beck as the 'risk society' is that risk is a by-product of the enhanced opportunities and choices that are available to us.[44] The repercussions of technological advance in chemistry, nuclear energy, genetic engineering or computer sciences have acquired a social dimension and the same will be no less true for ICT induced changes in the practice of democracy.

Recently, in the sphere of policymaking, the question of the security of cyberspace has acquired national security proportions.[45] Nowhere is this more the case than in the US. Therefore, it is not surprising that the US has also been the source of some of the most negative reactions to the possibilities for introducing online voting. Not only is it one of the most technologically dependent and advanced nations on earth but it also combines this with a reverential attachment, on the part of its citizenry, to its democratic institutions. Yet, what is deemed an acceptable risk in one society is not the same for another. And what holds true for the US may not be applicable to the EU or its member states. This is already true for environmental standards or for the public acceptance of genetically modified organisms, even when based on similar scientific evidence. There is no a priori reason to expect e-voting to be dissimilar. In many respects the risk dimension to e-voting is already being framed differently in the various national contexts where it has been the subject of discussion and public study. From a comparative public policy perspective this is hardly surprising, even societies that are similar in economic, social and political structures can produce radically diverging conceptualisations of risk, especially where the risk in question touches on issues that are deemed basic to a society's conception of itself.

In Chapter 8 Pratchett *et al.* address the social dimension to risk and also identify a fundamental design dilemma for e-voting, namely how to balance security while, at the same time, enhancing simplicity and convenience of use. They argue that achieving this balance is one of the fundamental problems facing the development of e-voting. There is a temptation, on the part of system designers, to build and develop ever more sophisticated security measures (such as biometric devices, firewalls and other measures to prevent hacking etc.) that virtually prevent all but the most determined attack. The problem, however, is that the designers of e-voting systems need to recognise that if widespread use is to be achieved, they must be simple and convenient. Not all voters have access to state of the art technology and many lack cognitive familiarity with complex security requirements.

Based on focus group research Pratchett *et al.* draw attention to the 'cognitive capacity' problem. The research findings that Pratchett *et al.* cite suggest that users may find the implicit rules and norms of computer systems difficult to absorb. For instance, clicking a mouse-button or using a tab or return key, while straightforward for those who use computers frequently, are much less obvious for those not accustomed to using computers. The lesson to draw from the focus groups is the importance of the principle of simplicity. The key to striking a balance, according to Pratchett *et al.*, is to distinguish between authentication on the one hand and verification, tally and audit on the other. While proponents and critics of e-voting have focused on authentication issues, Pratchett *et al.* argue that it is much better to put in place a strategy based on effective verification, tally and audit procedures that do not sacrifice simplicity in favour of sophisticated technical solutions. In fact, such a strategy more closely resembles current electoral procedures.

Similarly, in Chapter 7, Kies and Kriesi identify a further design dilemma that could significantly affect the democratic consequences of implementing e-voting. On the one hand, the introduction of e-voting is commonly justified in terms of increasing the *quantity* of participation. Yet, on the other hand, there needs to be a counterbalance to risks concerning the potential erosion of the *quality* of participation. From a democratic theory perspective there is a real danger that e-voting could signal a descent down a slippery slope towards push-button style democracy with voters becoming increasingly disconnected from the body politic and encouraged to vote according to their own individual interests. One way out of this conundrum for Kies and Kriesi is to introduce what they have labelled a 'virtual pre-voting sphere'. Indeed, they provocatively argue that, from a normative perspective, it is the only way to proceed if the introduction of e-voting is intended to increase not only the *quantity* of participation but also its *quality*.

Through the introduction of a pre-voting sphere, which would accompany the introduction of online voting, the authors hope to address fears of a potential decrease in the quality of the vote. In order to support their argument they draw on recent 'opinion formation' theories and employ Habermasian notions of the 'public space' as their normative reference point. Kies and Kriesi's basic thesis is that a pre-voting site has the potential to improve the quality of democratic choices by raising the quality of citizens' opinion formation through the provision of pluralistically organised information and opportunities for deliberative exchange. While the authors are keen to operate at a higher level of abstraction, their normative conceptualisation is especially pertinent to the plurilingual and multicultural context of the EU.

Institutional visions

In this last part we move beyond short-term effects and attempt to highlight some of the dynamic effects that could accompany the introduction of e-voting over the longer term. What are the institutional implications of greater e-democratic experimentation within an EU context and how will this affect our institutional visions for the future of the EU polity? These questions raise fundamental issues regarding the nature of the European integration process. In this section we will begin by identifying an ontological dualism in EU studies and then probe the implications of further e-politicking for each of these institutional visions. The ensuing discussion is contingent upon some rather major assumptions, namely that there is a drive towards further EU democratisation and that e-techniques are considered as potential solutions.

One of the major sources of the intellectual difficulties that surround discussions about the EU has been, at root, an ontological question. On the whole we are accustomed to organising phenomena in terms of classes or categories. The problem with the EU, however, is that it does not fit easily into any of the conventional frameworks for understanding political phenomena. It has features of a treaty-based international organisation, yet, unlike such bodies, it possesses a wide jurisdiction and its laws are supreme over its member states. It evidently carries weight in international politics but frequently does not speak with a 'single voice' and lacks the traditional instruments of force that are considered basic for exerting international influence. Moreover, it has certain institutional attributes that resemble the internal institutions of a nation state but lacks the most elementary attribute of a state – an enforcement apparatus of its own. It is not surprising then that some view the EU as a *sui generis* phenomenon and a unique political experiment. For others, however, the EU may have certain unique attributes but it is, nonetheless, a functioning political system with a set of formal rules, a separation of powers among its institutions and what some see as an emerging bicameral legislature in the forming. Hix, one of the leading exponents of this latter view, has stated the dualism as follows:

if the EU is a unique animal, it will be difficult to compare it to other creatures (and new theories will be needed to understand how it behaves). But, if it is only a strange variant of an already well under-stood species, it can be compared with other members of the species (and theories that explain how the species behaves will also apply to the EU).[46]

The key issue to underline here is that our empirical conception of the EU will affect our normative prescriptions – and, ultimately, our institutional visions. If the EU is but a strange or 'sick' variant of a well under-stood species we would profit from looking and perhaps even importing features of 'healthier' variants. This is the view of Hix, for whom the antidote is to introduce greater political competition. If, on the other hand, the EU is a new political species then we may need to envisage new conceptualisations of the member state/EU nexus and identify novel forms of horizontal linkages among EU actors including its citizens.

Let us now introduce the ICT and e-democratic element into this equation. It would seem that there is more scope for innovative e-democratic type experimentation if one favours the *sui generis* view. This is the institutional vision taken up by Schmitter, one of the leading proponents of this view, in Chapter 9. We will, therefore, focus on the first vision and try to imagine the e-democratic implications. For Hix[47] the solution lies in offering EU voters more choices. One of the missing 'democratic' components is the connection between EU level parties and voters, few of whom know of the existence of European level parties or their policy platforms. Furthermore, at no point do EU voters have the opportunity to choose between rival candidates for EU executive office or rival policy agendas, since the process of electing MEPs is not an electoral contest about the content or direction of EU policy but, instead, resembles mid-term judgements on the performance of incumbent national parties.[48] One of Hix's proposed institutional reforms is to introduce electoral competition by allowing, for example, EU voters to choose the Commission president, either directly or indirectly.[49] Other scholars, such as Papadopoulos, favour the introduction of more direct democratic mechanisms for the EU.[50] Unlike Hix, who favours the strengthening of party competition, Papadopolous draws on the Swiss case to argue for referendums and other direct democracy procedures, such as popular initiatives, for Europe-wide issues. Both these institutional visions stem from a similar ontological position concerning the reality of the EU political system and where to look for solutions to classic problems of legitimacy and accountability.

Though neither author mentions e-democratic tools explicitly, they could be relevant to the institutional visions of both. This does not in any way downplay the major obstacle of finding the necessary political will and consensus to institute such reforms. While Hix's vision could be more easily implemented without recourse to e-voting or other e-democratic tools (although we would argue that some of his ideas could certainly be facilitated by these), it is with regard to Papadopoulos' vision that e-democratic tools could be most useful and complementary. His institutional vision, if implemented, spans all the dimensions of e-democracy as we have presented it. A future in which pan-European popular initiatives and direct democratic votes are a prevalent feature of the EU political landscape is difficult to envisage without some corresponding increases in transparency (e.g. timely access to legislative proposals) and deliberation (e.g. a common public space for EU citizens to discuss the *same* issues). This institutional vision would certainly lend itself to the type of e-politicking that we have identified throughout this chapter.

In Chapter 9, Schmitter offers an institutional vision with features including novel democratic mechanisms for holding EU leaders accountable to their citizens. Schmitter focuses on what he refers to as 'e-politicking via ICT' and its potential for further democratisation of the EU. For him, ICT is such a powerful force that in the long term it will have to affect the practices and, eventually, the values of democracy in Europe at all its multiple levels. He begins by introducing some provisos that need to be addressed before an e-voting agenda can be properly advanced. These include progress on the resolution of security and digital divide issues as well as member state commitment to democratisation and some commonly agreed and coordinated rules for 'e-politicking'. With these in place, Schmitter identifies a series of e-politicking techniques including e-voting for elections and for referendums. The latter, he suggests, should be drafted by the European Parliament and need not be binding at an initial stage. e-Vouchers, which could help to foster new public spaces by allowing European citizens to express their intensities about passions and interests, could also be introduced. Finally e-contacting, where citizens reveal their identities and are informed or notified if certain issues come up, represents another potentially rewarding ICT facilitated mechanism. In sum, Schmitter argues that as we enter a more overt phase of European political integration there may be a willingness to resort to novel democratic mechanisms and that the properties of ICTs make it especially appealing for the EU context and for overcoming problems of scale, distance and the diversity of languages and cultures. Moreover, by e-politicking via ICT the EU would identify itself as a modern, innovative and forward thinking polity.

In the final chapter, Ladeur adopts a more sociologically oriented perspective. Echoing Manuel Castells' theorisation of the network society,[51] Ladeur's emphasis is on discontinuity. For him, the sphere of politics will not be immune to the dramatic transformations that are occurring in the social and economic realms. To this end, his chapter identifies some of those transformative changes that are affecting the way society and the economy are organised as network structures increasingly replace hierarchies. He argues that the implications for politics and the way governments and

citizens interact are equally profound. From Ladeur's perspective, introducing e-voting would constitute far more than the implementation of a
new voting procedure. Instead, it could form an integral component of an
instituted reform providing EU citizens with more strategic decision-making
power. More flexible voting methods would allow voters to assign a more
'informative' and complex message to their vote enabling a more differentiated communication flow between political parties and voters. Such new
flexible voting forms may generate a new interest in democratic participation, but also contribute towards the emergence of virtual constituencies as
a result of the devaluation of the territorial attachment of citizens.

Instead of conclusions: some *amuses-bouche*

It would be maladroit for us to offer 'conclusions' before allowing the
reader to savour the dishes our authors are about to offer. One certainly
does not serve *le dessert* before *le plat principal*. Instead, the purpose of this
introduction has been to describe what has whetted our appetites and
provide a flavour of the intellectual offerings each of the contributors has
brought to the table. We would not wish the reader, at this early stage, to
lose their appetite and therefore prefer to offer, instead of conclusions,
some modest *amuses-bouche*. Besides, a most welcome *digestif* is provided in
the Epilogue by Stephen Coleman.

We would like to highlight two areas that we believe are especially pertinent for current debates, the *variability of e-voting arrangements* and the *supply
and demand side* of the e-voting equation. With regard to the former, cross-
national variations in e-voting arrangements across the EU are to be
expected. There are many factors that could produce divergences not only
in the perceived feasibility of implementing e-voting and the type of
e-voting technique developed but also, crucially, in its political and social
effects. Differences in existing constitutional and electoral law provisions,
diverse political cultures and traditions of democracy, and varying degrees
of willingness to experiment with complementary forms of e-politicking,
are just a few examples of the factors that will impact on the type of
e-voting arrangements that could emerge. This explains why analysts,
including the contributors to this volume, disagree on the impact of
e-voting, such as its likely effect on turnout. The problem is that e-voting
in Democratic Primary elections in Arizona is not the same as e-voting in
UK local elections, which, in turn, is not e-voting in Geneva local referendums and will certainly not be e-voting for European Parliamentary
elections. Both the UK (May 2003 local elections) and the Geneva (Anières
and Cologny referendums in 2003) e-voting trials were spectacularly un-
inspiring with regard to the possibilities for using the internet as a platform
for promoting deliberative interactions among website visitors. This is
particularly surprising for the canton of Geneva, which had tested its system
on a sample of internet users and found that a sizeable majority were in

favour of more interactive elements.[52] Perhaps these rather unimaginative pilots are simply the product of the embryonic stage at which we find ourselves in connection with e-voting experimentation. The variability of solutions, multiplied by the variability of electoral, social, juridical, technological and political contexts leads to a very large number of possible outcomes, effects and developments. Any discussion about introducing e-voting for the European Parliamentary elections has to take this variable geometry into account.

Let us now underline the supply/demand side of the e-voting equation. As we have noted above e-voting pilots have been promoted in a top-down perspective. Public authorities, in close collaboration with private organisations, have supplied e-voting solutions in order to test the technological feasibility of the system and to measure e-voting's impact, especially on turnout. In addition, many governments have announced – rather prematurely, as it has turned out – their desire to implement e-voting for local, regional, national and EP elections.[53] There is a distinctive fad element to these hasty public announcements as governments strive to be seen at the vanguard of what Schmitter, in his chapter, refers to as 'politico-technological innovation'. Many of the governments that have promised to offer e-voting have very quickly realised the technical, logistical and political complexities that will need to be overcome and, in direct contrast to the very public displays with which the initiatives were announced, have quietly delayed the trials. The other side of the equation is, of course, the demand side. The big and rather elusive question is whether there is any popular demand for such e-techniques. Reliable data are hard to come by on this issue and what should be noted is that popular support for e-voting is not the same as demand. We can, however, look to the field of e-government in Europe. Some countries, such as Ireland and Finland, offer their citizens a wide array of possibilities for conducting online transactions with the state, despite the fact that only a minority of citizens use or even wish to be offered these solutions. In other countries, such as Belgium and the Netherlands, the situation is the exact inverse, where a popular demand exists that is above the EU average although the e-government offer is less developed than the EU average.[54] More prescriptively we would argue that the bottom-up demand aspects should be taken into account by the promoters of e-voting solutions. While it may be legitimate to offer new additional features in the absence of a strong demand, as the latter could self-generate once citizens are exposed to the measures, the inverse is sub-optimal. In contexts where a high demand for e-voting exists,[55] civic demand and the supply of policy outputs could, over time, be brought into congruence. As we have already noted above, this also applies to the refinement of e-voting systems, for example by providing more deliberation enhancing platforms when a demand for the latter can be clearly registered.

This book is about one of the latest changes in the 'technology of democracy' and how it may impact on one of the core mechanisms of democratic participation: voting. The idea of injecting a novel element into the process of election has predictably spawned controversies and speculations about the future of democracy. Positions have been taken and, as we have argued above, major fault lines have emerged. But this book has attempted to go further by expressly drawing attention to an EU dimension. To date, however, European citizens have not been offered the means for casting their vote in European Parliamentary elections via the internet. Indeed, for most observers the topic of e-voting and the EU is, in fact, a *non-sujet*. In this book, and this introductory chapter in particular, we have argued to the contrary and, whether member states knowingly intend it or not, e-voting is an issue likely to generate political attention at multiple levels of EU governance, from the local to the regional and from the national to the supranational. But, perhaps more importantly, the subject of e-voting has raised issues that go to the very core of contemporary governance and brought to our attention questions of democratic theory and legal scholarship as well as the social dimension to technological risk and the potential institutional impacts of political experimentation via ICT. How long e-voting for European Parliamentary elections will remain in the hypothetical realm only the future will tell us. It is plausible that in 2009, the next scheduled meeting of the European electorate, some voters will be able to cast their vote over the internet. However, it is just as plausible that this will not be the case. The goal of this volume is simply to prepare us for the journey by bringing together a number of authors who have thought about this journey very carefully by reflecting upon previous experiences. Undoubtedly, they have raised more questions than answers but then this is an inevitable, although not regretful, consequence of the multifaceted subject they are addressing.

Notes

1 Throughout this chapter we will use the term e-voting to refer to all forms of remote voting over the internet. Chapter 2 by Gibson addresses in greater detail all the major issues related to the definition of e-voting and its different forms.

2 See Norris, P. 'e-Voting as the Magic Ballot? The impact of internet voting on turnout in European Parliamentary elections', paper presented at the conference on e-Voting and the European Parliamentary elections, European University Institute Florence, May 2002.

3 Moravscik, A. (2002) 'In defence of the "Democratic Deficit": reassessing legitimacy in the European Union', *Journal of Common Market Studies*, 40 (4): 603–24.

4 See the Press Release of the Transnational Radical Party, the sponsors of the initiative. Available at: www.coranet.radicalparty.org/pressreleases/press_release.php?func=detail&par=1634.

5 See the UK's Electoral Commission's Recommendation, December 2003, for the electoral pilots at the June 2004 elections. Available at: www.electoralcommission.gov.uk.

6 For a similar argument see Coleman, S. (2002) *Elections in the 21st Century: From Paper Ballot to e-Voting*, London: Electoral Reform Society. Available at: www. electoral-reform.org.uk/publications/books/exec.pdf.

7 See Press Release of the Transnational Radical Party, op. cit.

8 We owe to Philippe Schmitter this insight concerning the notion of 'Information Rights' and its link to T.H. Marshall. Marshall laid out the three elements for developing what he described as full citizenship. These were civil rights (individual liberty, freedom, right to free speech, and the right to own property), political rights (the right to participate in the political process) and social rights (a degree of economic and welfare security based on 'prevailing' living standards). See Marshall, T.H. (1965) *Class, Citizenship, and Social Development*, Cambridge: Cambridge University Press.

9 See Bobbio, N. (1987) *The Future of Democracy. A Defence of the Rule of the Games*, Minneapolis: University of Minnesota Press.

10 See Whale, J. (2000) *Edmund Burke's Reflections on the Revolution in France*, Manchester: Manchester University Press.

11 Dahl, R.A. (1956) *A Preface to Democratic Theory*, Chicago: Chicago University Press.

12 See Schumpeter, J.A. (1976) *Capitalism, Socialism and Democracy*, London: Allen & Unwin (5th edn).

13 Sartori, G. (1973) *Democratic Theory*, Westport: Greenwood Press.

14 Barber, B. (1984) *Strong Democracy. Participatory Politics for a New Age*, Berkeley, Los Angeles and London: University of California Press.

15 Budge, I. (1996) *The New Challenge of Direct Democracy*, Cambridge: Polity Press.

16 Kriesi, H. (1998) *Le système politique Suisse*, Paris: Economica (2nd edn).

17 Elster, Jon (ed.) (1998) *Deliberative Democracy*, Cambridge: Cambridge University Press.

18 Fishkin, J. (1991) *Deliberation and Democracy. New Directions for Democratic Reform*, New Haven and London: Yale University Press.

19 Habermas, J. (1992) *Faktizität und Geltung: Beiträge zur Diskurstheorie des Rechts und des demokratischen Rechtsstaats*, Frankfurt am Main: Suhrkamp.

20 See, for instance, Nixon, P. and Johansson, H. (1999) 'Transparency through technology: the internet and political parties', in B.N. Hague and B.D. Loader (eds) *Digital Democracy*, London: Routledge; Davis, R. (1999) *The Web of Politics*, Oxford: Oxford University Press; Wilhelm, A.G. (2000) *Democracy in the Digital Age: Challenges to Political Life in Cyberspace*. New York: Routledge; Coleman, S. and John, G. (2001) *Bowling Together: Online Public Engagement in Policy Deliberation*. Available at www.bowlingtogether.net/about.html.

21 See Trechsel, A., Kies, R., Mendez, F. and Schmitter, P. (2003) 'Evaluation of the use of new technologies in order to facilitate democracy in Europe: e-Democratizing the parliaments and parties in Europe', European Parliament, STOA (Scientific and Technological Option Assessment) Report, Directorate-General for Research.

22 See Trechsel, A. *et al.*, op. cit.

23 For a useful critical overview of the White Paper see Scharpf, F. (2001) 'European governance: common concern vs the challenge of diversity', *Jean Monet Working Papers*. No. 6/01 Symposium: The Commission White Paper on Governance. Available at www.jeanmonnetprogram.org/papers/01/010701.html.

24 The Laeken Declaration is available at www.euconvention.be/static/Laeken Declaration.asp.

25 See the Futurum website www.europa.eu.int/futurum/index_en.htm.

26 See Trechsel, A. *et al.*, op. cit.

27 See Coleman, S. (2002) op. cit.

28 Marquand, D. (1979) *Parliament for Europe*, London: Jonathan Cape.
29 Mény, Y. (2003) 'De la démocratie en Europe: old concepts and new challenges', *Journal of Common Market Studies*, 41 (1).
30 Zweifel, T. (2002) '. . . Who is without sin cast the first stone: the EU's democratic deficit in comparison', *Journal of European Public Policy* 9 (6).
31 See Mény, op. cit., p. 9.
32 See Moravscik, A., op. cit.
33 See Chapter 9 by Schmitter.
34 See Norris, P. (2002) op. cit.
35 On the issue of trust and the state see in particular Giddens, A. (1990) *The Consequences of Modernity*, Stanford: Stanford University Press.
36 Nonetheless, according to the study by Trechsel *et al.* (2003) op. cit., the European Parliament has one of the highest scores in terms of the e-democratic potential of its parliamentary website.
37 For further information on the eEurope action plan see the Commission's website at www.europa.eu.int/information_society/eeurope/2005/index_en.htm.
38 For ongoing works on the topic of e-voting within the Council of Europe see the relevant integrated project 'Making democratic institutions work' at www.coe.int/t/e/Integrated_Projects/democracy/.
39 Birch, S. and Watt, B. (2004) 'Remote electronic voting: free, fair and secret?', *Political Quarterly* 75 (1).
40 See pp. 5–6 of the report by the UK Department of Constitutional Affairs on the implementation of e-voting. Available at: www.dca.gov.uk/elections/e-voting/pdf/e-summary.pdf.
41 See, for instance, Internet Policy Institute (2001) *Report of the National Workshop on Internet Voting*. Available at: www.nsf.gov; Public Administration Select Committee (2001) *First Report 2001–2002*, London: HMSO; see California Internet Voting Task Force (2000) *A Report on the Feasibility of Internet Voting*. Available at: www.ss.ca.gov.
42 See p. 7 of the Serve Study by Jefferson, D., Aviel, R., Simons, B. and Wagner, D. (2004) *A Security Analysis of the Secure Electronic Registration and Voting Experiment (SERVE)*. Available at: www.servesecurityreport.org/paper.pdf.
43 Dahl, R. (1991) *Democracy and its Critics*, New Haven and London: Yale University Press.
44 See Beck, U. (1986) *Risikogesellschaft. Auf dem Weg in eine andere Moderne*, Frankfurt am Main: Suhrkamp.
45 See the report, US Whitehouse (2003) *National Strategy to Secure Cyberspace*. Available at: www.whitehouse.gov/pcipb/cyberspace_strategy.pdf.
46 Hix, S. (1998) 'The Study of the EU II: the new governance agenda and its rival', *Journal of European Public Policy*, 5 (1).
47 For an extended and cogent discussion see Hix, S. (1999) *The Political System of the European Union*, Basingstoke: Macmillan.
48 See Hix, S. (2002) 'Why the EU should have a single president and how she should be elected', paper for the Working Group on Democracy in the EU for the British Cabinet Office. Available at: www.personal.lse.ac.uk/HIX/Working%20Papers/Why%20the%20EU%20Should%20Have%20a%20Single%20President.pdf.
49 See Hix, S. (2002) op. cit.
50 See Papadopoulos, Y. 'Democratising the European Union à la Suisse, or is the addition of some (semi) direct democracy to the nascent consociational European federation just Swiss folklore?', paper presented at the conference Towards a federal Europe?, European University Institute, Florence, June 2003. See also

Papadopoulos, Y. (2003) 'Cooperative forms of governance: problems of demo-cratic accountability in complex environments', *European Journal of Political Research*, 42 (4): 473–502.

51 Castells, M. (1996) *The Rise of the Network Society*, Cambridge: Blackwell Publishers.

52 The canton of Geneva tested its system on 449 internet users with the right to vote, a sizeable majority of whom were in favour of linking the e-voting plat-form to more political parties and public authorities via hyperlinks and in favour of hosting online forums on the official web site. See Christin, Th. and Müller, R. (2002) *Analyse quantitative du test Alpha Ter: Evaluation par questionnaire du système de vote par internet*, Geneva: c2d, University of Geneva. Available at: www.ge.ch/chancellerie/E-Government/doc/rapport_alphater_evoting.pdf.

53 A good example is the Estonian government's announcement, in 2002, to e-enable the 2003 General Elections. However, this project remained *lettre morte*.

54 See Trechsel, A. (2003) 'Perspektiven zur e-democracy in der EU', in H. Muralt-Müller, A. Auer and Th. Koller (eds) *E-voting*, Bern: Stämpfli, pp. 374 ff.

55 Such a demand could be gauged, for example, in a survey in the canton of Geneva. See Kies, R. and Trechsel, A.H. (2001) 'Le contexte socio-politique', in A. Auer and A.H. Trechsel (eds) *Voter par internet? Le projet e-voting dans le canton de Genève dans une perspective socio-politique et juridique*, Geneva, Basle, Munich: Helbing & Lichtenhahn. Available at: www.ge.ch/chancellerie/e-government/doc/Voter_par_Internet.pdf.

Part I
Political outcomes

2 Internet voting and the European Parliament elections

Problems and prospects[1]

Rachel K. Gibson

Introduction

Much of the rising fear about the performance of democracy in modern nation states is connected with reports of a decline in voter turnout. Parliamentary elections across Western Europe throughout the 1990s show a downward trend in voters going to the polls, almost without exception.[2] Levels of participation in European Parliament elections make for particularly gloomy reading with turnout falling again in 1999 to an average of 50 per cent across the EU-15 member states, a fall of over 10 per cent since 1984 within the EU-12. A number of countries, such as Germany and the UK, saw the numbers casting ballots falling to an all time low.[3] Across the Atlantic attention is also focused on the issue of voter abstention. In 1968 just over 7 per cent of registered voters did not vote in the US presidential election. By 2000 that figure had almost tripled to just under 19 per cent. Low turnout among younger voters has caused particular anxiety with only 36 per cent of 18 to 24 year olds reporting that they voted in the US Presidential elections of 2000.[4] A similar tale emerged in the recent British General election of 2001 where turnout dropped to its lowest level since 1918, with just over 60 per cent of those between 18 and 24 reportedly not voting.[5]

While such trends may be no more than temporary ebbs in longer term election cycles or simply reflect institutional change such as the enlargement of the EU,[6] they have clearly begun to ring rather loud alarm bells in the minds of policy makers, election administrators and media observers. In a post-election report on the 2001 general election, the UK Electoral Reform Society sounded the following warning note:

> A democracy in which the public does not participate is in trouble. Falling turnout at elections is a worry for all of us, because we know that voting is the most basic act of democratic participation; people who do not vote tend not to participate in other civic activities.[7]

The Minister for e-Commerce in the UK, Douglas Alexander echoed these concerns in a speech after the election when he commented that: 'High voluntary participation in elections is crucial for a healthy democracy. . . . The more people who vote, the stronger the legitimacy of the decisions taken by elected representatives.'[8] Falling rates of participation are particularly worrying for European parliamentarians given the perceived distance of the EU from most citizens' lives.

In looking for ways to engage people in the electoral process a number of options present themselves. Civic education programs within schools that teach children the values and responsibilities of citizenship are a perennial alternative. Arguably, however, American schools are some of the more advanced in this regard, with strong traditions of singing the national anthem, flying the flag and rote learning of the constitution from the earliest years. The consistently low level of turnout in the US, however, compared to that of countries with a less civically engineered curriculum does not bear strong testimony to the effectiveness of such methods. Alternatively, parties and politicians themselves could play a role by engaging in more meaningful debate during election campaigns and putting forward more distinctive programmes. A common complaint heard from voters is that the current system is too stage managed and the parties all sound the same as each other. Of course, the media would also need to lend a hand in this by concentrating on the issues and avoiding the 'horserace' type of reporting that characterises much of their election coverage.[9] Finally, institutionally speaking, elections could be made more open and thus potentially more competitive, with the rules being changed to ensure representation of a wider range of political groupings in parliament.[10] Party finance rules could also be redrawn to ensure a more egalitarian system that would encourage more grass roots and independent campaigns.

While such solutions may, indeed, help to increase citizens' interest in voting, from a practical and legal standpoint they are clearly rather complex and costly to deliver. In addition, even if they worked to create a more porous and vibrant system, the benefits to turnout would probably not be felt for some time, and politicians are notorious for thinking in terms of one election cycle at a time. It is not surprising, therefore, that the rising concerns over turnout have prompted governments to turn to a more immediately implementable and comparatively low-cost alternative – voting over the internet via home or work personal computers (PCs) or, even more conveniently, hand-held devices such as mobile phones. With data showing that two-thirds of non-voters in the UK would have been more likely to vote in the 2001 election if they could have done so by mobile phone,[11] and 57 per cent of Britons with internet access saying that they be willing to vote online,[12] the case for considering i-voting appears to have become unavoidable.

As shall be shown below, strong interest has emerged within the EU itself and many of its member states for moving parliamentary and legislative elections online. This chapter aims to assess how realistic such ambitions are for the European Parliamentary elections of 2009. It does so by first profiling the development of internet or i-voting as it is called here, and identifying the four main variants of the method that have been used thus far. The key arguments made for and against i-voting are then profiled in general, and examined for their particular relevance to EU parliamentary elections. Finally, conclusions are drawn about the appropriate pace of any move toward i-voting. While turnout may be boosted by a move to online elections, the financial, logistical, and legal ramifications of implementing such a system mean that any large-scale roll-out in the near future is highly problematic. Finally, attention is called to the need for further research into the 'mode' effects of the new voting technology. One of the points of contention to arise from this analysis is the lack of any empirical information on what the long- or even short-term consequences of using i-voting might be for peoples' political attitudes and behaviour. Given its widening implementation around the world, systematic investigation of any such effects has become both timely and relevant.

The development of internet voting

Internet voting or i-voting is the casting of a secure and secret electronic ballot that is transmitted to officials over the internet.[13] As such, i-voting is a sub-type of electronic voting or e-voting which refers to the casting of a ballot via a broader range of electronic telecommunications technology including telephones, cable and satellite television, and computers without internet connections. e-Voting has been used widely in elections around the world, mainly through direct recording electronic voting (DRE) devices such as touch screen computers at the polling station.[14] The practice of i-voting is far less common. One of the earliest political uses of the technology was in 1996 when the US Reform Party allowed members to select its presidential nominee by casting an online ballot from their PC. Many of the subsequent experiments in i-voting have also taken place in the US. In Alaska, the Republican Party primary elections of 2000 were trialled on the internet, but the results were disappointing, with only 35 votes being cast online, (less than 1 per cent of eligible voters). Later, in November 2000, voters in three counties in California and Arizona were allowed to cast a vote for president in a non-binding trial of the technology. Probably the most widely publicised and well-known example of i-voting to take place to date, however, was the Arizona Democrats' online primary in March 2000.[15] This marked the first use of i-voting in any large scale and legally binding manner for nomination to public office.[16] While no other states as yet have adopted it for election of major office-holders, the federal government has since shown strong interest in expanding its use in the 2004 presidential election as part of its Federal Voting Assistance Program

(FVAP). In July 2003 it was announced that the i-voting experiment run in the previous presidential election for military personnel overseas was to be extended to civilians and include electors in more states. While only 350 people were eligible to use the technology in 2000, officials anticipated these changes could mean over 100,000 foreign-based Americans could vote online by 2004.[17]

European initiatives in i-voting

The Arizona primary also served to stimulate the interest of governments outside the US in using internet-based technologies for elections. Placing itself ahead of the curve, the UK government, in conjunction with Election. com (the company responsible for the Arizona primary), and British Telecom piloted a series of i-voting systems for local elections in 2002 and 2003. This resulted in a total of nine authorities in 2002 experiment-ing with some type of new ICT-enabled voting in selected wards. The options trialled included interactive digital TV and SMS via mobile phones, as well as home PCs and internet-connected public kiosks in libraries and supermarkets.[18] These experiments were heralded by Robin Cook, the former leader of the House of Commons, as the first steps toward an online general election in 2006, an event that he viewed as vital in signalling the continuing relevance of government to people's lives.[19] Warming to his theme, Mr Cook poked fun at the antiquities of the current system, saying for those under 40, polling day was possibly the only time when they would face using a pencil stub and this was why it was tied to a piece of string: 'it's so rare and they might pocket it as a souvenir.'[20] The programme for 2003 proved even more ambitious with a total of 17 local authorities offering some form of new electronic means of voting at an estimated cost of £18.5 million,[21] a five-fold increase on the figures reported from the year before, and beyond the projected £10 million allocated by the Chancellor in 2002.[22] The UK May 2003 pilots are dealt with more fully in the Norris contribution to this volume.

A number of other European countries have also declared their inten-tion to introduce i-voting for local and general elections within the next decade. Otto Schily, the German Interior Minister, at a conference on electronic democracy in early 2001 indicated that the government would like to see i-voting fully operational for the 2010 general election, with a more limited form being introduced in 2006.[23] According to media reports of Germans' views on the topic, take-up should not be too much of a problem, with more than half of those polled by a commercial advertiser in mid-2002 indicating they expected the option to become available in the near future. Internet users, of course, showed a greater level of enthu-siasm than those not online, with approximately three-quarters of the former group saying they were in favour, and only one-third of the latter.[24]

In France, government attitudes toward the need for i-voting has proved somewhat less positive. While i-voting was offered in a referendum held in Brest in 2000, and e-voting and internet-based transmission of votes was organised by an American company in two towns in the lead up to the Presidential elections of 2002, the legal framework to recognise any votes cast in this manner as binding has, thus far, not gained approval from the National Assembly.[25] Other countries such as Sweden and Switzerland have established formal inquiries into the possibilities for i-voting. At the local level, however, the Swiss town of Aniéres was reported to have allowed its citizens to vote online in elections held in January 2003.[26]

While individual countries have experimented with local polls and mock elections for particular towns or within universities, one of the main initiatives in the area of i-voting within Europe has come from the EU itself with the launch of the 'CyberVote' project by the European Commission in September 2000.[27] The aim of the project is to develop and demonstrate an online voting system that can be used by member countries for local, national and European elections. The system envisaged is one that permits use of the internet from fixed sites (i.e. home voting from PCs) alongside mobile devices (i.e. mobile phones and hand-held devices). Pilot schemes in selected locations in Germany, France and Sweden were carried out during December 2002 and January 2003.

Initiatives in i-voting are not the exclusive province of Northern and Western Europe, however. The Estonian government has announced plans to implement i-voting for the 2003 general elections. Its London ambassador brushed aside any concerns about the problems of the low level of internet use among the mass of the population by pointing to the availability of other methods.[28] Estonia's enthusiasm follows the example of its Baltic neighbour Latvia which saw a mock election for the Mayor of Riga take place on the internet, four days before the actual event. The event itself was run by Delfi the major ISP in the region, however, not the Latvian government.[29] In Poland, enthusiasm for moving to an internet-based voting system is also in evidence, with the state electoral commission equipping 10 per cent of local polling stations with computers and internet access during 2002. While not allowing citizens the chance to vote online, the transmission of final results to the commission's central server was planned to take place via the internet, with results being publicised on a website on a rolling basis during the course of the evening.[30] Even further afield, investigation of the online option for elections has been carried out by several countries in the Asia-Pacific region where levels of internet use are high. A government taskforce set up in New Zealand concluded that i-voting would have a positive effect on numbers voting and argued for a target date of 2005, for it to be offered at the polling place. Finally, in Japan, the Centre for Political Public Relations offered poll site internet voting in the 2001 gubernatorial elections in Hiroshima.[31]

Models of i-voting

Given this growing interest in the use of i-voting across Europe and world-wide, assessment of its implications has clearly become very timely. In order to review the costs and benefits of applying the new technology to elections it is first necessary to specify exactly how i-voting takes place. Although much discussion has focused on people using personal computers (PCs) at home and work, this is only one of the ways in which i-voting could be introduced at elections. There are essentially four models of i-voting that have been practised in elections and they are based, in turn, around two distinct logics or approaches:[32]

1   Internet Voting at the Polling Place (IV@PP) – votes are cast at official polling stations and transmitted via the internet to election officials;
2   Remote Internet Voting (RIV) – votes are cast in any location with an internet connection and transmitted via the internet to election officials.

The crucial differences between the systems from an administrative perspective are that: (1) voter authentication in the IV@PP model is done at the polling place by election officials, whereas for RIV it is done through a pre-arranged Personal Identification Number (PIN) or digital signature; and (2) the infrastructure or voting platform (machine and environment) is not controlled by officials for RIV at any outlet. These distinctions give rise to the following models of i-voting represented in diagrammatic form in Figure 2.1.

As presented here, IV@PP is the most traditional model in that it simply replaces the existing equipment such as paper ballots or punch cards with

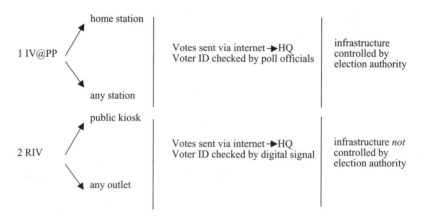

Figure 2.1 Models

Note: Models adapted from the California Internet Voting Task Force Report 'A Report on the Feasability of Internet Voting' (op. cit.), p. 14. This adaptation first appeared in Gibson (2001/2) *Political Science Quarterly* 116 (4): 566.

a machine that records the votes locally and then transfers those votes via the internet to a central tally centre. At the other end of the spectrum, RIV from any outlet represents the most radical departure from existing practice, offering voters the possibility of voting from any machine that is connected to the internet. Voters log on to the election website from their PC at home or work, or through their digital TV or mobile phone to cast a vote. Intermediary options vary from maintaining polling station voting but allowing voters to use any site to cast their vote, to opening kiosk-style outlets that are owned and managed by the election authority, but can be located in a variety of public places such as post offices, libraries and shopping malls.

These four models form a useful reference point to assess the implications of i-voting, since they offer a somewhat different reconciliation of the costs and benefits associated with the method. While RIV carries a far higher risk of outside interference and compromise to security, it offers far greater potential benefits in terms of freeing up the voting process and allowing people to participate from unconventional locations, that are most convenient for them. IV@PP on the other hand, while reducing the risks of any malicious sabotage and keeping voters under the watchful eye of election administrators, obviously does not change much from the individual voter's perspective, other than providing a new computerised context for casting their vote. The controversy that greeted the Arizona Democrats experiment in i-voting is hardly surprising, therefore, given that they opted for RIV from any location, the most radical of the options on offer. Criticisms poured in, ranging from heightened security fears to the possibility of violation of democratic rights due to the unequal distribution of computers across the state, and the trivialisation of the voting act if people could do so 'in their pyjamas'. Based on the claims made in the Arizona Democrats' i-voting experiment, and the debate it sparked, the main arguments offered by the proponents and opponents of i-voting are summarised and expanded upon below.

In support of i-voting

The arguments for i-voting generally rest on three central claims: that it (1) increases participation; (2) enhances administrative efficiency; and (3) forms a natural or logical progression in existing practice and resistance to it is driven largely by inertia or ignorance.

Increasing participation

Boosting the numbers of people that vote is one of the principal arguments offered by those who advocate i-voting. This is certainly the case for the EU in their Cybervote Project. According to the Press Release issued in October 2000 the first objective stated is: 'an improvement of the democratic process by increasing voter participation and thereby increasing the number of votes. On-line voting should lead to an increase of citizens taking part in numerous types of elections.'[33]

In the UK, the move to adopt i-voting was explicitly promoted as a means to reverse the disastrous decline in turnout seen in the 2001 general election.[34] In a government statement released prior to the local elections of May 2003, Local Government minister Nick Raynsford said: 'The electoral pilots aim to improve turnout, in particular among key groups of people who might otherwise be excluded, such as people who are working away from the area, younger voters, the elderly and people with mobility problems.'[35]

Why should this be the case? The primary explanation offered is inc-reased *convenience*. i-Voting would allow voting to be spread over a series of days, affording voters greater flexibility in terms of when they can vote. While IV@PP would also give voters a choice over which polling station to attend, RIV would offer an even greater ease of access, allowing people to vote from wherever they have access to the internet. In so doing, RIV would have the added benefit of helping those voters who might find it difficult to make it to the polling station, to cast their ballot. People with mobility restrictions, for instance, the disabled, the ill and the elderly, would be able to vote from home or a kiosk near to their residence. Those in transit for work or holiday, or those living in remote rural locations, and expatriates living in another country would also find it much easier to vote. In addition, with i-voting the authorities could also target areas with low participation rates. Strategically placed kiosks in libraries, schools, supermarkets and bus stations, staffed by election officials, might be able to draw in more people from more disadvantaged groups such as the poor and ethnic minorities.

Beyond convenience there is also an argument that i-voting would also increase turnout due to the 'pull' of the internet itself. This argument is considered particularly relevant for young people who tend to be less attracted to voting in its traditional form but are also at the high end of users of digital technologies. This is particularly exciting for governments given the high levels of apathy and disinterest evinced by young people in the political process.

Increasing administrative efficiency

As well as reducing costs for voters, moving to i-voting offers considerable efficiency gains for administrators at all stages of the election. As with other forms of e-voting, ballot production and distribution expenses are elimin-ated along with the inevitable wastage of over-production – an environ-mental plus! RIV would reduce staffing costs for polling stations and voting machines. In addition to monetary savings, i-voting could reduce errors in the voting process on the part of voters and electoral administrators. Voters could be prevented from making mistakes on their ballot entry, particularly if the ballot is long and complicated. Intelligent software could prevent them from over-voting or skipping a contest for instance. Online help could be made available to aid voters when completing the ballot in different languages. Approved summary information on each of the candidates could also be provided for voters to consult as required. Finally, if all votes were cast electronically, errors in the count and the time taken to produce the final tally would be significantly reduced, as vote totals would be produced at the click of a button.

Logical progression

A final argument presented by the proponents of i-voting is that most, if not all election administration uses digital technology at some point in the process, be it in the pre-election stage of compiling the voter roll and registering voters or the post-election phase of ballot counting. Offering voters the opportunity to vote via their computers, therefore, simply pulls the 'public' face of elections administration into line with its 'private' or internal face. A senior elections administrator in Australia, for instance, went on record to argue that 'just about every electoral transaction could be conducted over the internet, from enrolment to voting to displaying the results, and everything in between'.[36] In the US this argument carries particular resonance since voting machines have long been a feature of the electoral landscape. In the UK, the case for i-voting has been directly linked to the wider wiring of the elections process in a government consultation paper issued by the office of the e-envoy in the UK during 2002.[37] After advancing the case for a limited roll-out of i-voting, the document went on to outline plans for an online electoral register, voter registration, postal vote application and electronic counting and collating of results.

Given the 'logic' supporting this line of argument for i-voting, any criticism of its implementation can be cast as the modern day form of luddite-ism or techno-fear. Politicians and pundits that object are seen as afflicted by basic unwillingness to embrace new technology, either due to fear, ignorance or an inherent conservatism toward changing established practice, particularly where it involves a significant outlay of expenditure. As the manufacturers of these voting systems are at pains to point out, all new electoral methods attract opposition and suffer teething pains, and no method is free from error or the risk of fraud. Mail-in ballots, for example, are far from 100 per cent secure and the state of Oregon took ten years to move the proposal from the legislative agenda to full implementation. However, this now constitutes the principal method of casting ballots in the state.

Arguments against i-voting

Objections to i-voting are generally based on three main lines of argument: (1) the negative consequences for equality of voter influence; (2) the potential for violations of security and voter privacy; and (3) the reduced quality of participation.

Equality of voter influence

A major criticism of the use of the internet by public bodies is that it is not yet a truly public medium. Figures on net usage around the world show that, even in the more advanced industrialised democracies, it is generally only a minority of the population that have access to, and are using the new medium regularly.[38] In terms of voting, such discrepancies carry serious consequences since they make it easier for some people to cast their vote than others, thereby potentially providing them with greater influence over the election outcome. Given that studies of internet users consistently show that they are younger, more affluent and more educated than non-users, switching to i-voting runs the risk of actually widening the existing participation gap between the more and less advantaged sectors of society. Of course, such problems emerge only if RIV or self-administered kiosks are used, since IV@PP would maintain the fixed opening hours and locations of polling stations.

Security

While social and political concerns about equality of voter influence are important in this debate, arguments about security and the potential for violation of voter privacy have become increasingly salient. These concerns have been highlighted in a series of reports issued by government appointed agencies or independent policy institutes during the past two years that have assessed the feasibility of i-voting (see also the chapter by Pratchett *et al.* in this volume).[39] While not dismissing the possibility of i-voting entirely, they recommend strongly against any use of RIV specifically on security grounds. With voters and the voting infrastructure removed from the watchful eye of the elections administration staff there are just too many opportunities for compromising the outcome. Even with IV@PP there are heightened security risks, since the ballot has to travel across a publicly accessible network and so is open to external interference and manipulation. In general, security objections cover three main aspects of the voting process:

1   Authentication – ensuring that the voter is who they claim to be.
A major concern in any election is ensuring that voters are properly identified. For the remote types of i-voting some kind of electronic identification

is necessary. In Arizona a combination of PINs and personal information was used and in the UK local elections a 16-digit voter ID number was matched with a 4-digit PIN. Such measures, however, are seen by some as too weak to thwart a determined attack, which would be far more likely in the case of a nationwide general election than in the context of small-scale local elections. Ben Fairweather, at De Montfort University, a member of the research team commissioned by the Government to investigate the possibilities for e-voting in local and national elections made this point in press reports prior to the May 2002 elections, saying that in 'piloting [i-voting] at the local level you're not facing the challenges you'll face in the real thing'. The temptations offered to saboteurs by a general election, he argued, were far stronger, given the greater magnitude of any disruption caused, and the implications of any changes to the outcome that might be achieved.[40] A digital roll call and digital signatures using biometric data have been offered as a potential solution, however, such measures would still not be able to prevent the unauthorised use of another person's ballot. The remote voting environment permits a greater degree of voter coercion and bribery than can occur at the traditional polling place.[41] Such criticisms can, of course, be lodged against other methods such as absentee or mail-in votes. The effects of any instances of fraud in these systems, however, would arguably be more localised and less compromising to the validity of the elections process.

2   Privacy/secrecy – ensuring that the voter's ballot is anonymous.
Another key concern in an election is that votes remain secret, a requirement that clearly runs counter to the need for voter authentication. While this tension exists in all election systems, it is particularly acute for i-voting given its more stringent identification requirements. The use of PINs and digital signatures offer election officials an electronic trail linking voters to their vote in a manner that is not possible with conventional paper methods. Remote methods of i-voting create further problems in this regard since it makes possible interception and monitoring of one's vote by a range of unauthorised parties. Voting from work, for instance, on a PC connected to a local area network (LAN) allows your system manager to spy on, and retain a copy of, your ballot. Although software to protect the secrecy of your ballot could be made available, the level of computer literacy necessary to download and install such anti-surveillance software may well prove beyond the capability of many voters if it was offered as a 'DIY' option.

3   Integrity – ensuring the voter's ballot is not subject to interference.
In addition to properly identifying voters and maintaining the secrecy of how they voted, any legitimate election must ensure that that vote is an accurate reflection of the voter's intention. Votes should not be tampered with or changed in any way from the time of their being cast to the point where they are counted. All forms of e-voting face acute problems in this

regard since automation means that one successful instance of fraud could invalidate the entire vote count. Electronic ballot images are typically stored on flash memory cards which, if accessed, could be changed en masse. The chances of such infiltration are markedly increased, however, with i-voting given its reliance on an open network. While these risks can be limited for IV@PP by configuring machines to store ballots and upload them to the central server at intervals in batch mode, such protection does not extend to RIV. Some of the more serious methods of interference include distribution of so-called 'Trojan horse' viruses to users' PCs via web or email downloads. Such programmes, when activated, could rearrange the ballot such that parties' or candidates' voting boxes are moved around and a false vote sent back, without the user detecting the mistake.

Quality of participation

A third major criticism of i-voting is that it will erode the significance of voting which will, in turn, lead to a further decline in levels of political engagement among the public (see also the chapter by Kies and Kriesi in this volume). This claim is centred on the understanding that voting is an important act that cements civic life, and requires a public ritual to instil and perpetuate it. If casting one's vote is reduced to the equivalent of checking email or buying a book online then this reduces its salience and significance in individuals' lives.

In turning to new ICTs as a means of improving falling participation rates governments are seen as falling victim to the lure of 'the modern fix' which is that 'if something isn't working, throw some technology at it'.[42] Far from revitalising the body politic, however, these critics argue i-voting may actually prove to be 'one more way people are disconnecting from the body politic'.[43] The act of voting becomes 'privatised' and people are encouraged to weigh their own individual interests above those of the body politic. The consequences for social cohesion within a country need to be carefully considered argues Richard M. Schum, project director of the Internet Policy Institute workshop that examined i-voting. The act of voting is 'far more than simply a means by which to elect officers of government' he argues, 'For this one moment, all citizens who enter the voting booth are of equal stature – each casts one vote notwithstanding their differences in race, education, occupation or net worth'. RIV, however, allows a select group 'to opt out of going to the polls', with negative consequences for the community as a whole.[44] Worse still, once instituted for elections, i-voting can then be used to run referenda on a more frequent basis, which for some is the death knell to deliberative politics.[45] Increasingly, interest groups will hold sway, leading to a situation of 'accelerated pluralism' as Bruce Bimber described it, whereby a cacophony of highly specialised interests, clamour to be heard.[46] At worst, one might see groups and individuals putting forward a stream of proposals to voters to vote up or down from the comfort of their own homes, with democracy descending into little more than a game show.

One additional concern about democratic quality that should be introduced here too, is the potential threat that e-voting poses to electoral choice. While smart software can prevent voter error it also allows the authorities far greater power to constrain voter choice by determining permissible responses. Ballots could be constructed to prevent individuals from spoiling their ballots or leaving them blank. Such measures would leave governments with considerably more power to control levels of protest voting, therefore.

Assessing the evidence

The question we now turn to is how far these claims stack up with regard to any move to i-voting in the European Parliamentary elections of 2009. At this point, conclusive empirical data based on real world instances of i-voting is in somewhat short supply, given its limited roll-out (again the chapter by Norris in this volume is a notable exception). However, evidence from Arizona as well as other trials worldwide, such as the UK pilots, do provide some useful indications as to the credibility of the various arguments presented above. In addition, while not behavioural in nature, useful sources of information can be found in a number of recent surveys in Europe and the US that have been conducted on people's willingness to engage in i-voting and online politics more generally.

Turnout claims

In the Arizona primary, one of the most dramatic features of the election was the jump in turnout compared to previous years.[47] A record number of votes for a Democratic primary in Arizona were cast (85,907), this figure representing a 600 per cent increase in turnout compared with 1996. Although not all of this increase can be directly attributed to i-voting, it did prove to be the most popular method of voting, accounting for 46 per cent of total votes cast (5 per cent of votes being cast via internet at the polling booth and 41 per cent from remote locations). While the increase can be explained in part by the increased competitiveness of the race in 2000 (in 1996 Clinton ran unopposed), it was still far higher than the average increase across the 30 states holding Democratic primaries in 2000 which was up by just 41 per cent compared with 1996.[48] Data on younger voters provided a more unambiguous cause for celebration, however, since although voting was lower among 18–24 year olds (2.1 per cent of all votes cast), three-quarters of those who said they had voted, reported having done so online.[49]

Results from the UK pilot schemes in 2002 and 2003 provided a more muted endorsement for i-voting as a means to expand participation. Clearly, there was some evidence of an internet effect in 2002 with the three wards in Sheffield that trialled the new ICT-enabled voting seeing an average increase of 6 per cent in voter turnout, and one ward in Liverpool experiencing a 12 per cent jump. Two other much poorer inner city wards, however, saw only marginal increases of around 2 per cent. These results also need to be set against the remarkable gains that were achieved in those areas where all-postal ballots were introduced. Following the dramatic successes in 2000 when a majority of the seven authorities introducing all-postal voting saw turnout increase by 50 per cent or more,[50] the option was expanded to include 13 councils in 2002. Surveying the outcomes of the various pilots held in 2002, the Electoral Commission explicitly noted this differential effect, arguing that while voter feedback suggested the convenience of the electronic methods was attractive, unlike those councils that ran all-postal ballots 'the evidence in relation to turnout remains unconvincing at this stage'.[51] By May 2003, however, the technology was seen to be offering slightly more promising results. In its report *The Shape of Elections to Come* that the Electoral Commission produced following the trials it noted that 'there is some evidence that turnout can increase slightly due to electronic voting', (up to about 5 per cent) and that within the range of alternatives offered i-voting had proved the most commonly used, with an average of 12.6 per cent of those with the remote web access option, having used it. In addition, public opinion research conducted by MORI indicated high levels of satisfaction among those using the internet option, largely due to its ease of use and convenience.[52] However, again the all-postal vote system, which had been expanded to include 32 councils in 2003 produced even more dramatic gains. Every one of the all-postal pilots witnessed an increase in votes cast, with some councils such as Sunderland seeing a doubling of their previous turnout figures. Overall, the average turnout in all-postal districts stood at 49 per cent, in marked contrast to the national average of 35 per cent.[53]

Results from the EU CyberVote pilots in localities in Sweden, France and Germany offer some additional evidence to weigh up i-voting's impact on participation. These trials did not carry the official electoral weight of their US and UK counterparts, however, the rate of uptake among participants was still considered disappointing, particularly in Germany. The experiment run at Bremen University was organised to allow for i-voting in elections for various internal governing bodies. Despite being a highly computer literate environment and i-voting being available for three days, only 47 voters were recorded as having utilised the facility. The report on the trial concluded with a comment on how the results reflected the 'severe acceptance' problems facing e-government in general, and the need to overcome a worrying level of mistrust.[54]

Overall, therefore, the evidence from these mock and 'real world' experiments in i-voting offer a decidedly mixed verdict on whether it can increase participation. The Arizona primary clearly provides a ringing endorsement for the proposition. However, one should also note that it was accompanied by unprecedented levels of worldwide media attention that no doubt served to increase voters' willingness to be involved. The real test of the turnout argument then would seem to be one that can only be answered over time. Once the novelty has worn off, and the press coverage declines, can the technology serve to keep voters engaged?

The idea that the medium itself can galvanise non-voters into action is one that in general, attracts little support. As Bill Thompson, a technology consultant in the UK and frequent opiner on the impact of the internet on society, noted in a report for the BBC, 'people want an alternative, not just new ways to engage with an old and discredited system. It is not clear how putting draft bills online or forcing councils to conduct internet referenda will really change this'.[55] Much of the empirical evidence relating to people's engagement in even the most limited types of online political activities such as information gathering, has served to underscore this point. The webcasting of the British Parliament, for instance, which began in January 2002 was reported to have received less than 4,000 hits on its first day of operation. While not an entirely insignificant number, it compares very poorly with the nearly 1 million visitors per hour that crashed the 1901 UK Census site later in the year. As *Guardian* correspondent, Charles Arthur put it: 'The inescapable conclusion is that people are more interested in where their Edwardian relatives lived than in what MPs get up to – by a factor of about 10,000 to one.'

Such a conclusion was perhaps inevitable, he continues, given that BBC radio broadcasting of parliament has long since been moved to long wave 'on the basis that it drew a tiny audience. Nothing, he concludes rather gloomily, seems to have changed'.[56] Research conducted by the Pew Centre for People and Press in the US during the 1996 and 2000 presidential elections has offered an even more pessimistic view on the ability of the internet to sustain its attraction as a political medium, with figures showing that the proportion of online users visiting party or candidate websites actually declined between the two time points.[57] Evidence from the UK and studies of young people present a rather more positive outlook, however, Gibson, Ward and Lusoli in their study of online participators in the UK found that after controlling for education, income and gender, the strongest predictors of involvement in e-politics was age and familiarity with the internet. These results were seen to indicate that a skill set existed for online participation that was not necessarily linked to the resources typically required for offline participation.[58] Similarly, Owen found that the scope and frequency of online activities among young adults that could be seen as precursors to civic engagement, were far more strongly linked to skills acquired in the online environment than more traditional resources relating to socioeconomic status. Such findings were seen as suggesting that the medium itself, whether due to its convenience factor or its greater immediacy and multi-media functionality, did offer a new 'hook' to entice certain non-traditional participators to become more involved.[59] Whether this appeal is wide enough and can be sustained long enough to expand the pool of non-traditional participators in the longer term, however, is clearly the important next question that such research must address.

In addition to support for the idea that the internet might be able to draw new faces into the pool of politically active, the evidence from surveys of voters' attitudes toward i-voting should also be considered. Large majorities of people from countries where internet access levels are high say that they would use i-voting in an election, if it were offered. A Rasmussen Research poll in September 2000 of 1,598 American adults, for example, revealed that 60 per cent would use i-voting if it were available for the presidential election,[60] a rise of over 10 per cent from the previous year.[61] More significantly, 63 per cent of respondents said they would vote more if online voting were available, a figure that rose to 74 per cent of those in the 25- to 34-year-old age group.[62] A post-election survey in Arizona revealed that a third of those who had voted via the internet said they would be more likely to vote in future elections if the option were available. This compared with just 9 per cent of those who had not voted online.[63] In the UK a MORI poll conducted in 2001 revealed that 53 per cent of respondents would support new methods of voting, including voting via the internet. A further 21 per cent indicated that they would be encouraged to vote in the next general election if internet voting from home were available.[64] In explaining this endorsement, voters were most quick to point to the convenience factor of i-voting, with 52 per cent of respondents in the MORI poll citing this as their reason for supporting the introduction of the new method. Set against the rather mixed reception given to i-voting in the trials to date, these results suggest that voters may need to be further convinced of cost reduction associated with the new method, before it results in any significant boost to turnout.

Equality concerns

A major issue to have emerged in terms of the appropriate pace of moving to i-voting and the model to be adopted is the differential ability of citizens to access the technology. While it may be the case that in the longer term, as the above research suggests, internet-related politics does invite more non-traditional actors into the process, current conditions mean that in the short term, an online voting environment offers an advantage to certain groups in terms of increasing the ease for them to cast their ballot.

Despite the EU's commitment in the Lisbon Council meeting of 2000 to the *e*Europe Action Plan which aims to make the EU 'the most dynamic knowledge based economy in the world by 2010', comparative statistics

Table 2.1 Population online in the EU member countries

Country	% Online
Sweden	66.5
Denmark	59.4
The Netherlands	53.8
Finland	51.4
United Kingdom	46.7
Luxembourg	42.7
Austria	36.9
Germany	36.6
Ireland	36.6
Italy	28.0
France	26.6
Belgium	25.6
Spain	25.0
Greece	15.1
Portugal	14.8
E-15 Average	35.1

Sources: 'European citizens and the media: National Reports' issued by the Directorate-General Press and Communication, Opinon Polls of the European Commission, May 2003. Based on data from Eurobarometer 56 August/September 2001. Report available at www.europa.eu.int/comm/public_opinion/archives/eb/ebs_158_media.pdf.

show a wide range of levels of access to the internet, with no country even coming close to universal access among its citizens. According to figures published by the European Commission itself in May 2003 in a report entitled 'European Citizens and the Media' (see Table 2.1), most European countries still have significant numbers of people that do not use the internet.

Overall, approximately one-third of EU citizens (35 per cent) report using the internet and only four countries, Sweden, the Netherlands, Denmark and Finland can claim to have a majority of their population online. At the other end of the spectrum, Greece and Portugal have less than one in five of their population online. While these differences in access across countries do not create any inequalities of influence between countries within the European Parliament as a whole, they do mean that the benefits of installing i-voting would be far greater for citizens in some member states than others. Probing these figures further to identify who the people are in each country that are using the technology, problems of unequal influence do emerge as Table 2.2 shows.

There is a clear and uniform bias across the 15 member states in the levels of internet access between younger and older citizens, as well as between those with different levels of education, and men and women.

Table 2.2 Demographic and socioeconomic characteristics of internet users across EU member states

Country	Gender		Age			Education			
	Male	Female	15–24 yrs	55 yrs+	Up to 15 yrs	16–19 yrs	20 yrs+	Still studying
Sweden	72.5	60.8	98.3	27.9	40.6	72.4	79.6	93.9
Denmark	60.9	57.9	97.6	19.5	30.4	64.0	79.4	98.8
The Netherlands	61.0	46.7	88.2	20.7	28.1	59.1	71.0	96.3
Finland	54.3	48.8	87.0	11.8	23.9	46.0	76.2	88.8
UK	53.7	40.2	73.8	14.6	11.5	40.4	79.2	90.2
Luxembourg	55.4	31.3	86.7	10.6	15.9	43.4	85.9	90.8
Austria	42.8	31.6	77.0	8.2	16.9	38.5	59.4	89.3
Germany	41.9	28.0	60.6	9.9	11.0	34.4	55.3	73.6
Ireland	36.6	36.4	69.4	8.6	7.7	33.1	73.5	84.9
Italy	34.4	21.9	36.1	3.6	10.5	45.5	58.6	66.0
France	28.2	25.1	57.1	4.2	8.4	18.7	62.0	77.8
Belgium	29.0	22.0	56.0	2.5	5.7	24.3	53.9	69.2
Spain	29.1	21.2	51.2	3.1	5.7	35.7	65.7	67.4
Greece	18.9	11.6	46.7	0.9	3.3	14.6	39.0	62.3
Portugal	18.4	11.6	40.8	1.4	2.4	37.9	70.6	61.0

Sources: 'European citizens and the media: National Reports' issued by the Directorate-General Press and Communication, Opinon Polls of the European Commission, May 2003. Based on data from Eurobarometer 56 August/September 2001. Report available at www.europa.eu.int/comm/public_opinion/archives/eb/ebs_158_media.pdf.

Essentially, younger males with a higher education background are more likely to be able to access the web and email. The disparity in access is not quite as pronounced in those countries with the most widespread use of the technology, such as Sweden, which indicates that as usage increases, previously excluded groups are catching up in rates of 'take-up'. However, they show that educational attainment and age are still very significant determinants of internet access, a trend that has also been identified in data reported from the US.[65] Thus, any immediate instituting of i-voting for European parliament elections would result in a significant section of the population being excluded from i-voting, particularly if it was implemented in its remote form.

Examining the data collected thus far on the series of i-voting experiments that have taken place, it is not surprising, therefore, that a distinct bias toward more socioeconomically advantaged groups is observed. Post-election analysis from the Arizona primary at both the individual and aggregate level, for instance, has revealed a significant relationship between education, age and online voting.[66] Survey data gathered by the three councils that ran online voting in the 2002 UK local elections, reported by the BBC, revealed that despite the youth appeal of the technology, the typical internet voter was more likely to be male, aged 35–54, and middle class. The news report concluded that such a bias, along with the lack of any significant expansion in the numbers voting meant that it was highly unlikely that the technology would redress inequities of participation.[67]

In addition, although the finding that younger people were more willing to vote if they could do so online has been seen as a ray of hope for those arguing against the reinforcement and normalisation thesis of web-based politics, such findings also clearly point to the possibility of exclusion or disadvantage for older voters. The Swedish pilot of the EU Cybervote scheme in Kista, Stockholm is interesting in this regard since it was specifically targeted at older voters with the process being turned into more of a social event around public access kiosks. Despite these efforts, however, the report issued subsequently warned that 'much work would be needed to attract and motivate' involvement among this group, since most of these people were technically highly inexperienced.[68]

Overall, therefore, should these divergences in access persist until the 2009 EP elections, any move to offer i-voting, particularly in its remote form, would serve to advantage citizens of higher socioeconomic status by providing them with more convenient opportunities to cast their vote. Any moves to allow i-voting, therefore, would, at the very least, have to allow for a range of methods to be utilised.

Administrative efficiency

It is difficult to estimate precisely the costs and benefits that would be delivered by switching to an online voting system. While the infrastructure and monitoring of the process would remain in the hands of the national authorities, new bureaucracy in the shape of an EU Election Adminis-tration Commission would no doubt need to be established. Prior to any election, decisions would be required about the standards to be used for software and hardware, along with the level of security to be observed, and perhaps even ballot design and user interface. Security standards for vendors would need to be agreed upon in advance and a list of approved companies offered to countries. Questions about the types of platform that would be acceptable (i.e. PCs, kiosks, digital TV) would need to be resolved, as well as the number of operating systems to be supported (i.e. Windows, Linux, MacOS) and types of web browsing software (i.e. Netscape, Opera, Internet Explorer) that could be used. The need to ensure the broadest compatibility possible would mean that the process would quickly become a very complex and costly one. Meeting the costs of these contracts might necessitate some system of subsidisation for poorer countries since allowing security standards to be dictated by available resources would not be an acceptable option. Vendors would need to make sure there was interop-erability between their systems since the ability of countries to switch between suppliers would be important for maintaining market competi-tiveness and the most up-to-date equipment.

From a legislative perspective, new laws would be necessary to tackle the security threats outlined earlier including malicious attacks, unauthor-ised workplace surveillance, political coercion, and automated vote selling. Legal questions also arise about how the EU could respond if those attacks came from abroad. Would the perpetrators be pursued by the EU or national level justice systems? In addition, new rules on web campaign-ing by parties and candidates would be necessary in order to recreate the insulated environment of the polling station. Whereas now voters are free from electioneering as they cast their ballot, voting via remote access means they are exposed to political messages right up to the point of choice. Would direct email from the parties during the voting period have to be banned? Could, and should voters be stopped from independently accessing political sites just prior to voting?

In financial terms, establishing and running online elections would be a costly endeavour for the EU and its member states. Even if savings were realised in the long run on expenditure for ballots and staffing costs, the upgrades required in hardware and software to protect against viruses and attacks would introduce significantly higher ongoing costs. Also, if extending the voting period meant that poll sites had to be kept open longer then staff requirements would not necessarily be reduced. Finally, massive voter education programmes would be necessary to teach people about how to cast their vote and also download software to protect their home PC from hackers or viruses. Specific projections of the costs for running a national election online have not yet been published. Election.com and the Arizona Democrats have consistently refused to disclose exactly how much their online experiment cost and who paid for what. Media speculation, however, estimated Election.com absorbed huge losses to run the primary (in excess of $1,000,000).[69] The EU Cybervote project that is exploring the possibility of i-voting and running a number of trial schemes has already cost over 3 million euros to pilot. Estimates of the expenditure by the British government on the IT upgrade necessary for just 30 councils in the 2002 local elections was reported to be around three and a half million pounds,[70] with the Chancellor committing a further 30 million pounds for rolling out the technology in local pilots leading up to the next general election in 2006.[71] The cost of an EU-wide initiative in i-voting, therefore, would clearly be many times that and, if imposed centrally, would no doubt lead to legal wrangles about which level of government (EU or nation state) would pay the bill for implementation.

Security

The post mortem report issued by the UK Election Commission following the 2003 trials of i-voting proved to be fairly upbeat on issues of security, with no major breaches being publicly identified. However, from the discussion of security and fraud issues within the document it is clear that the 2003 pilots were treated more as 'test cases' for identifying the possible flaws in the system rather than testing how watertight the established procedures actually were. The recommendations produced by the newly formed government body, the Communications-Electronics Security Group (CESG) regarding the proper procedures for the conduct of online voting were treated very much as such, with some authorities not implementing the very stringent pre-encrypted ballots solution. As the report states, officials did not see the elections as a high risk event with 'the *development* of national e-voting security standards [being] among the main objectives of this year's pilots' (emphasis added).[72]

In the Arizona Democratic primary, initial reports also proved fairly optimistic about security provisions. Most of the violations identified were problems to do with voter authentication or sporadic instances of service denial. Some voters reported that their PIN had not been received or accepted, while others failed to access the election website due to disabled cookies and outdated browsers. On the whole it was estimated that only 4 per cent of registered Democrats who tried to vote over the internet were unsuccessful.[73] As time has gone by, however, criticisms have mounted of the security operation, given the continued failure of Election.com to reveal details about the precise measures they put in place. Election.com have defended their silence by saying that to offer details of their procedures would compromise their procedures for future elections. Critics, however, have dismissed such reasoning as obfuscation, with the following analogy being offered:

> If I take a letter, lock it in a safe, hide the safe somewhere in New York, then tell you to read the letter, that's not security. That's obscurity. On the other hand, if I take a letter, lock it in a safe and then give you the safe along with the design specifications of the safe and a hundred identical safes with their combinations so that you and the world's best safecrackers can study the locking mechanisms – and you still can't open the safe and read the letter – that's security.[74]

Given that this was one of the biggest tests to date of the new voting technology it does seem surprising that there has not been more transparency about the internal procedures used in Arizona and also in the British pilots. All forms of e-voting, in removing paper records from the election process mean that watertight process auditing and error-free software are necessary. In i-voting these needs are particularly acute given its greater vulnerability to external interference and higher security risk. Allowing for independent auditing and for software source code to be made public are, arguably, the most important steps in this regard. Although publishing of source code does furnish interested third parties with greater knowledge of how to attack the system, it also leads to more rigorous testing of the programming and thus discovery of weaknesses.[75] The recent decision by the US National Security Agency to switch to Linux, an open source operating system bears strong witness to the greater security attached to open source code.[76] Any implementation of online voting for EU elections, therefore, would require serious debate among vendors and the authorities regarding the level of transparency to be reached.

In addition to not releasing details of their internal security measures during the period of vote casting, Election.com also failed to release a post-election report systematically cataloguing instances of fraud, error and attempts to gain unauthorised access to the system. While again, some of these data may be sensitive and reveal only minimal problems, failure to make it public simply fuels the suspicions of opponents that major breaches occurred. This is particularly pertinent given a report issued by the joint MIT and California Institute of Technology Voting Project in March 2001 that investigated the error associated with different modes of voting. The team of researchers compared five different voting systems for the numbers of spoiled or incomplete ballots in all presidential elections since 1988. The report concluded that ballots that were counted by hand and required manual marking by the voter had the lowest incidence of such error, whereas punch cards and DRE devices resulted in significantly higher numbers of uncounted ballots.[77]

Even if the most watertight security provisions were put in place, however, election administrators and governments still face the additional pressure of building public confidence in the new method. If most people do not see i-voting to be a secure means of casting their ballot, then any infractions, however slight, may mean the whole election outcome is thrown into question. Given the chaos surrounding the vote count in the US presidential election of 2000, any problems emerging from the use of the new technologies could see levels of public trust in the elections process slipping to worryingly low levels.

Overall, the public do appear to have concerns about the security associated with the use of i-voting for public elections, these being notably higher in the US than elsewhere. The Rasmussen poll of US voters in September 2000 reported that nine out of ten respondents were concerned about the possibility of election fraud if voting took place online (two-thirds reported that they were very concerned).[78] The evidence from Europe indicates that security concerns are not so salient for voters. In the 2001 pre-election MORI poll of British voters discussed above, only 31 per cent of those who did not support the use of new technologies for voting indicated that the possibility of fraud was a reason for their opinion. More general evidence from non-users of the internet within Europe supports this picture of a less alarmist attitude, with only 3 per cent of non-users saying that security concerns prevent them from going online (see Table 2.3).

In addition, more objective evidence of this relaxed approach to internet security within Europe emerges from an EU commissioned report into security of servers. The study, which compared countries in terms of the number of servers equipped with secure socket layer (SSL) for data encryption, noted that no country in the EU had even half the number, per capita, that were found in the US.[79]

Quality

What of the arguments about how i-voting will compromise the value of voting and further erode levels of civic responsibility among the public? While it is too early to assess whether i-voting is inflicting serious damage on the body politic, there do appear to be a sizeable number of voters who believe this to be the case. The MORI poll in the UK found that among the third of the electorate who did not support using the new voting methods, the main reason given was that they believed people should make an effort to go to the polling station (46 per cent). This lay ahead of security concerns and disproportionate levels of access to a computer. While we do not have comparable data from other European countries on opposition to i-voting in particular, we do have data indicating why individuals do not use the internet in general (see Table 2.3). This evidence suggests a similar story of refusal. Although not having a PC at home was the most common reason cited by Europeans in not using the internet (39 per cent), the second most important reason (26 per cent) was that they were simply not interested (see Table 2.3). Probing these results a little further, however,

Table 2.3 Why people don't use the internet, by country (%)

Country	Not sure what it is	No time	No computer at home	Cost of internet connection	Cost of computer	Too complex	Content no use	Not secure	No interest
Belgium	10	8	41	13	14	13	9	3	24
Denmark	12	6	50	11	10	9	10	5	15
West Germany	5	10	37	14	12	16	14	5	26
Greece	18	12	28	6	6	7	6	2	35
Italy	11	9	36	5	6	9	6	3	28
Spain	12	15	33	11	8	9	8	1	30
France	7	10	47	15	20	10	11	5	22
Ireland	9	7	41	8	9	10	4	2	23
N. Ireland	5	11	46	5	9	5	4	2	22
Luxembourg	12	9	31	13	13	9	6	3	24
Netherlands	6	5	40	15	10	17	19	3	19
Portugal	19	11	30	13	9	9	2	2	29
UK	6	9	38	10	11	11	7	4	29
East Germany	3	9	37	15	16	13	11	4	28
Finland	2	5	53	13	13	7	9	1	16
Sweden	7	8	50	8	16	15	8	6	15
Austria	3	10	39	12	10	11	11	3	31
EU-16 average	9	10	39	11	11	11	8	3	26

Source: Eurobarometer 55.2 May/June 2001. Question asked was, 'Why do you not use the internet?'.

it is interesting to note that citizens from those countries with the lowest levels of access (Greece, Portugal and Spain) also displayed the highest level of disdain for the new medium. People from countries with the highest rate of access (Sweden, Denmark and Finland), on the other hand, were more likely to offer technical or logistic reasons for not using the technology. Thus, although resource-based arguments might help explain lower levels of internet use in the countries of southern Europe, there also appears to be some cultural reluctance driving adoption rates across the region. In addition to the 'have-nots', there also appear to be a substantial group of 'want-nots' in these countries when it comes to the internet – people who actively choose not to use the internet or simply see it as unimportant to their everyday lives.

Overall, therefore, these findings suggest that the EU may face resentment and even resistance in certain countries or pockets of the electorate if it were to institute a system of i-voting in the near future. Some people, in fact, may flatly refuse to use the technology, seeing it as devaluing a time honoured ritual. Of course, such arguments need to be balanced against the aggregate needs of a changing society. As the report on i-voting issued by the Electoral Reform Society in the UK noted, social and economic life in Britain, as in many other European nations, is undergoing rapid change with people demanding more flexible business and working hours. Extending this flexibility to the political environment would seem to be a reasonable step to take. Indeed, to argue that only those people who are prepared to walk to the polling station to cast their vote should be allowed to 'fails to recognise the logistical complications of modern lifestyles'.[80]

Conclusions

Assessing the arguments for and against i-voting presented here, it would seem that two key questions arise for politicians and election administrators at any level of government to address, before any move to i-voting is considered: (1) Is it workable? How far can i-voting meet the standards of privacy, accuracy and fairness required for any legitimate election?; and (2) Can it promote democracy by helping to engage more people in the political process? On the first question, it would seem that a consensus has been reached that i-voting, in its more radical form at least, does not meet the workability standards for any large-scale national election. Such an event would be too vulnerable to fraud and/or internal collapse. Such problems, however, are generally seen as resolvable with the advance of time and technology. Questions about the impact of i-voting on the democratic system more broadly, however, encounter a far more divided range of opinion. Such a diversity of views is hardly surprising, however, since the answer depends on what we understand democracy to mean, and the link between it, and the act of voting.

If one sees democracy as a directly participatory and communitarian experience, then one would no doubt regard any effects of i-voting as largely negligible. Indeed, one might even be inclined to see it as simply the latest tired gimmick produced by an elite, desperate to prop up their creaking and antiquated system of representation. However, if the act of voting is seen as a stepping stone – a crucial first step in the process of binding people to the state and inculcating citizenship – as the opening quote from the Electoral Reform Society argues, then i-voting may make a great deal of difference to democracy. Taking a positive view, one could argue that i-voting in attracting some new and particularly younger voters into the process and providing them with their first 'taste' of participation, however minimal, would build the stepping stone to future civic engagement. Taking a more critical view, however, one can argue that it is not simply the act of voting that cements this connection, but the way in which it is done. Can mouse clicking a box during a chat over your morning coffee, or texting your vote from the local pub really provide the same foundation to citizenship as being actively mobilised to go to the 'public space' of the polling station and mix with your political peers? Indeed, might these new methods serve to further downplay the significance of electoral choice in voters' minds, thereby leading to increased disengagement from the system?

While not wanting to endorse the more exaggerated fears of the i-voting sceptics, an important avenue for future research in this area, therefore, would appear to be nature and extent of any 'mode' effects associated with i-voting. Does the use of the new ICT-enabled methods actually result in any long-term decline in levels of voter attachment to the political system and their fellow voters, compared with other methods? Given the current mixture of methods in place, as more countries move toward trials of the new voting systems, the investigation of such questions has never been more practicable or relevant.

Notes

1 This chapter was written when the author was a stipendiat at the Mannheim Zentrum für Europäische Sozialforschung (MZES), Germany, under the EU funded TMR 'Representation in Europe' programme, directed by Hermann Schmitt.

2 See IDEA (2002) *Voter Turnout since 1945: A Global Report*, Stockholm: International IDEA; Wattenberg, M. (2000) 'Turnout', in R. Dalton and M. Wattenberg (eds) *Unthinkable Democracy: Parties without Partisans*, Cambridge: Cambridge University Press.

3 Schmitt, H. and Thomasson J. 'Euro-hostile Non-voting in European Parliament Elections', paper presented at the ECPR Joint Sessions of Workshops, Turin, March 2002.

4 For evidence about declining turnout in OECD countries. US election statistics see 'Voting and Registration in the Election of November 2000', US Census Bureau, February 2002, www.census.gov/prod/2002pubs/p20-542.pdf.

5 *Election 2001 The Official Results*, The Electoral Commission. London: Politicos, p.15, www.electoralcommission.gov.uk/publications_pdfs/chaptertwo.pdf.

6 Franklin, M.N. (2001) 'How Structural Factors Cause Turnout Variations at European Parliament Elections', *European Union Politics*, 2(3); Wessels, B. and Schmitt, H. (2000) 'Europawahlen, Europäisches Parlament und nationalstaat-liche Demokratie', in H.-D. Klingemann and F. Neidhart (eds) *Die Zukunft der Demokratie*, Berlin: Sigma.

7 'Elections in the 21st century: from paper ballot to e-voting' The Report of the Independent Commission on Alternative Voting Methods. February 2002. Electoral Reform Society, UK. www.electoral-reform.org.uk. Preface, p. 5.

8 Speech to 'Conference on Democracy in the Information Age' 25 November 2001. Available at: www.dti.gov.uk/ministers/speeches/alexander251001.html.

9 See Putnam, R. (2000) *Bowling Alone: The Collapse And Revival Of American Community*, London: Simon & Schuster for an extensive critique of the negative impact of the mass media on civic engagement.

10 See Norris, P. (1999) 'Institutional Explanations for Political Support', in P. Norris (ed.) *Critical Citizens: Global Support for Democratic Governance*, Oxford: Oxford University Press, pp. 217–35, for a comprehensive discussion of how institutional arrangements can strengthen public support for democracy.

11 Shillingfor, Joia, 'Don't 4get2 vote', *The Guardian, Online Supplement* 20 December 2001, p. 7.

12 'Is Britain on Course for 2005?' The third KPMG Consulting e-government survey. April 2002. Available at: www.kpmgconsulting.co.uk/research/othermedia/ps_egov2002.pdf. (accessed 18 August 2003).

13 This is the definition adopted by the California Internet Voting Task Force in its report, *A Report on the Feasibility of Internet Voting*. (Office of the Secretary of State for California: Sacramento, California, January 2000). The task force was established in January 1999 by the Secretary of State, Bill Jones to examine the feasibility of internet voting. The full report is available at www.ss.ca.gov/executive/ivote.

14 After production of a smart card or token, voters register their choices directly on the screen. Votes are stored on the local computer or network and then trans-ferred to an electronic database where they are cumulated and counted. Belgium, the Netherlands, and Brazil in particular, have been pioneers in this regard. Brazil, where voting is mandatory, has used computers to vote at polling stations since 1990. South Africa saw its second democratic election in June 1999 administered in part through a network of computers linking polling stations in remote villages and townships to a central headquarters in Pretoria. A number of local councils in the UK used touchscreen computers at the polling stations in their May 2000 elections.

15 Another political example of i-voting was the US Reform Party in 1996 which used it, along with mail-in voting to select its presidential candidate. i-Voting has also taken place for private elections within a variety of business and trade organisations such as PricewaterhouseCoopers, Boeing and the MSF in the UK, along with universities and online groups such as the Internet Corporation for Names and Numbers (ICANN).

16 See Gibson, R. (2002) 'Elections Online: Assessing Internet Voting in Light of the Arizona Democratic Primary', *Political Studies Quarterly*, 116(4).

17 'U.S. Expands Overseas Online Voting Experiment', *washingtonpost.com* July 20 2003: p. A04. Available at: www.washingtonpost.com (accessed 21 July 2003).

18 'UK Tests e-Voting System in Local Elections', *europemedia.net* 8 February 2002. Available at: www.europemedia.net/shownews.asp?ArticleID=8278.

19 Ashley, Jackie 'Cook Plans to Make UK First to Vote on Internet', *The Guardian*, 7 January 2002. Available at: www.guardian.co.uk/print/0,3858,4330373,00. html.

20 Tempest, Matthew 'Reformers Sceptical of Online Voting', *The Guardian*, 7 January 2002. Available at: www.guardan.co.uk/Archive/Article0,4273,4330711,00. html.

21 Parker, Simon 'Cross Culture' *The Guardian*, 30 April 2003 (Society section) pp. 2–3.

22 'Government Told Not to Rush Voting Online', *europemedia.net* 2 August 2002. Available at: www.europemedia.net/shownews.asp?ArticleID=11852.

23 'Germany Considers Internet Voting', *europemeda.net*, 4 May 2002. Available at: www.europemedia.net/shownews.asp?ArticleID=3106.

24 '50 Per Cent of Population Believe Online Voting Will Become a Reality', *europe media.net*, 30 August 02. Available at: www.europemedia.net/shownews.asp? ArticleID=12329.

25 'France to Consider e-Voting', *europemedia.net*, 2 April 2001. Available at: www. europemedia.net/shownews.asp?ArticleID=2333.

26 'Swiss Village Institutes e-Voting', *europemedia.net*, 23 January 2003. Available at: www.europemedia.net/shownews.asp?ArticleID=14580 (accessed 19 June 2002).

27 For further details see www.eucybervote.org.

28 'Estonia Plans for Internet Elections by 2003', *europemedia.net*, 29 March 2001. Available at: www.europemedia.net/shownews.asp?ArticleID=2276.

29 'Virtual Election of Riga Mayor to Take Place Today on Delfi Portal', *europemedia.net*, 7 March 2001. Available at: www.europemedia.net/shownews.asp? ArticleID=1789.

30 '2002 Elections to Gauge the Future for e-Voting', *europemedia.net*, 17 October 2002. Available at: www.europemedia.net/shownews.asp?ArticleID=13166 (accessed 19 June 2002).

31 Parliamentary Office of Science and Technology. Postnote May 2001 No. 155 'Online Voting', see www.parliament.uk/post/home.htm.

32 See Derek Dictson and Dan Ray 'The Modern Democratic Revolution: An Objective Survey of Internet-Based Elections' (SecurePoll.com, The Internet Voting Portal: Bryan, Texas, 2000). For further information see the authors' website www.securepoll.com.

33 European Commission Press Release, 'Vote in Total Confidence Via the Internet', 13 October 2000. For further details see www.eucybervote.org.

34 Wintour, Patrick 'Hi-tech Voting Aims to Raise Turnout', *The Guardian*, 23 November 2001. Available at: www.guardian.co.uk/internetnews/story/0,7369, 60427,00.html. Ashley, Jackie 'Cook Plans to Make UK First to Vote on Internet', *The Guardian*, 7 January 2002. Available at: www.guardian.co.uk/print/ 0,3858,4330373,00.html.

35 Parker, op. cit.

36 Phillip Green, Chief Electoral Commissioner for the Australian Capital Territory (ACT) 'Elections and Technology – Implications for the Future', paper presented at the Conference on Electoral Research: The Core and the Boundaries, (Adelaide, Australia, 1999) p. 6.

37 'In the service of democracy' (2002) A consultation paper on a policy for electronic democracy. HM Government and UK Online. Available at: www. edemocracy.gov.uk/downloads/e-Democracy-Policy.doc. (accessed 18 August 2003).

38 For recent statistics on net usage worldwide see the NUA website: www.nua.org.

39 'A Report on the Feasibility of Internet Voting', California Internet Voting Task Force, January 2000, available at: www.ss.ca.gov/executive/ivote/; 'Report of

the National Workshop on Internet Voting: Issues and Research Agenda', Internet Policy Institute, March 2001; 'Elections in the 21st Century: from paper ballot to e-voting', The Report of the Independent Commission on Alternative Voting Methods, February 2002, Electoral Reform Society, UK: www. electoral-reform.org.uk.

40 Parker, op. cit. The report 'Implementing electronic voting in the UK' was commissioned by the former Department for Transport, Local Government and the Regions (DTLR) and published in May 2002. It is available for download at: www.odpm.gov.uk/stellent/groups/odpm_localgov/documents/page/ odpm_locgov_605188.hcsp.

41 Kim Alexander and David Jefferson 'Internet Voting: Proceed Cautiously', 16 May 2000. Available at: www.sjmercury.com/premium/opinion/columns/ e-voting.htm.

42 Grossman, Wendy 'The Rise in Voter Apathy is Damaging to the Health of Democracy' *Electrical register*, 13 May 2002. Available at: www.new.independent. co.uk/digital/features/story.jsp?story=294585 (accessed 14 May 2002).

43 Anthony, Ted 'A Vote for Old Fashioned Ballots', 11 March, 2000. Available at: www.dailynews.yahoo.com/h/ap/200000311/el/one_voter_s_view_1.html.

44 Schum, Richard M. 'Internet Voting: Its Perils and Promise', in *Voting in the Information Age: The Debate over Technology*, p. 47. The Democracy Online Project. Available at: www.democracyonline.org/taskforce/booklet/p41_schum.pdf p.39.

45 'Report of the National Workshop on Internet Voting: Issues and Research Agenda', Internet Policy Institute (op. cit.) p. 29.

46 Bimber, B. (1998) 'The Internet and Political Transformation: Populism, Community, and Accelerated Pluralism', *Polity*, 31(1): 133–60.

47 Up till 1984 Arizona Democrats had used nominating conventions for their selection of presidential candidates, after 1984 the primary election method was adopted.

48 Solop, F.I. (2001) 'Digital Democracy Comes of Age: Internet Voting and the 2000 Arizona Democratic Primary Election', *PSOnline*, 34(2): 3 (www.apsanet. org).

49 'Voting Goes Online, Young People Go Elsewhere', 20 March 2000. Available at: www.mtv.com...chooseorlose/features/feature_0317.html). Lee, Lydia 'Vote Naked in the Privacy of your own Home!', 20 March 2000. Available at: www.salon.com/tech/view/2000/03/20/election/print.html.

50 Parliamentary Office of Science and Technology. Postnote May 2001 No. 155 'Online Voting' see www.parliament.uk/post/home.htm.

51 The Electoral Commission (2002) 'Modernising Elections: A strategic evaluation of the 2002 electoral pilot schemes', London, UK, p. 7.

52 The Electoral Commission (2003) 'The Shape of Elections to Come', London, UK, p. 66.

53 The Electoral Commission (2003) 'The Shape of Elections to Come', London, UK, p. 23.

54 'CyberVote: The Trials'. Available at: www.eucybervote.org/trials.html (accessed 19 June 2003).

55 Thompson, Bill 'Why e-Voting is a Bad Idea', 19 July 2002. Available at: news.bbc.co.uk/2/hi/technology/2135911.stm (accessed 13 September 2003).

56 Arthur, Charles 'First live webcast of parliamentary debate attracts just 3,500 visitors', *The Independent*, 15 January 2002. Available at: www.news.independent.co.uk/digital/news/story.jsp?story=114530.

57 'Youth Vote Influence by Online Information', issued by the Pew Internet and American Life Project, 3 December 2000. Available at: www.pewinternet.org/

reports/reports.asp?Report=27&Section=ReportLevel1&Field=Level1ID&ID=
94 (accessed 12 January 2001).

58 See Gibson, R.K, Lusoli W. and Ward, S.J. 'Online Campaigning in the UK:
The Public Respond', paper presented at the annual conference of the American
Political Science Association, Boston MA, 2001.

59 Owen, D. 'The Internet and Youth Civic Engagement in the United States',
paper presented at the ECPR Joint Sessions of Workshops, Edinburgh, March
2003.

60 'Portrait of America', Rasmussen Research/TechTV. Available at: www.portrait
ofamerica.com/html/poll-1237.html.

61 David Brady 'Netting Voters', 19 June 2000. Comment posted on the
SecurePoll.com Internet Voting Updates. Available at: www.SecurePoll.com. An
ABC News poll in July 1999 had reported that 48 per cent of Americans would
vote over the internet, if it was secure. The study also reported that 61 per cent
of 18–24 year olds indicated their support for this method.

62 'Survey: Voting Participation Would Increase Through Online Voting',
Government Technology – News, 26 October 2000. Available at: www.govtech.
net/news...phtml?docid=2000.10.26-2030000000000059226/10/00.

63 Solop, op. cit.

64 'Attitudes to the Voting Process', MORI 4 June 2001. Available at: www.
mori.com/polls/2001/elec_comm1–2shtml.

65 Nie, Norman H. and Erbring, Lutz (2000) 'Internet and Society: A Preliminary
Report', Stanford Institute for the Quantitative Study of Society: California. Data
gathered as part of a wider commercial survey in December 1999 by researchers
at Stanford University from 2,689 households showed that even in the US,
while race and income had ceased to be significant predictors in internet use,
education and age had not.

66 Solop, op. cit.; Alvarez, R.M. and Nagler, J. 'The Likely Consequences of
Internet Voting for Political Representation', paper presented at the Internet
Voting and Democratic Symposium at Loyola Law School, Los Angeles, 2000.

67 Cowling, David 'Analysis: Does e-Voting Work?', *BBC News*, 17 July 2003.
Available at: www.news.bbc.co.uk/1/hi/uk_politics/2122142.stm (accessed 16
July 2002).

68 'CyberVote: The Trials'. Available at: www.eucybervote.org/trials.html
(accessed 19 June 2003).

69 Ledbetter, James 'Virtual Voting Faces the Real World', 16 March 2000.
Available at: www.slate.msn.com/netelection/entries/00.03.16_77458.asp.

70 'May Elections to Trial Online Voting', Press Release Downing Street
Newsroom, 6 February 2002. Reported in SecurePoll Electronic Voting Update,
16 April 2002. Available at: www.securepoll.com.

71 Parker, op. cit.

72 The Electoral Commission (2003) 'The Shape of Elections to Come', London,
UK, p. 57.

73 Solop, op. cit., p. 3.

74 Schnier, B. (1966) *Applied Cryptography*, 2nd edn, New York: Wiley. Quoted in
Phillips, D. (2001) 'Setting the Standard for Election Integrity', in *Voting in the
Information Age: The Debate over Technology*, p. 47, The Democracy Online Project.
Available at: www.democracyonline.org/taskforce/booklet/p41_phillips.pdf.

75 Report of the National Workshop on Internet Voting, IPI, p.20.

76 Alexander, K. (2001) 'Ten Things I Want People to Know About Voting
Technology. Setting the Standard for Election Integrity', in *Voting in the Information
Age: The Debate over Technology*, p. 32, The Democracy Online Project.

77 Ward, Mark 'No Votes for Net Elections', 28 March 2001. Available at: www.news.bbc.co.uk/hi/english/uk_politics/newsid1245000/1245880.stm_. For full report see www.vote.caltech.edu/Reports/index.html.
78 Rasmussen Research, op. cit. 'Portrait of America'.
79 *e*Europe Benchmarking Report, 5 February 2002, EU Commission: Brussels, p. 9.
80 Electoral Reform Society 'Elections in the 21st Century: From Paper Ballot to e-Voting', Preface, p. 5, op. cit.

3 e-Voting as the magic ballot for European Parliamentary elections?

Evaluating e-voting in the light of experiments in UK local elections[1]

Pippa Norris

Introduction

As access to the new communication and information technologies have diffused throughout post-industrial societies, the idea of using electronic tools to modernise electoral administration has been widely debated, with potential benefits of greater efficiency, speed, and accuracy.[2] Perhaps the most important and influential argument concerns the claim that remote electronic voting will make the process more convenient and thereby strengthen electoral turnout and civic engagement, especially for the wired younger generation.[3] If citizens will not come to the polls, it is argued, why not bring the polls closer to citizens? This is especially pertinent for European Parliamentary elections where any potential gains in voting participation from new technology are particularly important for the European Union, given that only 49.2 per cent of all European citizens voted in the June 1999 elections, haemorrhaging from almost two-thirds (63 per cent) of the electorate just two decades earlier.[4]

Much speculation and industry-generated hype surround the virtues of remote electronic voting, yet until recently almost no systematic evidence derived from actual elections was available to evaluate this issue. Given the vital importance of maintaining public confidence in the legitimacy and fairness of the electoral process, and the potential for even small details to cause disruption (exemplified by Floridian hanging 'chads' and butterfly ballots), policymakers need careful, cautious, and critical evidence-based evaluations throwing light on the pros and cons of implementing remote e-voting.

Evidence to evaluate this question is drawn here from the results of a series of innovative experiments conducted by the UK Electoral Commission using 59 pilot voting schemes available to 6.4 million citizens (14 per cent of the English electorate) in the 1 May 2003 English local elections. These contests are characteristically low-salience campaigns, determining control of local town halls up and down the land, but commonly stirring minimal interest among the media and the public. Turnout, as with

European Parliamentary elections, is usually fairly low; for example, only one-third of the electorate voted in the previous year's contests. The most recent range of pilot schemes used by the UK Election Commission provides an exceptionally good test of the effects of modernising electoral administration and voting facilities. Implications can be drawn well beyond the particular context, as the electorate in each district cast legal votes with the outcome determining the election of local representatives and the partisan control of councils. These studies built upon the experience of the more limited pilot schemes tried in 2000 and 2002. In the May 2003 elections, 59 different English local districts tested alternative ways of facilitating electronic voting, including use of the internet from home and public access sites, interactive digital television, SMS text messaging and touch-tone telephones. Pilots also used all-postal ballots, getting electronic information to voters, extended voting periods and electronic counting.

The evidence from the election results, and from the survey conducted after the contest, confirms that use of all-postal voting facilities generated turnout of about 50 per cent, compared with average turnout of about 35 per cent in the same districts. All-postal voting also improved public satisfaction with the electoral process, as intended. Nevertheless, there are good reasons to be sceptical about claims that electronic technologies can automatically resuscitate electoral participation. Remote e-voting, in particular, may expand citizen choice, but it proved far less effective in improving turnout than the implementation of old-fashioned snail-mail (all-postal ballots). The age profile of who used different voting mechanisms provides an important clue to their effects. The UK Electoral Commission has evaluated the results of the trials and this analysis will contribute towards the government's proposed reforms of voting procedures in future UK elections. The July 2003 report issued by the UK Electoral Commission, *The Shape of Elections to Come*, recommended rolling out all-postal votes as standard practice for all local elections, with further evaluation before this practice is extended to other types of election.[5] With regard to electronic voting, the Commission reached far more cautious conclusions, suggesting these should continue to be tested, with the overall aim of using electronic voting as a way of providing citizens with more choice about how they cast their ballots, rather than of improving turnout.

The inference that can be drawn for the European Parliamentary elections from the UK experiments is simple: more fundamental structural reforms to the European Union, which could both maximise electoral choices and electoral decisiveness, are required to have major impact on strengthening turnout. Tinkering with e-voting is insufficient, the equivalent of fiddling while Brussels burns, unless elections are seen as relevant and important to people's lives. The most important role of information technology for democracy in the EU may, instead, lie in its potential capacity to strengthen the public sphere by expanding information resources, channels of communication, and networking capacity for many organised interest groups, social movements, NGOs, transnational policy networks, and political parties. The internet is already creating major challenges to the decision-making processes in the EU, exemplified by networks of activists protesting at EU summits. As such the debate about e-voting may well prove largely irrelevant to the primary political impact of the internet on democracy within the European Union.

To consider these issues, the first section of this chapter summarises what we know about the technological, social and practical barriers to electronic voting. The second section sets out the context of the UK local elections and describes the pilot schemes. The third section considers the macro- and micro-level evidence about the impact of modernising voting facilities on electoral turnout, comparing all-postal ballots with the use of a variety of electronic technologies. The conclusion, in the last section, summarises the results and considers the broader implications for the impact of new technologies on citizen participation and civic engagement in European Parliamentary elections.

The pros and cons of remote e-voting

The modernisation of electoral administration is often regarded as a logical extension of technological developments widely used in communications, commerce and government. One of the most common forms of moderni- sation concerns electronic voting, which can be sub-divided into two categories.

Remote electronic voting (or remote e-voting for short), is understood here as the transmission of a secure and secret official ballot to electoral officials via various electronic information and communication technologies at a site located away from the polling station, whether from home, the workplace or a public access point. Remote e-voting is sometimes thought to refer only to internet voting, but in this study we can compare many electronic devices which are capable of transmitting an electronic ballot, including computers, touch-tone terrestrial telephones, cell (mobile) phones, text messaging devices and digital televisions.

By contrast, *on-site electronic voting* technologies are used to vote within the traditional physical location of a polling station, exemplified by touch- activated screens, dedicated computer terminals, or electronic counting devices, as debated after the Florida debacle.

Proponents suggest many advantages that may come from implementing remote e-voting.

- The most important is the added convenience for citizens. By using a telephone, computer, palmtop device or digital television to cast a ballot from home or the workplace, citizens could reduce the time and effort traditionally required to participate in person at the polling station. This may help overcome problems of social exclusion, especially for those with limited mobility such as the elderly, caregivers confined to the home by dependent relatives or employees and shift-workers with little flexibility in their work hours, as well as for those who are travelling away from home and for overseas residents. The implementation of remote e-voting can be regarded in many respects as an extension of the use of other familiar and well-tested voting facilities already widely available in many countries, including the use of postal, absentee, oversees, or advance ballots.[6] In the June 2001 UK general election, for example, 1.3 million postal votes were cast, representing 5.2 per cent of all ballots.[7]

- Moreover, both remote and on-site electronic voting could potentially reduce the information costs of participation, and allow citizens to match their preferences more accurately to their electoral decisions, by providing relevant information at the time that people are casting their ballot, for example by incorporating an optional web page display of photos and standardised biographies linked to each candidate, or by providing a briefing synopsis explaining each side of a referendum issue.

- For officials, well-designed and effective electronic technologies, either remote or on-site, could potentially improve and streamline the process of electoral administration, by increasing the efficiency, speed and accuracy of recording and counting votes.[8]

For all these reasons, the idea of e-voting has been hailed by advocates, particularly those in the industry, as an automatic 'magic ballot' that could entice more people to vote, make citizens more informed and improve vote-counting.

Against these arguments, sceptics counter that many contemporary limitations – technological, socioeconomic and practical – combine to create substantial barriers to the effective implementation of e-voting.

Technological barriers

Democratic electoral systems must meet certain stringent standards of security, data-protection, secrecy, reliability, accuracy, efficiency, integrity and equality. Public confidence in the integrity of the electoral system must be maintained to ensure the legitimacy of the outcome. This makes the administrative challenges of e-voting more difficult than the implementation of many common forms of electronic government or commerce, even banking. If poorly implemented, citizens could be discouraged from voting via new technologies; for example, the design could prove difficult for the disabled, those with low literacy skills or the elderly. Electronic votes cast in a general election could be a high-profile target for malicious, publicity-seeking hackers. The bursting of the dot.com bubble, combined with the recent spate of disruptive viruses and the inundation of e-mail spam, may have depressed public confidence in the security of the internet. Critics claim that the technology required to authenticate voters, and to assure the accuracy and integrity of the election system, either does not exist at present, or is not sufficiently available, to prove equitable and effective. Task forces reviewing the evidence, such as the US NSF and the UK Electoral Reform Society, have proved doubtful about the technological, security and legal issues surrounding e-voting, suggesting that further exploratory pilot studies are required before adoption.[9]

When remote e-voting has been tried in small-scale pilot studies, so far the security and technological issues involved in casting hundreds of votes electronically have often proved problematic. In October 2001, for example, the residents of the Dutch towns of Leidschendam and Voorburg were given the chance to vote via the internet on the choices for the merged towns' new name. The vote was abandoned when it became obvious that more votes had been cast than there were electors.[10] The Arizona Democratic primary election, which also experienced many technical glitches, has been widely quoted, although it remains difficult to assess how far we can generalise from the particular circumstances surrounding this unique contest.[11] Government schemes for remote e-voting in official elections have been developed in the Swiss cantons of Geneva, Zurich and Neuchâtel, and first implemented officially in a Geneva referendum in January 2003.[12] Internet voting has also been employed as an option for shareholder elections by companies such as Chevron, Lucent Technologies and Xerox, as well as in student elections.[13]

It remains unclear whether the purely *administrative* problems revolving at present around the practical issues of security, secrecy and integrity might eventually be resolved in future by suitable technological and scientific innovations. Potential problems of voter fraud might be overcome by advances in biometric voice and retina scanning and fingerprint recognition, for example, or by the widespread use of 'smart cards' as identifiers with a computer chip and unique digital certificates.

Social barriers

Setting aside these important technical and security matters for the moment, another fundamental issue concerns the potential problems that could arise if remote e-voting serves to exacerbate existing structural inequalities in electoral participation. In democracies the electoral process has to be equally available to every citizen, without discriminating against any particular group. This important principle is widely recognised in locating traditional polling stations throughout local communities, or in translating the instructions for registration and voting into the languages spoken by minority populations. Critics charge that implementation of remote e-voting from home or work could violate the equitable principle, given the widespread existence of the familiar 'digital divide' in internet access. Making remote voting easier for those with access to electronic technologies could further skew who participates, and therefore political influence, towards more affluent and wired socioeconomic groups. While not actively harming poorer neighbourhoods, remote e-voting could still potentially privilege some social sectors.

This argument holds less force when it comes to remote voting through special dedicated public terminals located in the community, such as any voting facilities established in libraries, schools or even supermarkets, where similar principles would apply to those determining the location of traditional polling stations. But the argument becomes relevant if remote e-voting is available from any home or workplace computer terminal, which is the most radical and exciting application of this principle.

Official estimates suggest that by spring 2003 about half of the British population (54 per cent) had used the internet in the previous three months, and 60 per cent had used the internet at some time.[14] About 40 per cent of households had an internet connection, a higher proportion than the European average (see Table 3.1). Other common communication technologies remain far more widespread, however, including the availability of mobile phones, found in 65 per cent of households. Other technologies are also widely available throughout Britain, including digital TVs (in 35 per cent of households), VCRs, Teletext TV, satellite TV and fax machines.

Table 3.1 Trends in household access to communication technologies, UK, 1970–2002

	Telephone	Mobile phone	Video recorder	Satellite receiver[a]	Home computer	Internet connection
1970	35	–	–	–	–	–
1975	52	–	–	–	–	–
1980	72	–	–	–	–	–
1985	81	–	30	–	13	–
1990	87	–	61	–	17	–
1994–5	91	–	76	–	–	–
1995–6	92	–	79	–	–	–
1996–7	93	16	82	19	27	–
1997–8	94	20	84	26	29	–
1998–9	95	27	85	28	33	10
1999–2000	95	44	86	32	38	19
2000–1	93	47	87	40	44	32
2001–2	94	65	90	43	49	40

Sources: *UK Expenditure and Food Survey* www.statistics.government.uk/StatBase.

Notes: Percentage of UK households with durable goods 1970 to 2001–2. a Includes digital and cable receivers.

Many have expressed concern about the 'digital divide', the substantial differential in internet access between the information haves and have-nots, including between rich and poor, as well as between graduates and those with minimal educational qualifications, between the younger and older generations, as well as between countries.[15] The European digital divide in the mid-1990s presents a similar picture to that found in the US; in 1996, access was concentrated among the younger generations, more affluent households, university graduates, managers and white collar workers (as well as students) and, to a lesser extent, among men (see Table 3.2). By spring 2000 the social profile in Europe had not changed that much as the strongest rise in access has been among the most affluent households, the well educated, and among managerial professionals, although use has spread rapidly among the early-middle aged, as well as the youngest age group. Multivariate analysis in Table 3.3 confirms that

Table 3.2 Social profile of online community, EU-15 1996–2000

	Online Spring 1996 (%)	Online Spring 2000 (%)	Change 1996–2000
Age			
15–25	9	28	+19
26–44	7	28	+21
45–64	5	21	+16
65+	1	6	+ 5
HH income category			
– –	4	12	+ 8
–	3	15	+12
+	5	24	+19
++	10	44	+34
Age finished education			
Up to 15	1	7	+ 6
16–19 years	4	19	+15
20+	9	38	+29
Gender			
Male	6	25	+19
Female	4	21	+17
Occupational status			
Manager	14	44	+30
Other white collar	8	29	+21
Manual worker	3	15	+12
Home worker	2	8	+ 6
Unemployed	3	10	+ 7
Student	13	44	+31
All EU-15			
All	5	22	+17

Sources: Eurobarometer 44.2 Spring 1996; 53.0 Spring 2000.

Table 3.3 Models predicting use of the internet, EU-15 1996 and 2000

	1996			2000		
	B	S.E.	Sig.	B	S.E.	Sig.
Demographics						
Age	−0.035	0.002	0.000	−0.025	0.002	0.000
Gender	0.588	0.052	0.000	0.230	0.048	0.000
Education	0.783	0.040	0.000	0.627	0.038	0.000
Income	0.303	0.020	0.000	0.252	0.019	0.000
Class	0.827	0.066	0.000	0.919	0.062	0.000
Nation						
Sweden	1.01	0.188	0.000	1.10	0.112	0.000
UK	0.966	0.186	0.000	0.003	0.131	0.984
Finland	0.784	0.189	0.849	−0.121	0.118	0.391
Netherlands	0.578	0.190	0.012	0.966	0.107	0.000
Denmark	0.573	0.190	0.003	0.727	0.110	0.000
Ireland	0.359	0.221	0.104	−0.620	0.120	0.000
Austria	0.020	0.210	0.923	−0.602	0.120	0.000
Germany	−0.035	0.187	0.012	−0.832	0.106	0.000
Italy	−0.507	0.201	0.002	−0.534	0.120	0.000
Portugal	−0.563	0.224	0.000	−1.42	0.166	0.000
Belgium	−0.628	0.254	0.013	−0.584	0.117	0.000
France	−0.774	0.202	0.000	−1.04	0.132	0.000
Spain	−1.02	0.217	0.000	−1.33	0.146	0.000
Greece	−1.43	0.257	0.000	−2.11	0.179	0.000
Constant	−5.3			−2.968		
N	65178			16078		
With internet access (%)	5.0			22.4		
Cox-Snell R^2	0.073			0.187		
Nagelkerke R^2	0.209			0.293		
Correct (%)	94.5			81.0		

Source: EuroBarometer 44.2bis Spring 1996, EuroBarometer 53.0 Spring 2000.

Notes: The table reports the beta coefficients predicting use of the internet based on logistic regression models. Use of the internet and use of party websites are each measured as a dichotomy where 1 = yes, 0 = no. Luxembourg, as closest to the overall mean, was excluded from the national list in both surveys. Age: years; Education: age finished FT education; Income: harmonized HH income scale; Class: manual (0)/non-manual HoH; Gender: male (1) female (0).

by 2000 the digital divide remained significant by age, gender, education, income and class, as well as showing the marked contrasts in access between the countries of Northern and Southern Europe. The age effects turn out to be very important for turnout, as discussed later.

This familiar pattern suggests that if remote e-voting, via computer terminals in the home or workplace, were introduced within the next few years into UK elections (including those for the European Parliament),[16] then the digital divide will probably reinforce, or even widen, many of the familiar socioeconomic disparities in electoral participation that already exist, including those of social class, education, gender and income.[17] Yet, there is one important qualification to this conclusion, as remote electronic voting could encourage younger people to take advantage of this opportunity.

Of course this argument does not apply to other forms of remote e-voting, such as via public kiosks at traditional polling stations, or in public access locations such as libraries, town halls, schools and community centres. On the other hand, the real advantages of using electronic voting are reduced through these channels, because people would still have to travel to a public location, while the disadvantages of electronic over paper-ballots for administrative security remain.

Practical barriers

But for the purposes of exploring the arguments further let us assume for the moment that the familiar digital divide in society is in the process of shrinking, as access to the wide range of new communication and information technologies, including text-messaging mobile phones, teletext digital television and the internet, gradually diffuse throughout affluent societies. If the issues of technological security and of socioeconomic equality are resolved, the key question then arises whether the introduction of remote e-voting would actually facilitate participation.

There are many reasons to remain sceptical about this claim. The theory that we can use to understand electoral participation, developed more fully elsewhere, suggests that the incentives motivating citizens to cast a ballot represent a product of three factors (see Figure 3.1):[18]

- *Electoral costs* involved in registering to vote, sorting out relevant information, deciding how to vote, and then actually casting a ballot;
- *Electoral choices*, determined largely by the range of parties, candidates and issues listed on the ballot paper; and
- *Electoral decisiveness*, influenced by how far votes cast for each party, candidate or issue are thought to determine the outcome.

Electoral costs

The theory assumes that rational citizens will be less likely to vote if they face major electoral costs of participating. This includes registering as electors, becoming informed about the issues, parties and candidates, and finally casting a ballot to express their voting choice. Standard rational choice theories suggest that, all other things being equal, the deterrent of higher costs reduces electoral participation.

Holding elections on a weekend or holiday, or over a series of days, rather than on a workday can reduce costs. Registration procedures are often believed to be an important hurdle. In many countries, including

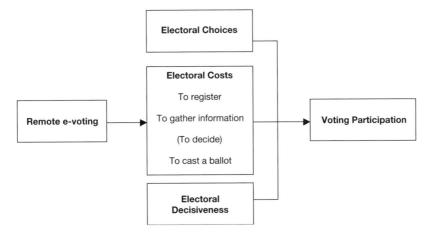

Figure 3.1 Model of voting participation

Britain, Sweden and Canada, registration is the responsibility of the government, conducted via a door-to-door canvas or annual census, so most eligible citizens are automatically enrolled to vote. In others, including the US, France and Brazil, citizens have to apply to register, often well ahead of the election, and complicated, time-consuming or restrictive practices can depress participation levels.[19]

In this regard, the use of remote e-voting can be seen as essentially similar in principle to other remote voting facilities in common use for casting a ballot, exemplified by the widespread availability of special arrangements for mobile populations, including the use of mail, proxy, absentee or overseas votes, as well as polling facilities for the elderly and disabled in nursing homes and hospitals.[20] But casting the ballot is only the last step in the electoral decision-making process, and not necessarily the most significant one if people lack the sense that they have electoral choices matching their preferences, and that voting counts towards the outcome.

Electoral choices

Electoral choices are determined by broader characteristics of the political system including the options available on the ballot, notably the range of parties and candidates contesting elected offices, and the policy alternatives listed for referenda issues. In turn, these options can be related to the type of electoral system, the party system and other basic political institutions such as parliamentary or presidential executives.

Rational voter theories suggest that in general, all other things being equal, the greater the range of choices available on the ballot, the more the public will find an option (a party, candidate or referenda issue) that reflects their own viewpoint, preferences and interests and, therefore, the stronger the incentive to vote. In elections to the European Parliament, citizens are presented with a range of parties on the ballot paper in each member state, but in so far as there is little difference between the parties on some of the major issues facing the future of the European Union, then citizens face a restricted choice in European elections.[21] Remote e-voting is unlikely to have an impact on any of these factors.

Electoral decisiveness

Electoral decisiveness is also important; meaning the political benefits anticipated from casting a ballot in determining the composition of parliament, government and the public policy agenda. In elections that are anticipated to be close (on the basis of past results, opinion polls or media commentary), citizens are likely to feel a greater incentive to get to the polls than in those where the outcome appears to be a foregone conclusion. Of course, the actual benefits of casting a single vote may, on purely rational grounds, be illusory, because one vote is unlikely to decide the outcome of an election, but this is not to deny the psychological belief that in close elections, each vote is believed to count for more than in safe contests. Hence, for example, British studies have found that the closer the difference in the national shares of the vote between the two major parties, the higher the level of electoral participation during the postwar era.[22] The marginality of British constituencies has also commonly been found to be one of the best predictors of turnout in each seat.[23]

There are trade-offs between electoral choices and electoral decisiveness. Widening the range of choices on the ballot paper may allow citizens to find a closer match to their interests. But if the party system becomes too fragmented with multiple choices, then casting a vote for smaller parties will be even less likely to influence the outcome, whether for parliament, government or the policy agenda. Moreover, a wider range of choices also simultaneously increases the costs of becoming informed about alternative candidates, parties and issues.

Given this understanding, this study hypothesises that the introduction of remote e-voting from the home or workplace would probably marginally reduce the costs of casting a ballot at a polling station (see Figure 3.1). But e-voting would be unlikely to affect other important costs, such as the significant cognitive demands required to sort out the relevant information in deciding how to vote, nor would it influence electoral choices and electoral decisiveness. As such, the internet cannot be regarded as a magic panacea for all the ills of European elections, which are the result of more deep-seated problems in how far voters feel that they can determine the outcome of European Union politics through casting a ballot in European elections.

Evidence for evaluating remote e-voting

What evidence would allow us to evaluate these issues? Here, we can turn to the British case, which has gone further than any other country in testing the impact of a wide variety of remote e-voting technologies using official ballots cast during actual elections.

Concern about electoral participation has risen in Britain. During post-war general elections, UK turnout (measured as the proportion of the voting age population casting a valid vote) has seen a broad picture of trend-less fluctuations (see Figure 3.2). But the 2001 UK general election saw turnout plummet, from 71.5 per cent to 59.4 per cent of the electorate, the lowest level since the 'khaki' election of 1918. Moreover, this followed a series of local elections from 1998 to 2000 that witnessed historically low levels of turnout, reaching the nadir of one-quarter (27 per cent) of the electorate bothering to vote in 2000 (see Figure 3.3). If unchecked, this pattern is worrying for democracy as the legitimacy of the electoral process, and the mandate of the government, might eventually be undermined.

The Labour Government has proposed modernising electoral administration in the attempt to re-engage the electorate. Recent changes enabled

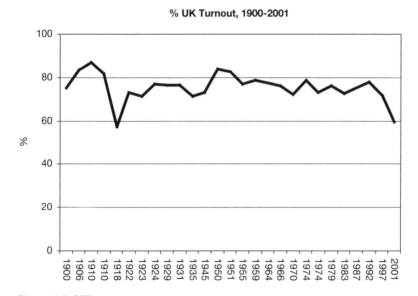

Figure 3.2 UK turnout

Sources: Rallings, C. and Thrasher, M. (2000) *British Electoral Facts 1832–1999* (Aldershot: Ashgate); Norris, P. *The British Parliamentary Constituency Database, 1992–2001.* Available at: http://ksghome.harvard.edu/~pnorris/data/data.htm.

Note: UK turnout is based on the number of votes cast as a proportion of the eligible electorate.

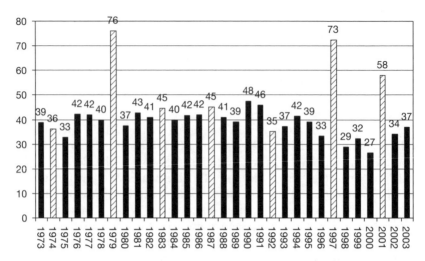

Figure 3.3 Turnout in UK local elections, 1973–2003

Sources: Rallings, C. and Thrasher, M. (2000) *British Electoral Facts 1832–1999* (Aldershot: Ashgate).

Note: Turnout is defined here as valid votes cast as a percentage of the eligible electorate. The highlighted (striped) columns are general election years. When both contests are held simultaneously, local election turnout rises sharply. When held separately, turnout is closer to the local election average.

by the *Representation of the People Acts* 2000 and 2001 include universal postal voting (available on request without needing a reason), an extension of the traditional polling hours, and more modern methods of how citizens can cast their ballots, including the possible use of telephone and internet-based voting.

The UK Electoral Commission is the official agency charged with implementing the process of modernisation and advising the Deputy Prime Minister about the most effective options in electoral administration. Innovations in polling places, polling hours, and all-postal ballots were tested in 38 pilot schemes used among 3.5 million eligible electors in the May 2000 local elections. All-postal ballots remove the need for citizens to apply for a mail ballot; instead, local authorities provide all citizens on the electoral register in an area with the automatic ability to cast a mail ballot during an extended period of about two weeks prior to election day. These initiatives were followed in the May 2002 local elections by 30 more pilots tried among 2.5 million eligible electors with a greater range of innovations directed at improving turnout, counting and the provision of information. The Commission concluded that these generated interesting preliminary results, with significant increases in voting turnout (particularly from all-postal voting schemes), no significant technical problems of implementation or electoral management, and no evidence of fraud. Following evaluation, the government signalled its desire to use electronic voting by the next general election after 2006,[24] and the Spending Review allocated substantial resources to fund further pilot studies conducted at local government level. Nevertheless, many significant questions remained concerning variations in turnout among wards, the best methods of avoiding electoral fraud, and issues of scalability across whole councils. The Commission concluded that the initial lessons needed to be tested more extensively, especially facilities for remote e-voting using multiple technologies.[25]

The May 2003 pilot schemes

Accordingly, a further series of 59 pilot schemes were conducted in the May 2003 local elections, the focus of this chapter. In total, 17 of the 2003 pilot schemes explored innovative ways of remote electronic voting using a range of technologies including mobile phone text message services, touch telephones, local digital television, on-line internet voting using home computers, terminals in local libraries and council-run information kiosks. For comparison, the Electoral Commission also continued to examine the use of all-postal ballots in over half the pilot schemes.[26] The map in Figure 3.4 illustrates the location of the pilot local authority areas, selected from across all of England. Examples of the May 2003 initiatives included the following:

- Chorley offered electors all-postal ballots, internet and telephone voting throughout their area, and used electronic counting.
- Ipswich offered citizens internet, telephone and SMS text messaging ballots.
- Shrewsbury and Atcham used all-postal voting, internet, telephone, and digital TV voting, as well as electronic counting.
- Sheffield used voting via public kiosks, internet, telephone and mobile phone text messaging.
- Medway, and Windsor and Maidenhead extended traditional voting hours.

Other pilots used electronic counting, mobile polling stations and extended polling hours. Timing is believed to be important: most countries hold their elections on a single day, usually at the weekend, which makes it easier for employed people to visit a polling station. In a few countries, however, elections are spread over more than one day. Franklin compared average turnout 1960–95 in parliamentary elections in 29 countries and found that compulsory voting, Sunday voting and postal voting facilities all proved important predictors, along with the proportionality of the electoral system, although not the number of days that polls were open.[27]

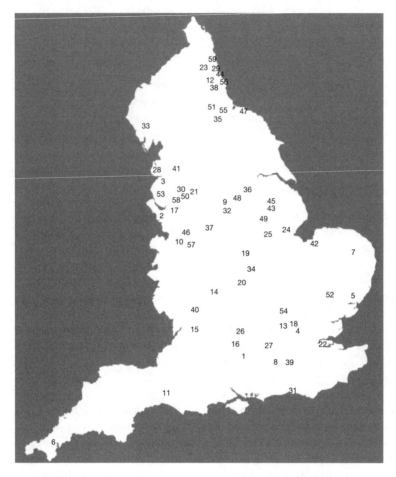

Key to map:

e-Pilot
1 Basingstoke and Deane
2 Chester
3 Chorley
4 Epping Forest
5 Ipswich
6 Kerrier
7 Norwich
8 Rushmoor
9 Sheffield
10 Shrewsbury and Altcham
11 South Somerset
12 South Tyneside
13 St Albans
14 Stratford on Avon
15 Stroud
16 Swindon
17 Vale Royal

Administrative innovations
18 Broxbourne
19 Charnwood

20 East Northamptonshire
21 Manchester
22 Medway
23 North East (Chester-le-Street, Derwentside and Wear Valley)
24 North Kesleven
25 North West Leicestershire
26 South Oxfordshire
27 Windsor and Maidenhead

All-postal
28 Blackpool
29 Blyth Vlley
30 Bolton
31 Brighton and Hove
32 Chesterfield
33 Copeland
34 Corby
35 Darlington
36 Doncaster
37 East Staffordshire
38 Gateshead

39 Guildford
40 Herefordshire
41 Hyndburn
42 King's Lynn and West Norfolk
43 Lincoln
44 Newcastle
45 North Lincolnshire
46 North Shropshire
47 Redcar and Cleveland
48 Rotherham
49 Rushcliffe
50 Salford
51 Sedgefield
52 St Edmundsbury
53 St Helens
54 Stevenage
55 Stockton-on-Tees
56 Sunderland
57 Talford and Wrekin
58 Trafford Borough
59 Wansbeck District

Figure 3.4 Location of English local authorities holding pilot schemes in May 2003
Source: The Electoral Commission, UK.

The political context of the May 2003 local elections

The political context of the UK local elections in May 2003 concerned a mid-term contest with elections to the Scottish Parliament and the Welsh Assembly, as well as local government elections in Scotland and England (outside of Greater London). The last time the English councils came up for election, in 1999, the Conservatives gained 1,300 seats, many from Labour, despite these results failing to translate into any substantial progress for the Conservative Party in the 2001 general election. In May 2003, in a low-key campaign, it was widely expected that Labour would experience some electoral damage, after being in power for six years and during a period of public disquiet about the perceived lacklustre delivery of public services, as well as massive opposition to Blair's support for the Iraq war. The question before the election was which opposition party would benefit most from Labour's mid-term blues in terms of gains in the share of votes, seats and councils.

On election night, the Conservatives won 35 per cent of the local council vote, a modest (+1 per cent) rise from 2002. Nevertheless, they enjoyed net gains of 566 seats, winning control of an additional 31 councils. The Liberal Democrats also had a successful night, with an estimated 27 per cent of the vote, making net gains of 193 seats and 5 councils.[28] The far right anti-immigration British National Party achieved a controversial local triumph by fielding a record 221 candidates (many in the north-east and north-west), gaining 11 seats, becoming the second largest party in Burnley. Labour were the main losers in the English council elections, with 30 per cent of the vote (down 3 per cent from 2002), suffering a net loss of 883 seats and 28 councils. This was a substantial loss, although not outstanding historically for a mid-term period. At the same time, Labour retained a working majority in the Welsh Assembly, and they were returned again as the biggest party in the Scottish Parliament.

Two sources of evidence are available to analyse the patterns of turnout. First, we can examine the change in the macro levels of turnout in the local authority districts using the pilot schemes in May 2003 compared against the level of turnout in the last benchmark election in these same areas.[29]

Moreover, to understand the micro-level behaviour of voters, and the reasons behind patterns of electoral participation, we can analyse the post-election survey conducted by MORI on behalf of the Electoral Commission in these districts. MORI interviewed a representative sample of approximately 200 adults aged 18+ in 29 of the 59 authorities that were piloting new voting arrangements at the May 2003 elections. A total of 6,185 interviews were conducted. Quotas were set by age, gender and work status with *c*.100 voters and 100 non-voters interviewed in each authority. Data are weighted by age, sex, working status to the known profile (using 2001 Census data) and by turnout on 1 May 2003. Aggregate data are also weighted by the population size of each pilot authority. Fieldwork took place between 2 May and 12 May 2003.[30]

The impact of e-voting

There were many reasons, both long-term and short-term, to expect that electoral participation would fall further in these contests. In Britain, power has gradually drained away from town halls, as more and more attempts have been made by both Conservative and Labour administrations to curtail local fiscal autonomy and control the standards of public service delivery in local areas. People may also be suffering increasingly from voter fatigue and 'election overload': compared with previous decades, there are now a regular series of European elections, Mayoral elections, Scottish/Welsh regional elections and occasional referenda, as well as general elections and local elections. As with other new assemblies, the first elections to the Scottish Parliament and Welsh Assembly could also be expected to attract higher than average turnout through a 'honeymoon' effect, and participation would be likely to fall in subsequent contests.

The particular May 2003 election was also a low-key affair. Since they came to power in 1997, Labour had enjoyed a continuous lead over the Conservatives in the national monthly opinion polls (with one minor blip). Usually in British elections, the safer the government's lead, the lower the turnout.[31] In addition, since Labour moved back into the centre of the political spectrum in the mid-1990s, British party competition has moderated. Voters, at the time, perceived few major contrasts between the main parties on most issues, with Labour under the leadership of Tony Blair bang in the centre of the political spectrum, the Liberal Democrats under Charles Kennedy close to the centre-left, and the Conservatives flailing away under Iain Duncan Smith somewhere towards the right.[32] The local election campaign also had fairly fuzzy issues: there was little conflict over the issues of taxes and spending, education and health, and nothing to compare with the way that the issue of the Conservative Poll Tax mobilised voters during the early 1990s. The public and the news media had paid even less attention than usual to the local campaign in the run up to polling day, with events in Iraq dominating the headlines. In the run up to the election, most of the editorial speculation about domestic politics had surrounded who might replace the Conservative leader, Iain Duncan Smith, in the event of a poor result for Tory Central Office, and whether the nationalists would do well in Scotland.

Given this context, not surprisingly the overall level of turnout in May 2003 was 49 per cent in Scotland (down 9 per cent from 1999, the inaugural election for the Scottish Parliament), and 38.2 per cent in Wales (down 8 per cent). In England, however, despite expectations, local government turnout was 37 per cent, a rise of 5 per cent from 1999 and a rise of 3 per cent from 2002. How far was the increase in the English local elections due to the pilot initiatives?

Table 3.4 shows the districts where all-postal voting was used, the most comparable previous election, the turnout in May 2003, and the change in turnout. The results illustrate the outstanding success of all-postal ballots: on average, turnout increased from one-third (34 per cent) to almost half (49.3 per cent) of the electorate in these districts. The increase was even more remarkable in some of the northern areas that had been lowest in turnout, almost doubling voting participation in Blyth Valley, for example, as well as Rotherham, Sunderland and Blackpool. By contrast, there were more modest increases registered in most councils, and only three cases with any slight fall. The fact that a 15 per cent increase in turnout was also found in the 2002 all-postal pilots confirms the consistency and robustness of these results. The Electoral Commission also found very limited evidence that the use of all-postal ballots led to any increase in fraud or electoral offences. Of course, part of the rise in turnout there could be due to a one-off 'Hawthorne effect', if local authorities mounting these initiatives publicise the opportunities to vote by mail more actively than usual, and if voters respond to the publicity and to the novelty-value. On the other hand, the fact that the rise in turnout was fairly substantial and reasonably consistent across many different types of urban and rural areas, as well as parts of England, suggests that at least some of the benefits of postal voting are likely to persist if used more widely in future local elections.

By contrast, the districts using electronic voting showed a far more mixed picture of turnout, as illustrated in Table 3.5 and Figure 3.5. Overall only about 9 per cent of the electorate in these districts used the electronic technologies to cast a ballot, with most of the public opting for traditional methods of voting. Three districts using electronic voting (South Salisbury, Shrewsbury and Atcham, and Vale Royal) did experience a rise in turnout of 9–12 per cent, but two of these also used all-postal voting as well. Overall, two-thirds of the areas experimenting with electronic voting registered a modest fall in turnout, not any rise, disappointing the hopes of the reformers.

Both all-postal voting and remote electronic voting share certain important features, both offering voters additional convenience over traditional in-person visits to the polling station. So why should areas using these facilities generate such different patterns of macro-level turnout? Here we need to turn to the micro-level survey data to understand more fully how the public responded to these opportunities, and which social groups used the all-postal and electronic voting facilities. In particular, even if the electronic facilities generated no positive effects in aggregate turnout that were evident at district level, there could still be differential patterns in which certain social groups took greatest advantage of the new voting facilities. In particular, it is important to monitor whether younger people – who are both the most wired generation and also the group least likely to turnout using conventional methods – might prove more likely than average to use the electronic voting facilities. Figure 3.6 shows the familiar curvilinear pattern of reported voting by age (in years): as a multitude of studies have found,

Table 3.4 Impact of all-postal voting in the 1 May 2003 UK local election pilot schemes

Name of authority	Year of last comparable election	Turnout at last comparable election (%)	Type of election this time (whole/3rd)	Start of polling date	Total turnout May 2003 (%)	Change in turnout since last comparable election (%)
Blyth Valley BC	1999	27	Whole	15 Apr	52.00	25
Rotherham MBC	2002	27	Thirds	17 Apr	51.30	24
Sunderland City C	2002	22	Thirds	17 Apr	46.46	24
Herefordshire CC	1999	38	Whole	15/17 Apr	61.00	23
Blackpool BC	2000	29	Whole	17 Apr	50.43	22
St Helens MBC	2002	26	Thirds	17 Apr	48.00	22
Stockton-on-Tees BC	1999	31	Whole	13 Apr	52.00	22
Derwentside, Chester-le-Street and Wear Valley	1999	31	Whole	17 Apr	52.40	21
Lincoln City C	2002	26	Thirds	17 Apr	47.33	21
Telford and Wrekin	1999	28	Whole	10 Apr	48.65	21
Darlington BC	1999	34	Whole	14 Apr	51.54	18
Doncaster C	2002	29	Thirds	16 Apr	47.00	18
Newcastle City C	2002	32	Thirds	17 Apr	49.83	18
North Lincolnshire	1999	33	Whole	15/16 Apr	51.28	18
Wansbeck DC	1999	32	Whole	17 Apr	50.20	18
Chesterfield BC	1999	35	Whole	18 Apr	51.69	17

	Year		Whole/Thirds	Date		
Copeland BC	1999	39	Whole	14 Apr	55.70	17
Guildford BC	1999	37	Whole	11 Apr	54.00	17
Hyndburn BC	2002	36	Thirds	17 Apr	51.47	16
Salford City C	2002	25	Thirds	14 Apr	41.00	16
Redcar and Cleveland BC	1999	37	Whole	17/21 Apr	51.50	15
Rushcliffe BC	1999	40	Whole	19/22 Apr	54.00	15
Sedgefield BC	1999	30	Whole	14 Apr	44.15	14
Corby BC	1999	31	Whole	12/14 Apr	43.00	12
East Staffordshire BC	1999	34	Whole	10/11 Apr	44.97	11
King's Lynn and West Norfolk BC	1999	36	Whole	15 Apr	47.66	11
North Shropshire DC	1999	33	Whole	17 Apr	43.80	11
Bolton MBC	2002	32	Thirds	15 Apr	42.00	10
Brighton and Hove City C	1999	38	Whole	15 Apr	45.96	8
St Edmundsbury BC	1999	38	Whole	19/22 Apr	38.50	1
Stevenage BC	2002	53	Thirds	16 Apr	52.20	–1
Trafford MBC	2002	53	Thirds	14 Apr	52.39	–1
Gateshead MBC	2002	57	Thirds	17 Apr	54.65	–2
Average		34			49.34	15

Source: The UK Electoral Commission.

Note: Turnout is based on the number of votes cast as a proportion of the eligible electorate. The most comparable election depends upon whether whole (1999) or one-third (2002) elections are used in each district. BC = Borough Council. MBC = Metropolitan Borough Council. DC = District Council. C = Council.

Table 3.5 Impact of remote electronic voting in the 1 May 2003 UK local election pilot schemes

Name of authority	Year of last comparable election	Turnout at last comparable election (%)	Type of election this time (whole/3rd)	Total number of votes cast	Total turnout in May 2003 (%)	Change in turnout from last comparable election (%)	Number of votes cast using e-channels	Electorate using e-channels (%)	Turnout using e-channels	Notes
Vale Royal	1999	30.8	Whole	40,904	43.6	12.8	9,752	10	23.8	
Shrewsbury and Atcham	2002	43.2	Thirds	22,039	54.5	11.3	4,090	10	19.0	(i)
South Somerset	1999	38.0	Whole	53,311	46.9	8.9	8,428	7	15.8	(i)
St Albans	2002	38.1	Thirds		43.4	5.3				
Basingstoke and Deane	2002	29.0	Thirds	28,317	30.9	1.9	3,442	4	10.7	
Norwich	2002	35.3	Thirds	33,866	35.8	0.5	20,845	12	37.0	
Sheffield	2002	29.7	Thirds	110,988	29.5	-0.2	10,189	7	25.0	
Swindon	2002	31.2	Thirds	40,812	29.8	-1.4	6,699	10	29.1	
Chester	2002	35.5	Thirds	22,482	34.0	-1.5	14,683	27	95.0	
Epping Forest	2000	30.0	Thirds	15,431	28.4	-1.6	2,760	6	15.0	
Rushmoor	2002	34.7	Thirds	18,345	31.0	-3.7	3,374	5	15.0	
Kerrier	1999	32.2	Whole	17,662	28.3	-3.9	4,176	8	20.4	
Stroud	2002	42.6	Thirds	20,441	36.7	-5.9	6,183	9	21.7	
Ipswich	2002	39.0	Thirds	28,516	31.9	-7.1	6,008	5	11.5	
South Tyneside	2002	54.7	Thirds	52,368	46.1	-8.6				(i)
Stratford-on-Avon	2002	44.6	Thirds	21,669	35.6	-9.0	4,176	7	19.0	
Chorley	2002	61.5	Thirds	32,900	49.9	-11.6	3,072	6	9.0	(i)
Average		38.2			37.4	-0.8	22,270	8.8	24.5	

Source: The UK Electoral Commission.

Notes: Turnout is based on the number of votes cast as a proportion of the eligible electorate. (i) Includes all-postal ballots.

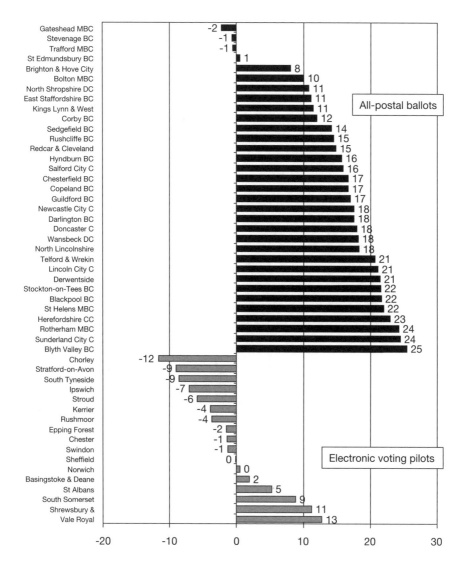

Figure 3.5 Percentage change in turnout in the May 2003 UK local election pilot schemes

Source: The UK Electoral Commission.

Note: Turnout is defined here as valid votes cast as a percentage of the eligible electorate. For details, including the date of the previous election used for calculating the per cent change in turnout in each district, see Tables 3.4 and 3.5.

Table 3.6 Reported voting participation, by age group

Type of pilot	Age group	Did not vote	Reported voting		Voted by post	
			Voted at a polling station	Voted electronically	No.	(%)
Combined pilots	Younger	84	N/a	8	8	100
	Middle aged	61	N/a	9	30	100
	Older	25	N/a	7	68	100
All-postal pilots	Younger	81	N/a	N/a	19	100
	Middle aged	58	N/a	N/a	42	100
	Older	29	N/a	N/a	71	100
Electronic pilots	Younger	84	10	5	1	100
	Middle aged	70	20	8	3	100
	Older	47	38	8	8	100

Source: MORI post-election survey of 6,185 electors 2–12 May 2003 in 29 local authorities piloting new voting arrangement. The survey results were weighted by wtfinal. For further details see: www.mori.com/polls/2003/electoralcommission.shtml.

Notes: Younger (18–29 years old), Middle aged (30–59), Older (60+ years old). N/a not applicable in pilot area.

younger people are persistently less likely to participate, with voting rising to a peak in late middle-age, until there is a fall among the over-70s, who often have difficulty in getting out to the polls.

The sample is not large enough to be able to monitor reliably each of the specific technologies used, such as text messaging or the internet, but respondents in the MORI survey can be divided into three major categories according to whether the type of pilot scheme used in their district was either combined, any electronic pilot, or all-postal pilot. Table 3.6 shows the breakdown of reported voting by the type of pilot areas and by major age groups.

The combined pilot areas allowed people to vote automatically by a postal ballot, or alternatively by some form of electronic technologies (whether by telephone, internet, text messaging or digital TV). In these areas there were enormous disparities in reported voting participation by age group: 84 per cent of young people said that they did not vote, compared with only one-quarter of the over-60s. Just fewer than one in ten in each of the age groups used the electronic channels of voting, and this pattern was fairly similar among young and old. But postal voting proved by far the most popular among the older group, who often have limited mobility.

The all-postal ballot pilots generated similar age differentials to the combined pilot areas: only one-fifth of the younger group reported voting compared with almost three-quarters of the elderly.

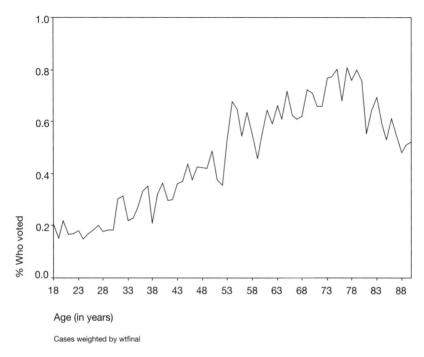

Figure 3.6 The age profile of voters in UK local authority elections pilot areas

Source: MORI post-election survey of 6,185 electors 2–12 May 2003 in 29 UK local authorities piloting new voting arrangements. The survey results were weighted by wtfinal. For more details see: www.mori.com/polls/2003/electoralcommission.shtml.

Note: Reported voting by age (in years) in all UK local authority pilot areas.

The last category of pilot schemes allowed people to cast a ballot either electronically or by traditional in-person polling stations. In these areas, electors could also opt for postal vote by application, but this process was not automatic. This category saw an intriguing pattern: as we have seen aggregate levels of turnout actually fell in some of these areas, and overall across all these pilot schemes turnout did not increase. One of the main reasons uncovered by this analysis is that without all-postal voting (where the local authority *automatically* sends everyone the option to cast a mail ballot) the elderly are less likely to vote either in person at polling stations or electronically through new technologies. And in these areas, while younger people do use the new electronic voting channels, nevertheless, they remain less likely to vote than the older generation. Figure 3.7 confirms this pattern, where age (in years) is regressed on reported turnout in each category of pilot schemes. Compared with other pilots, the strength of the age regression coefficient is reduced in the electronic pilot schemes, but this effect occurs mainly by depressing the participation of the elderly, rather than by boosting the participation of the young.

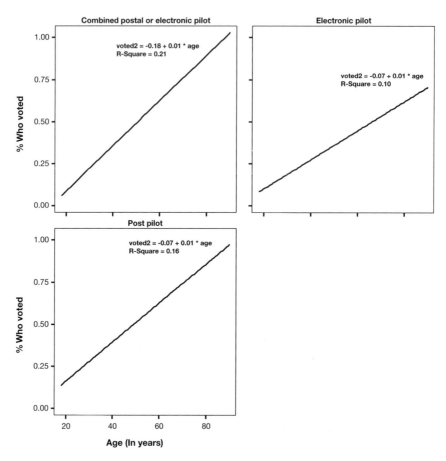

Figure 3.7 The age profile of voters in UK local authority elections, by type of pilot scheme

Source: MORI post-election survey of 6,185 electors 2–12 May 2003 in 29 UK local authorities piloting new voting arrangements. The survey results were weighted by wtfinal. For more details see: www.mori.com/polls/2003/electoralcommission.shtml.

Note: The lines represent the linear regression of age (in years) by reported voting.

Multivariate analysis, introducing controls for gender, race and class into logistic regression models of voting participation in each category of pilot schemes, confirmed that the effect of age remained consistently significant even after applying controls, and that the age effect diminished most under the electronic pilot schemes (see Table 3.7). This suggests that the use of electronic voting technologies combined with in-person voting in traditional polling stations alone, *if they are not supplemented by the simultaneous employment of automatic postal ballots*, would not bolster turnout. Quite simply, the elderly generation remain the least comfortable using new

Table 3.7 Regression models predicting turnout in UK local elections

Type of pilot scheme in area	B	S.E.	Sig.
Combined postal + electronic pilots			
Gender (Male = 1)	−0.88	0.18	0.000
Ethnicity (White = 1)	0.64	0.82	0.434
Logged age (Years)	6.65	0.65	0.000
Class (4-cat)	0.09	0.08	0.257
Constant	9.89		
Nagelkerke R^2	0.31		
Correctly predicted (%)	72.80		
No. of cases	1,125		
Electronic pilots			
Gender (Male = 1)	0.30	0.10	0.002
Ethnicity (White = 1)	0.17	0.29	0.554
Logged age (Years)	4.59	0.33	0.000
Class (4-cat)	0.17	0.04	0.000
Constant	7.87		
Nagelkerke R^2	0.15		
Correctly predicted (%)	70.00		
No. of cases	2,416		
Postal pilots			
Gender (Male = 1)	−0.45	0.08	0.000
Ethnicity (White = 1)	0.12	0.20	0.552
Logged age (Years)	5.35	0.26	0.000
Class (4-cat)	0.09	0.04	0.012
Constant	8.35		
Nagelkerke R^2	0.21		
Correctly predicted (%)	68.70		
No. of cases	2,444		

Source: MORI post-election survey of 6,185 electors 2–12 May 2003 in 29 local authorities piloting new voting arrangements. The survey results were weighted by wtfinal. For further details see: www.mori.com/polls/2003/electoralcommission.shtml.

Note: Binary logistic models predicting reported turnout in the UK local elections, May 2003.

technologies, having not grown up in the world of micro-chips, mobiles and text messaging that is now ubiquitous among the younger generation. And the older generation is the social sector with the strongest habits of voting, and yet the least physical mobility, who are therefore most motivated to take advantage of opportunities to cast a ballot by mail. The theory developed earlier suggests that reducing the costs of voting helps, but in order to participate citizens also need the sense that they have genuine electoral choices, and that casting a ballot will have an important impact through electoral decisiveness. Convenience in casting a ballot therefore only facilitates action if citizens are motivated through broader political considerations.

Conclusions

Modern lifestyles mean that younger generations have become increasingly comfortable with the security of on-line banking, shopping and stock market trading, so advocates of e-voting hope that this process could generate similar levels of trust and confidence. The use of electronic technologies in elections can be regarded as building upon other increasingly common electoral and political uses of internet for information and communications, such as the use of websites and e-mail by parties, candidates and interest groups, the publication of election results on-line, the provision of voter registration facilities and the use of the internet for the submission, collection and disclosure of campaign finance.

Nevertheless, the evidence presented in this chapter suggests that at present, even if the technical and social equality issues could be overcome, there are few grounds to believe that adopting remote e-voting from home or work on a wide-scale basis would radically improve turnout. The introduction of remote e-voting would probably have a modest impact upon the younger generation, if judged by the available evidence from the British pilot studies. And automatic postal ballots are far more effective in improving participation among the older generation, as well as being cheaper and more efficient to administer. Remote e-voting is, therefore, unlikely to prove a 'magic ballot'. Technological quick fixes, while superficially attractive, cannot solve long-term and deep-rooted civic ills. Yet, this does not mean that we should abandon all hope of modernising elections; the impact of all-postal voting proved positive and highly significant. For the simple price of a postage stamp, snail-mail proved very effective at boosting turnout, and the MORI survey of attitudes showed that postal voting also generated high levels of trust, satisfaction and a sense of security among citizens.[33]

This is not to argue that the internet fails to serve many other important functions during election campaigns, including for civic engagement. Content analysis of party websites suggests that the internet provides a more level playing field for party competition, serving information and communication functions that are particularly important for minor and fringe parties.[34] American surveys show that on-line communities can serve both 'bridging' and 'bonding' functions strengthening social capital.[35] Experimental evidence demonstrates that party websites on the internet do, indeed, promote civic learning, and in this regard information on the internet is analogous to campaign information from newspapers or television news.[36] Nevertheless, survey evidence from those Americans who use the internet during campaigns in the US strongly suggests that e-voting would be used most heavily primarily by people who are already most likely to participate, thereby still failing to reach the apathetic and disengaged.[37]

Perhaps the primary impact of the internet on democratic life concerns its ability to strengthen the public sphere by expanding the information resources, channels of electronic communication, and the networking capacity for many organised interest groups, social movements, NGOs, transnational policy networks, and political parties and candidates (such as Howard Dean's run for the Presidency) with the technical know-how and organisational flexibility to adapt to the new medium.[38] The impact of the internet on intermediary organisations across Europe is evident from the way that it facilitates networks of activists concerned to challenge the decision-making processes in the EU. As such, the debate about e-voting may well prove largely irrelevant to the primary political impact of the internet on democracy within the European Union. How the European Parliament and European Commission respond to these new demands, and thereby use the potential of new technologies to widen and deepen the democratic processes, represents one of the key challenges of governance for the twenty-first century. Elections need to matter, and there needs to be an effective range of real choices on the ballot for citizens to believe that they can make at least a symbolic difference to the outcome through casting a vote. If European elections are widely regarded as largely irrelevant to the policy outcome, or if people do not feel that they are presented with choices which represent their interests, then no matter if casting a vote becomes as easy as clicking a mouse, participation levels will, unfortunately, probably remain miserably low.

Notes

1 Many thanks are due to the UK Electoral Commission, especially Ben Marshall, Kate Sullivan and David Maher, for generous help in providing the MORI data and for background briefing papers, as well as to the BBC Political Research Department, particularly Giles Edwards, who also provided invaluable research papers.

2 Further details analysing these issues can be found in Norris, P. (2001a) *Digital Divide*, New York: Cambridge University Press; Norris, P. (2002a) *Democratic Phoenix: Political Activism Worldwide*, New York: Cambridge University Press; Norris, P. (2004) *Electoral Engineering: Electoral Rules and Voting Choices*, New York: Cambridge University Press. Details are available at: www.pippanorris.com.

3 Stratford, J.S. and Stratford, J. (2001) 'Computerized and networked government information', in *Journal of Government Information* 28 (3): 297–301; Börgers, T. (2000) 'Is internet voting a good thing?', in *Journal of Institutional and Theoretical Economics*, 156 (4): pp. 531–47.

4 van der Eijk, C. and Franklin, M. (eds) (1996) *Choosing Europe? The European Electorate and National Politics in the Face of the Union*, Ann Arbor: University of Michigan Press; Norris, P. (2000) 'Blaming the messenger? Political communications and turnout in EU elections', in *Citizen Participation in European Politics*, Demokratiutredningens skrift nr 32. Stockholm: Statens Offentliga Utredningar. For details of turnout in elections to the European Parliament see: www.europa. eu.int.

5 See Electoral Commission (2003) *The Shape of Elections to Come*, London: UK, Electoral Commission, 31 July 2003, at: www.electoralcommission.org.uk.

6 For details of the availability of these facilities see www.ACEproject.org.

7 House of Commons Library Research Paper (2003) *UK Elections Statistics 1945–2003*, 03–59, July 2003, p. 17.

8 See, for example, Arterton, C.F. (1987) *Teledemocracy*, Newbury Park, CA: Sage; Schwartz, E. (1996) *Netactivism: How Citizens Use the Internet*, Sebastapol, CA: Songline Studios; Budge, I. (1996) *The New Challenge of Direct Democracy*, Oxford: Polity Press; Rash, W. (1997) *Politics on the Net: Wiring the Political Process*, New York: W.H. Freeman; Rheingold, H. (1993) *The Virtual Community: Homesteading on the Electronic Frontier*, Reading, MA: Addison Wesley; Barber, B.R. (1998) 'Three scenarios for the future of technology and strong democracy', in *Political Science Quarterly*, 113 (4): pp. 573–90.

9 Internet Policy Institute for the National Science Foundation (2001) *Report of the National Workshop on Internet Voting*, March 2001, at: www.internetpolicy.org/research/e_voting_report.pdf; The Independent Commission on Alternative Voting Methods (2002) *Elections in the 21st Century: From Paper-Ballot to e-voting*, Electoral Reform Society, January 2002, at: www.electoral-reform.org.uk/sep/publications/books/exec.pdf.

10 www.news.bbc.co.uk/hi/english/in_depth/sci_tech/2000/dot_life/newsid_1746000/1746902.stm.

11 Gibson, R. (2002) 'Elections online: Assessing internet voting in light of the Arizona democratic primary', in *Political Science Quarterly*, 116 (4): pp. 561–83; Solop, F.I. (2001) 'Digital democracy comes of age: internet voting and the 2000 Arizona Democratic primary election', in *PS-Political Science & Politics* 34 (2): pp. 289–93.

12 Auer, A. and Trechsel, A.H. (eds) (2001) *Voter par Internet? Le projet e-voting dans le canton de Geneve dans une perspective socio-politique et juridique*, www.helbing.ch. See also the Geneva system described at: www.geneve.ch/chancellerie/e-Government/e-voting.html.

13 Dictson, D. and Ray, D. (2000) *The Modern Democratic Revolution: An Objective Survey of Internet-Based Elections*, www.Securepoll.com.

14 National Statistics Omnibus Survey (2003) 'Individuals accessing the internet', in *Access to Internet from Home – Expenditure and Food Survey*, January to March 2003.

15 Norris, P. (2001) *Digital Divide*, New York: Cambridge University Press.

16 Of course, none of this provides any evidence concerning the potential use of voting electronically via text messaging, using conventional or mobile telephones, since this is not measured in the Eurobarometer surveys under comparison. The widespread access of telephones in European societies could mitigate some of the social inequalities of internet voting, although of course this does not necessarily overcome, and may even exacerbate, the concerns about security.

17 For an analysis of the social disparities in turnout see Norris, P. (2002a) op. cit., Chapter 5.

18 See Norris, P. (2002a) op. cit.; Norris, P. (2004) op. cit.

19 Katz, R. (1997) *Democracy and Elections*, New York: Oxford University Press, Table 13.2. It should be noted that under other less democratic regimes, citizens face far more serious barriers, such as in the recent presidential election in Zimbabwe where electors stood in line at polling stations despite delays of up to 50 hours and the serious threat of intimidation, violence and coercion.

20 The best discussion of the administrative arrangements for registration and balloting found around the world can be found at www.ACE.org developed by International IDEA and IFES. For further details see Maley, M. (2000) 'Absentee voting', in Rose, R. (ed.) *The International Encyclopedia of Elections*, Washington, DC: CQ Press. See also entries by Blais, A. and Massicotte, L. (1981) 'Day of election'. See also Crewe, I. 'Electoral participation', in Ranney, A. and Butler, D. (eds) *Democracy at the Polls*, Washington, DC: AEI Press; Powell, G.B. (1986)

'American voter turnout in comparative perspective', in *American Political Science Review*, 80 (1): pp. 17–43; Jackman, R.W. (1987) 'Political institutions and voter turnout in industrialised democracies', in *American Political Science Review*, 81: pp. 405–23; Jackman, R.W. and Miller, R.A. (1995) 'Voter turnout in industrial democracies during the 1980s', in *Comparative Political Studies*, 27: p. 467 and p. 492; Blais, A. and Dobrzynska, A. (1998) 'Turnout in electoral democracies', in *European Journal of Political Research*, 33 (2): pp. 239–61; Lijphart, A. (1997) 'Unequal participation: democracy's unresolved dilemma', in *American Political Science Review*, 91: pp. 1–14.

21 For further argument and evidence along these lines, see Franklin, M., van der Eijk, C. and Oppenhuis, E. (1996) 'The institutional context: turnout', in van der Eijk, C. and Franklin, M. (eds) *Choosing Europe? The European Electorate and National Politics in the Face of Union*, Ann Arbor, MI: University of Michigan Press.

22 See the discussion in Heath, A. and Taylor, B. (1999) 'New sources of abstention?', in Evans, G. and Norris, P. (eds) *Critical Elections: British Parties and Voters in Long-term Perspective*, London: Sage.

23 See, for example, Whiteley, P. (2001) 'Turnout', in Norris, P. (ed.) *Britain Votes 2001*, Oxford: Oxford University Press.

24 Office of the e-Envoy (2002) *In the Service of Democracy*, July, www. edemocracy.gov.uk.

25 The Electoral Commission (2002) *Modernising Elections: A Strategic Evaluation of the 2002 Electoral Pilot Schemes*, London: The Electoral Commission, at: www. electoralcommission.org.uk.

26 One evaluation of the experience of all-postal ballots in Oregon found that this had a modest effect on electoral turnout, particularly in low-salience contests. But the main impact was to increase voter participation among the groups already most likely to vote, thereby increasing socioeconomic inequalities in turnout. See Karp, J.A. and Banducci, S. (2000) 'Going postal: how all-mail elections influence turnout', in *Political Behavior*, 22 (3): pp. 223–39.

27 Franklin, M. (2002) 'Electoral participation', in LeDuc, L., Niemi, R.G. and Norris, P. (eds) *Comparing Democracies 2: Elections and Voting in Global Perspective*, London: Sage.

28 These estimates are derived from the House of Commons Library Research Paper (2003) *UK Elections Statistics 1945–2003*, 03–59, July. It should be noted that the BBC estimates suggested that the Liberal Democrat share of the vote was slightly higher (30 per cent).

29 It should be noted that the particular benchmark year varies by the type of authority, with some councils elected in whole and others by thirds.

30 It should be noted that there were serious limitations in what could be analysed using the MORI survey data because of a number of design flaws. In particular, there was no 'control' sample of voters in non-pilot districts. There were none of the standard attitudinal measures used for analysing turnout, such as political efficacy and partisanship. Many of the questions were filtered so that they were only asked of sub-samples in different pilot areas, preventing comparison across areas. Moreover, the way of classifying 'pensioners' into the DE class skewed the age profile in this category, making class analysis unreliable. There were also too few ethnic minorities to allow reliable analysis by racial group.

31 Heath, A. and Taylor, B. (1999) 'New sources of abstention?', in Evans, G. and Norris, P. (eds) *Critical Elections: British Parties and Voters in Long-term Perspective*, London: Sage.

32 Norris, P. and Lovenduski, J. (2004) 'Why parties fail to learn: electoral defeat, selective perception and British party politics', in *Party Politics*, 10 (1).

33 For further details about public attitudes monitored in the MORI survey, not discussed here, see UK Electoral Commission (2003) *The Shape of Elections to Come*, London: UK Electoral Commission, 31 July, at: www.electoralcommission. org.uk. See also, MORI polls (2003) 'New ways to vote' 1 August, at: www. mori.com/polls/2003/electoralcommission.shtml.

34 Norris, P. (2003) 'Preaching to the converted? Pluralism, participation and party websites', in *Party Politics*, 9 (1): pp. 21–45.

35 Norris, P. (2002b) 'The bridging and bonding role of online communities', in *The Harvard International Journal of Press-Politics*, 7 (3): pp. 3–8.

36 Norris, P. and Sanders, D. (2003) 'Medium or Message? Campaign learning during the 2001 British general election', in *Political Communications*, 20 (3): pp. 233–62.

37 Norris, P. (2001b) 'Who surfs? New technology, old voters and virtual democracy in US elections 1992–2000', in Kamarck, E. (ed.) *democracy.com*. Washington, DC: Brookings Institute, (revised edition).

38 For further details of this argument, see Norris, P. (2001a) op. cit.

4 Second-order elections to the European Parliament

Is e-voting the solution?

Hermann Schmitt

European Parliament elections as second-order national elections

Direct elections to the European Parliament were first held in 1979. Although they were contested, in most member states, by the same parties that also compete in first-order national elections, they were different. Efforts to summarise these differences emphasised a few central points. First and most importantly, European Parliament elections lacked any of the usual dramatic consequences of the electoral process. No government was formed after election day. No head of government – be it a Prime Minister, a Chancellor, or whoever – was dependent on the strength of political groups in the newly elected parliament.

More important than the European consequences of European Parliament elections were their national implications. Whether or not a national government could be said to be reaffirmed by the election result; whether or not the opposition could draw support from it in its quest for national political power; these were the questions that political actors were dealing with. Consequently, European Parliament elections have been described as second-order national elections.[1] As such, they appeared to be similar to mid-term elections in the US; *Landtagswahlen* in Germany; by-elections in Britain; and so on.[2] Specific to this type of second-order national elections is that their immediate, arena-specific political significance is inferior compared to their indirect meaning to the main political arena, the national polity.

The political stature of the European Parliament has changed since 1979 when it was first directly elected. While its budgetary powers were substantial early on, its legislative powers have been growing significantly. Following the Single European Act of 1987, the European Parliament, for the first time, was formally involved in the legislative process of the European Community through the co-operation procedure between Council, Commission and Parliament. This involvement was further extended by the establishment of a co-decision procedure in the Treaty on the

European Union (Maastricht Treaty) in 1993. Since Maastricht the European Parliament is among the most powerful players in the institutional system of the European Union.[3]

Maastricht also provided the Parliament with a say in the investiture of the European Commission. While the treaty does not authorise it to elect a President of the Commission and an accompanying set of Commissioners, it can now decline a Council proposal for the formation of the incoming Commission. This clause of the Maastricht Treaty is seen by some as a first step in the direction of a European Union government being dependent upon, and therefore responsible to, the European Parliament. However, it clearly cannot establish a link between the European Parliament election result and the formation of a European government.

As crucial as this would be in view of the constantly growing policy reach of the legislative *apparatus* of the Union,[4] the increase in the powers of the European Parliament over the last two decades does not yet translate into electoral politics. European Parliament elections are still not about alternative leadership proposals and campaign platforms of competing trans-national electoral alliances of political parties. And that is why *there still is* (or, seems to be) *less at stake in European Parliament elections*, and why European Parliament elections are still best described as second-order national elections.

In view of the election result, the second-order character of European Parliament elections has three major consequences. First, turnout is expected to be lower than in first-order elections. Second, government parties – that is, parties participating in national government – are expected to lose support compared to their first-order standing. And third, small parties – and that involves many new and/or ideologically extreme parties – are expected to win in comparison to what they obtain in first-order elections, again in relative terms.[5]

These propositions are based upon the assumption that the second-order character of European Parliament elections ('less at stake') impinges on the behaviour of political actors involved. First of all, political parties will pay less attention and they have been found to 'fight' their national campaigns half-heartedly.[6] Often, they do not even exhaust their campaign funds.[7] In an age of personalisation of mass communication, professional communicators lack the 'faces' that could signify the electoral alternatives. As a consequence, mass-media attention to this non-event is restricted, and their coverage is moderate at best.[8] Voters are not enthused. Many do not bother to participate.[9] Those who go and vote still seem to be impressed by first-order arena considerations rather than by European Union politics,[10] which is not to say that European Parliament elections would not be capable of representing voters' preferences in parliament.[11]

How can e-voting change the picture?

If we concentrate on the behaviour of voters, the specificity of second-order elections – European Parliament elections in our case – is that fewer turn out and that those who do choose differently from among the parties on offer than voters would in first-order elections. This latter phenomenon most likely is caused by an unknown mix of two different processes, one being differential mobilisation (which refers us back to the turnout aspect), and the other being that voters apply different criteria for determining which party to endorse.[12]

Given these particularities of European Parliament elections, in what way, if any, could e-voting alter the picture? e-Voting is understood here as the opportunity for voters to cast a ballot not in person in the voting booth, but electronically, e.g. from home or wherever they might be on election day (see the chapter by Gibson in this volume for a taxonomy of e-voting systems). It is difficult to envisage how e-voting could possibly affect the second-order election-specific calculus of the vote. But it might reduce some of the 'costs' of electoral participation and thereby raise the second-order election-specific low level of turnout. The cost factor that might be reduced is the time and effort that it takes to go to the electoral office and cast a vote in person. However, there are other cost factors involved in electoral participation, most noteworthy among these are the time and effort that it takes to acquire subjectively sufficient information to cast a ballot. Those other costs will tend to remain unaffected by e-voting. In addition, low levels of electoral participation in European Parliament elections might be related to factors that are independent of participation costs. For example, abstentions could be motivated by Euro-hostile attitudes. Such motivations would also remain unaffected by e-voting.

In order to assess the likely impact of e-voting on the result of European Parliament elections we will pursue two strategies in this chapter. The first is to determine the amount of Euro-hostile non-voting – because this portion of abstentions is unlikely to be reduced by e-voting. The second is to explore what role the internet already plays for voters during the campaign preceding European Parliament elections.

How important is Euro-hostile non-voting in European Parliament elections?

For politicians and the media alike, participation rates in European Parliament elections are seen as a crucial indicator of political support for the European Union. When the first direct election was called in 1979 the European Parliament launched a broad non-partisan mobilisation campaign in all the Member States.[13] Those efforts have been repeated in subsequent elections. In spite of this, turnout was widely considered

Table 4.1 Participation in European Parliament elections 1979–99
(figures are percentages)

	1979	1984	1989	1994	1999
Austria				68[c]	49
Belgium	**92**	**92**	**91**	**91**	**90**
Denmark	47	52	46	53	50
Finland				60	30
France	61	57	49	53	47
Germany	66	57	62	60	45
Greece	**79a**	**77**	**[80]**	**71**	**70**
Ireland	[63]	48	[68]	44	[51]
Italy	**86**	**84**	**82**	75	71
Luxembourg	**[89]**	**[87]**	**[87]**	**[89]**	**[86]**
Netherlands	58	51	47	36	30
Portugal		72[c]	51	36	40
Spain		69[b]	55	59	[64]
Sweden				42[c]	38
UK	32	33	36	36	23
EU-9	62				
EU-10	64	59			
EU-12		61	56	57	
EU-15				57	50

Sources: www.europa.eu.int; Statens Offentliga Utredningar 2000; Grundberg, G., Perrineau, P. and Ysmal, C. (eds) (2000) *Le vote des quinze. Les élections européennes du 13 juin 1999*, Paris, Presses de Sciences Po.

Notes: a Election of 1981; b Election of 1987; c Election of 1995. Bold figures signify elections under compulsory voting; figures in [ ] indicate that national elections were held concurrently with European Parliament elections.

disappointingly low in 1979, and has declined since. The trend generally points downwards, EU-wide participation dropped from some 60 per cent in 1979 and 1984, to around 55 per cent in 1989 and 1994, and down again to 50 per cent in 1999 (Table 4.1).

This decline in turnout is probably less alarming than it might seem at first sight. To some degree, it is the consequence of successive enlargements of the Union with countries where factors promoting high turnout are absent or weak. As a case in point, the proportion of the EU citizenry 'operating' under conditions of compulsory voting has declined.

In addition to compulsory voting, turnout is also affected by the timing of European Parliament elections relative to that of first-order national elections. Turnout is highest when European and national elections are held concurrently. It is lowest immediately after a first-order national election, and increases slowly with the passing of the domestic electoral cycle. The effects of these factors are not immediately apparent, but they generate problems of comparability with respect to 'raw' turnout figures.

When composition effects (i.e. the decline of the proportion of citizens under compulsory voting) and timing effects (i.e. the unequal closeness to national first-order elections) are removed, participation in European Parliament elections is relatively stable.[14] But although turnout may be stable, it is nonetheless particularly low. This brings us to our question of Euro-hostile abstentions in European Parliament elections. Do voters abstain from European Parliament elections because they are hostile towards the politics of the European Union? If so, offering e-voting mechanisms will not alter turnout.

Past research is somewhat inconclusive with regard to Euro-hostile abstentions. Schmitt and Mannheimer, in their 1991 analysis of the 1989 European Election Study data, find that participation in European Parliament elections is virtually unrelated to attitudes about European integration. In 1989 at least, electoral participation was mostly a matter of habitual voting – 'people went to the polls because they are used to doing so on election day'.[15] Later analyses based on the same 1989 European Election Study included, in addition to individual level factors, systemic and contextual characteristics and their interaction with individual-level variables.[16] While this strategy of research meant quite a step forward (accompanied by a considerable increase in the variance explained), attitudes towards European integration and the European Community were, again, found to be virtually unrelated to electoral participation.

By contrast Blondel, *et al.* in their 1994 participation study conclude:

> voluntary Euro-abstention to be significantly affected by attitudes to European integration, by attitudes to the European Parliament, and by attitudes to the parties and candidates in the election, and that it is not significantly affected by second-order considerations and calculations.[17]

While this obviously conforms much better with conventional wisdom of politicians and journalists,[18] the validity of those claims has to be questioned.

Blondel *et al.* call *voluntary Euro-abstainers* those respondents who, in the course of the interview, gave one or more of the following reasons for their abstention: 'Lack of interest, distrust of or dissatisfaction with politics and politicians, lack of knowledge and dissatisfaction with the European Parliament electoral process.'[19] Two objections can be made to such a self-reporting intentions methodology. First, survey respondents are, themselves, not the most reliable source of information about the causes of their behaviour.[20] Second, the approach yields non-falsifiable and therefore non-scientific propositions as it is impossible to assess whether the same causes (i.e. Euro-hostile attitudes) exist among those who do not manifest the expected effect (i.e. who report to have turned out). Put somewhat differently, Blondel *et al.* may be seen to have 'stacked the deck' because they defined (i.e. selected) the category of respondents that was found to be 'dissatisfied with the European Parliament electoral process' on the basis of this very characteristic.

Although we are sceptical about the validity of the conclusions of Blondel *cum suis*, we still cannot rule out that things might have changed since we first explored the issue for the 1989 election. Over the last decade the public appearance of the European Union has changed in many important ways. National sovereignty has been further transferred to Union institutions and authorities (e.g. in the currency domain). The political consequences of EU policy making are more widely felt (like during the BSE crisis and the Foot and Mouth Disease epidemic). Last but not least, the dynamics of EU membership (like Eastward enlargement as approved by the Nice Treaty) is a source of concern for many citizens. These and other developments may have changed the relation between mass political orientations towards the European Union and electoral behaviour in European Parliament elections. Euro-hostile abstentions in European Parliament elections might have become more numerous and, hence, strategic non-voting in the EU more important than in the past. The question that we will try to answer, in a diachronic analysis covering the three elections from 1989 onwards, is whether this is, indeed, the case.

Data base and strategy of analysis

Our data base is the European Elections Studies of the 1989, the 1994 and the 1999 elections. Three sets of independent variables have been included in every EES post-election survey since 1989 that can be employed here, two structural and one attitudinal. On the structural side, there are the social-structural position of respondents[21] and their general political involvement.[22] These structural factors will be used to isolate the true effects of Euro-hostile attitudes on turnout. Two basic indicators of respondents' support for Europe and the European Union[23] will then be utilised to determine the evolution of Euro-hostile abstentions. When it comes to the dependent variable, respondents have been asked in each study whether they participated in the preceding election and which party they voted for. The format of these questions differs slightly from study to study; but that would probably be of greater concern if we were estimating levels of participation rather than identifying causes of abstention.

A strategy for determining the effects of EU attitudes on participation in three consecutive European Parliament elections must be both theoretically grounded and empirically parsimonious. With regard to theory, we refer to the conventional wisdom that non-voters are 'peripheral' socially[24] and politically.[25] Both these peripheral locations are of a structural – i.e. not election-specific – nature. They are supposed to impact on turnout no matter what kind of election is analysed. The potential relevance of support for Europe and the European Union, by contrast, is of an attitudinal nature and is very election-specific. While both structural position and political attitudes may be interlinked, we decided – with an eye on parsimony – to control for structural factors first and then move on and assess the behavioural relevance of EU attitudes. This can be done by a procedure known as block-recursive regression. Stepwise logistic regressions are performed with electoral participation as the dependent variable. Social-structural factors are entered first, and their explanatory power is determined by the pseudo-R square measure.[26] Indicators of political involvement are entered second, and the proportion of additional explanatory power is determined. Attitudes about Europe and the European Union are entered third and, again, their explanatory power is determined (together with the goodness of fit of the overall model).

Findings

We move on and consider the evolution of Euro-hostile abstentions over time. Did the phenomenon increase, or decrease, or was there not much of a change? Are there particular country patterns standing out? And what about the evolution of structural determinants of electoral participation? Some of these questions can be answered on the basis of information provided in Table 4.2. The first observation is that attitudes about Europe and the European Union do not play much of a role for the decision to go and vote, or to abstain, after structural determinants of electoral participation have been considered. This is so across the board; no country is really standing out as exception to the rule – although Sweden in 1999 comes close to that. And we do not find much development over time either.

Could it be that controlling for the two structural dimensions conceals a stronger direct ('gross') association between turnout and (lack of) support for Europe and the European Union? This could happen if structural characteristics and European attitudes co-vary strongly, in which case controlling for one effect would, at the same time, diminish the other. In such a case, the net effect – the one that is computed after structural characteristics are controlled for – of European attitudes on electoral participation could be very modest, while the gross effect – i.e. the unconditional correlation – could still turn out to be quite substantial. Table 4.3 compares gross and net effects of European attitudes on electoral participation. It appears that there are, indeed, examples where social integration and political involvement shield a strong 'gross' effect of European attitudes on participation in European Parliament elections. Sweden in 1999 is one of the prime examples of that class of cases. On average, however, 'gross' and 'net' effects of political support for Europe and the European Union do not differ much – mainly because the 'gross' effects are very modest themselves.

Do people stay home because they disagree with the European Union and European integration? The answer, in a nutshell, is no. Nowhere do

Table 4.2 Participation in European Parliament elections: the effects of social structure, political involvement and attitudes towards Europe (figures are Nagelkerke's pseudo-R-squares and R-square changes from logistic regressions)

Election year	1989				1994				1999			
Country	A	B	C	C − B	A	B	C	C − B	A	B	C	C − B
Austria									0.09	0.15	0.16	0.01
Belgium	0.09	0.18	0.22	0.04	0.06	0.08	0.10	0.02	0.08	0.15	0.20	0.05
Denmark	0.12	0.20	0.20	0.00	0.15	0.25	0.26	0.01	0.07	0.17	0.17	0.00
Finland									0.13	0.26	0.28	0.02
France	0.18	0.23	0.24	0.01	0.20	0.28	0.28	0.00	0.08	0.12	0.12	0.00
Germany	0.05	0.20	0.22	0.02	0.09	0.19	0.21	0.02	0.13	0.18	0.18	0.00
Greece	0.20	0.23	0.24	0.01	0.24	0.25	0.26	0.01	0.06	0.10	0.11	0.01
Ireland	0.13	0.16	0.16	0.00	0.07	0.15	0.15	0.00	0.15	0.16	0.16	0.00
Italy	0.03	0.16	0.17	0.01	0.03	0.05	0.08	0.03	0.03	0.15	0.15	0.00
Luxembourg	0.07	0.07	0.10	0.03	0.17	0.29	0.33	0.04	0.11	0.28	0.31	0.03
Netherlands	0.07	0.14	0.16	0.02	0.18	0.24	0.26	0.02	0.13	0.22	0.23	0.01
Portugal	0.08	0.15	0.15	0.00	0.12	0.25	0.25	0.02	0.06	0.15	0.15	0.00
Spain	0.11	0.21	0.21	0.00	0.12	0.21	0.23	0.02	0.12	0.18	0.21	0.03
Sweden									0.19	0.31	0.37	0.06
UK	0.15	0.26	0.28	0.02	0.11	0.20	0.21	0.01	0.17	0.21	0.21	0.00
Country average	0.11	0.18	0.19	0.01	0.13	0.20	0.22	0.02	0.11	0.19	0.21	0.02

Source: *European Election Studies* 1989, 1994 and 1999.

Note: In the above table headings, 'A' symbolises the variation in turnout explained by social structural factors; the sex of respondents, their age, education, marital status (single vs. not), union membership and church attendance are used as predictors in this block. 'B' stands for a model where, in addition to social structural factors, those of political involvement are entered; political involvement is measured as interest in politics and party attachment. 'C' represents a model where, in addition to social structural factors and factors measuring political involvement, a third block of variables has been entered: attitudes towards European unification (for/against unification) and the European Union (is EU membership of one's country good or bad?); note that in 1999, the unification question has been asked in a somewhat different form than in the earlier surveys. Note that regressions following the ordinary least squares (OLS) algorithm produced identical findings.

Table 4.3 Attitudes towards Europe and participation in European Parliament elections: direct impact and effect when social structure and political involvement are controlled for (figures are Nagelkerke's pseudo R-squares from logistic regressions)

Election year	1989		1994		1999	
Country	R^2	ΔR^2	R^2	ΔR^2	R^2	ΔR^2
Austria					0.02	0.01
Belgium	0.01	0.04	0.02	0.02	0.07	0.05
Denmark	0.01	0.00	0.03	0.01	0.01	0.00
Finland					0.03	0.02
France	0.03	0.01	0.02	0.00	0.00	0.00
Germany	0.05	0.02	0.07	0.02	0.03	0.00
Greece	0.01	0.01	0.01	0.01	0.01	0.01
Ireland	0.00	0.00	0.00	0.00	0.00	0.00
Italy	0.01	0.01	0.02	0.03	0.00	0.00
Luxembourg	0.01	0.03	0.04	0.04	0.03	0.03
Netherlands	0.04	0.02	0.06	0.02	0.02	0.01
Portugal	0.01	0.00	0.01	0.02	0.01	0.00
Spain	0.01	0.00	0.03	0.02	0.04	0.03
Sweden					0.12	0.06
United Kingdom	0.04	0.02	0.05	0.01	0.01	0.00
Country average	0.02	0.01	0.03	0.02	0.03	0.02

Source: *European Election Studies* 1989, 1994 and 1999.

Note: In the above table heading, pseudo-R^2 symbolises the gross effect of attitudes towards European unification (for/against unification) and the European Union (is EU membership of one's country a good or bad thing?) on electoral participation; note that in 1999, the unification question has been asked in a somewhat different form than in the earlier surveys. ΔR^2 symbolises the net effect of these same variables – after the effect of social structural factors (sex, age, education, marital status [not available in 1999], union membership and church attendance) and political involvement (interest in politics and party attachment) has been removed.

Euro-hostile attitudes play a major role in the decision to participate in or abstain from European Parliament elections.

This in a way is good news. Growing levels of abstention in European Parliament elections are not the result of a growing alienation with the EU political system or hostility towards the politics of European integration. Instead, they seem to result from the fact that those who used to vote on election day – the socially integrated and politically involved – stay at home in ever greater numbers when the members of the European Parliament are elected. The lack of excitement that comes with these elections, which itself is largely a function of the lack of political consequences that can be associated with the election result, may be the main reason for this phenomenon. The second-order logic of European Parliament elections, thus, seems to accelerate the decline of participation.

The current importance of the internet for European Parliament elections

For the time being e-voting does not exist for the European Parliament elections. Therefore, the only role the internet can play in these elections is to provide access to all sorts of information, most notably to the home-pages of EU political institutions as well as to those of national and trans-national political parties. Do the citizens of the European Union use this new technology in the weeks preceding election day to inform them-selves about the upcoming elections and the 'supply' of voting options? In the questionnaires of the 1999 European Election Study's post-election survey, the internet figured for the first time as a source of pre-electoral information alongside the more traditional ones like talking to friends, watching TV news, reading newspapers and attending a public meeting. The proportions of eligible voters engaging in these information-seeking techniques are displayed in Table 4.4.

In all EU member countries, speaking with friends, watching TV and reading papers are the major sources of information. On average, about two-thirds of national citizens use these sources. Attending public meetings

Table 4.4 Sources of pre-electoral information: European Parliament elections of 1999 (figures are percentages)

Country	Talked to friends	Watched TV news	Read newspaper	Attended a meeting	Visited a website
Austria	73	87	76	4	3
Belgium	73	64	54	6	5
Denmark	71	57	60	4	6
Finland	57	53	67	6	6
France	60	53	57	6	1
Germany	74	85	73	5	6
Greece	72	71	45	11	5
Ireland	72	58	65	5	5
Italy[a]	70	60	54	24	13
Luxembourg	71	75	75	16	13
Netherlands	62	58	66	2	3
Portugal	67	91	52	3	0
Spain	53	49	43	12	2
Sweden	73	59	70	5	4
United Kingdom	47	48	54	3	5
EU average[b]	66	65	61	8	5
EU average without Italy[b]	66	65	61	7	5

Source: *European Election Study 1999*. Figures are based on weighted data (political weight 1, var006).

Notes: a Unlike the others, the Italian survey was realised in a tele-panel which might distort the level estimate of internet usage. b Arithmetic mean of country scores (without national election study findings).

and exploring the world-wide web are much less popular. An average proportion of only 5 per cent of national citizens claims to have accessed the web in search of pre-electoral information. Having said that, it is astounding that the traditional form of 'high cost' participation in election campaigns – attending public meetings – is almost at the same level (an average proportion of 8 per cent) than the most likely solitary internet search (namely, bowling alone!). In some countries – like Denmark, the UK, Germany and the Netherlands – we even find somewhat more voters checking the web than participating in a public meeting.

Nevertheless, the proportion of citizens using the internet as a source of information ahead of European Parliament elections is small. There are at least two plausible explanations for this finding. One is that the internet is not a suitable channel for citizens to seek political information ahead of elections; if this holds true, levels of internet usage for pre-electoral information should be the same, no matter what kind of election is at stake. The other explanation is that active information seeking – and that is what browsing the internet adds up to – is not a very common activity in this kind of low stimulus election; if that is true, levels of internet usage for pre-electoral information should be considerably higher in first-order national elections. We can test these alternative explanations by comparing information-seeking patterns in European Parliament elections with those observed in recent national first-order elections in two of the member countries of the Union, France and Germany.[27] The result of this comparison is rather straightforward (see Table 4.5). Information-seeking activities are more frequent in first-order national election campaigns than they are ahead of European Parliament elections. This holds for any of the five activities considered, including the internet. With respect to first-order national elections, one in ten (France) or even one in six citizens (Germany) report to have used the web in order to acquire information deemed to be relevant for the election. In both countries, this again amounts to about the same proportion of citizens who attended public meetings – the other 'active' information seeking device mentioned in our questionnaire.

We return to the use of the internet during European Parliament elections and attempt to explore its possible social-structural contours (Tables 4.5 and 4.6). Those contours are less pronounced than one would expect. The young are somewhat closer to the web than older citizens, about 7 per cent of the up to 35 year olds are using the internet as a source of pre-electoral information as compared to 4 per cent of those over 65. But this only holds for the average of the country scores, and there is no regular pattern that would present itself in each and every country under study.[28] Education also plays a role, with an average of 7 per cent of the highly educated accessing the web for election material as compared to 3 per cent of those with only basic education. Here again, there are differences and in most of the countries no clear trend is emerging.

Table 4.5 Sources of pre-electoral information: European Parliament elections of 1999 and subsequent first-order national elections compared (figures are percentages)

	Talked to friends	*Watched TV news*	*Read newspaper*	*Attended a meeting*	*Visited a website*
France					
EP election 1999	60	53	57	6	1
Presidential election 2002	88	87	74	10	10
Germany					
EP election 1999	74	85	73	5	6
Federal election 2002	92	97	88	14	17

Source: *European Election Study 1999* and CSES II post-election surveys in France and Germany.

Notes: Data are weighted to improve representivity. Figures indicate proportions of eligible voters who engaged in any of the activities 'often' or 'sometimes'. Identical questions have been included in representative telephone surveys following the European Parliament election in 1999, the presidential election in France in 2002 and the election of the members of the federal parliament in Germany in 2002.

Table 4.6 Internet as a source of pre-electoral information, according to the age of voters (figures are percentages)

Country	*18–34*	*35–49*	*50–64*	*65 +*	*Overall*
Austria	4	3	4	3	3
Belgium	5	6	5	2	5
Denmark	7	7	5	4	6
Finland	15	2	8	5	6
France	2	1	2	1	1
Germany	8	4	6	7	6
Greece	4	8	3	5	5
Ireland	7	5	3	5	5
Italy[a]	16	10	14	12	13
Luxembourg	28	9	9	2	13
Netherlands	4	4	1	1	3
Portugal	0	1	1	0	0
Spain	1	2	4	2	2
Sweden	4	6	3	2	4
United Kingdom	5	6	4	4	5
EU average[b]	7	5	5	4	5
EU average without Italy[b]	7	5	4	3	5

Source: *European Election Study 1999*. Figures are based on weighted data (political weight 1, var006).

Notes: a Unlike the others, the Italian survey was realised in a tele-panel which might distort the level estimate of internet usage. b Arithmetic mean of country scores.

Table 4.7 Internet as a source of pre-electoral information, according to the education of voters (figures are percentages)

Country	Low	Middle	High	Overall
Austria	3	2	6	3
Belgium	2	5	7	5
Denmark	1	5	8	6
Finland	4	3	10	6
France	2	1	2	2
Germany	7	5	6	6
Greece	5	2	8	5
Ireland	6	6	4	5
Italy[a]	11	12	13	12
Luxembourg	2	14	21	13
Netherlands	2	2	4	3
Portugal	0	1	0	0
Spain	1	2	3	2
Sweden	0	3	6	4
United Kingdom	4	3	10	5
EU average[b]	3	4	7	5
EU average without Italy[b]	2	4	7	5

Source: *European Election Study 1999*. Figures are based on weighted data (political weight 1, var006).

Notes: a Unlike the others, the Italian survey was realised in a tele-panel which might distort the level estimate of internet usage. b Arithmetic mean of country scores.

Table 4.8 The use of internet as a source of pre-electoral information and reported electoral participation (figures are percentages of those indicating to have participated)

Country	Internet not used (a)	Internet used (b)	Overall (c)	Difference (b − a)	Correlation[b]
Austria	61	67	61	+06	–
Belgium	96	100	96	+04	–
Denmark	57	73	57	+16	0.08
Finland	41	65	42	+24	0.12
France	70	71	70	+01	–
Germany	59	63	60	+04	–
Greece	89	96	89	+07	–
Ireland	57	67	58	+10	–
Italy[a]	86	92	87	+06	–
Luxembourg	94	97	95	+03	–
Netherlands	33	57	33	+24	0.09
Portugal	58	100	59	+42	–
Spain	84	90	84	+06	–
Sweden	46	78	48	+36	0.11
United Kingdom	30	36	31	+06	–
EU average[c]	64	77	65	+13	
EU average without Italy[c]	63	76	63	+13	

Source: *European Election Study 1999*. Figures are based on weighted data (political weight 1, var006).

Notes: a Unlike the others, the Italian survey was realised in a tele-panel which might distort the level estimate of internet usage. b Pearson correlation; coefficients significant above p = 0.05 are shown. c Arithmetic mean of country scores.

Finally, what does the use of the internet as a source of pre-electoral information mean for electoral participation? The message seems to be clear: internet usage goes hand in hand with elevated electoral participation. There is not one EU member country in which voters who claim to have used the internet would not report in greater numbers to have voted than those who did not use the web (Table 4.8). In four countries – that is, in Finland, Sweden, Denmark and the Netherlands – this association is even statistically significant, despite the small numbers of cases involved. The causal structure of this association, however, is anything but obvious.[29]

On the future importance of the internet for European Parliament elections: summary and perspectives

We began by restating the concept of second-order national elections that was elaborated in an effort to understand the results of the first direct election to the European Parliament back in 1979. The European Union has changed significantly since, but elections to the European Parliament are still 'second order' – because there is, or seems to be, less at stake. This has consequences for the political actors involved, not least for the voters. In second-order elections, voters are expected to abstain in greater numbers, and they are expected to arrive at characteristically different vote choices because their choice criteria ('calculus of the vote') are different.

e-Voting, should it be introduced, would have hardly any bearing on the choice criteria of voters. But it might affect the likelihood of voters participating in European Parliament elections. This would be the case if non-voting would largely be a function of the 'costs' of physical participation. These costs could be reduced by allowing the voters to participate virtually. But there are additional 'costs', e.g. for information, which e-voting as such does not help to reduce. In addition, non-voting could be motivated by Euro-hostile attitudes the effect of which, also, would not be affected by e-voting.

In order to determine the likely impact of e-voting on European Parliament election results, we therefore first explored the degree of Euro-hostile non-voting in European Parliament elections over time. What we found is encouraging for the introduction of e-voting, and discouraging at the same time. It is encouraging because there is not much Euro-hostile non-voting, and there never was. This disqualifies a possible cause of Euro-abstentionism that would have been immune to the blessings of e-voting. It discourages e-voting because it appeared, in the course of the analysis, that non-voting is almost as frequent among the integrated as among the isolated; among the interested as among the uninvolved; which seems to suggest that it is simply the lack of excitement that stems from the fact that European Parliament elections still do not deliver any of the dramatic consequences of the electoral process that the citizenry is used to from first-order electoral politics. e-Voting cannot do much about that as it provides no cure against electoral boredom.

A second route of empirical analyses explored the current use of the internet as a source of pre-electoral information in European Parliament elections and in first-order national elections. It appeared that the proportion of citizens using the internet is very small. But other pre-electoral information activities are pretty rare as well. Astonishingly enough, the internet on average is almost as 'popular' as public meetings – which once were one of the most typical forms of electoral campaigning of European political parties (at least of those of the mass-integration variety). Younger and better educated citizens were found to use the internet in somewhat greater numbers but the contrasts, while in the right direction, appeared to be rather modest. Finally, internet users were found to participate in greater numbers than those who do not use it – whatever the causal structure might be here.

Last but not least, we compared the pre-electoral role of the internet in European Parliament elections to that in presidential elections in France and in federal elections in Germany. There, we found considerably elevated proportions of citizens using the internet in the weeks ahead of an election. This seems to be a clear indication that participation in European Parliament elections cannot be cured by the introduction of e-voting. It is not the 'cost' of electoral participation that causes people to abstain. It is the lack of excitement and of visible consequences. In the title of this chapter we asked: Is e-voting a solution? The answer at the end is: probably not. Consequential elections, a close race, real electoral alternatives to choose from – these would probably be better measures to fight low turnout.

Notes

1 See Reif, K. and Schmitt, H. (1980) 'Nine Second Order National Elections: A Conceptual Framework for the Analysis of European Election Results', *European Journal of Political Research*, 8: 3–44; Reif, K. (1984) 'National Electoral Cycles and European Elections', *Electoral Studies*, 3: 244–55; Reif, K. (ed.) (1985a) 'Ten Second-Order Elections', *Ten European Elections*, Aldershot: Gower; Curtice, J. (1989) 'The 1989 European Election: Protest or Green Tide?', *Electoral Studies*, 8: 217–30.

2 Christopher Anderson and Daniel Ward, when analysing German *Landtagswahlen* and British *by-elections* have used the term 'barometer elections' to describe second-order national elections. See Anderson, C.J. and Ward, D.S. (1997) 'Barometer Elections in Comparative Perspective', *Electoral* Studies, 15: 447–60.

3 See Wessels, B. and Schmitt, H. (2000) 'Europawahlen, Europäisches Parlament und nationalstaatliche Demokratie', in H.-D. Klingemann and F. Neidhart (eds) *Zur Zukunft der Demokratie*, Berlin: Sigma.

4 See e.g. König, T. (1997) *Europa auf dem Weg zum Mehrheitssystem*, Opladen: Westdeutscher Verlag; Pinder, J. (1998) *The Building of the European Union*, Oxford: Oxford University Press (3rd edition); Hooghe, L. and Marks, G. (2001) *Multi-level Governance and European Integration*, Lanham, MD: Rowman & Littlefield Publishers.

5 See Reif and Schmitt, op. cit.

6 See Reif, K. (ed.) (1985b) *Ten European Elections*, Aldershot: Gower. There is actually very little positive knowledge about what European Parliament election

campaigns are about. Little has been done after the 1979 'Campaign Study' in the framework of the first European Election Study. A content analysis of the Euromanifestos of political parties which is currently being undertaken will provide more information on this (see www.mzes.uni-mannheim.de/projekte/manifestos/).

7 In a country like Germany, where the state is refunding campaign costs on a flat rate basis, a considerable part of the money granted to the parties is saved for more important political events to come.

8 See Blumler, J.G. and Fox, A. (1983) *The European Voter: Popular Responses to the First Community Election*, London: Policy Studies Institute; Blumler, J.G. (1983) *Communicating to Voters. Television in the first European Parliamentary Elections*, London: Sage. This literature emerged from a study of the 1979 European Parliament elections. Twenty years later, the European Election Study 1999 was again a mass communication study. It involves an analysis of party manifestos (see note 6), a content analysis of mass-media news broadcasts, and a representative mass survey conducted shortly after the election in each of the member countries. See Van der Eijk, C., Franklin, M.N., Schönbach, K., Schmitt, H., Semetko, H. *et al.* (2002) *European Elections Study 1999: Design, Implementation and Results*, (Computer File and Codebook), Amsterdam: Steinmetz Archives. The forthcoming results of this study will put the 1979 findings in perspective.

9 See Schmitt, H. and Mannheimer, R. (1991) 'About Voting and Non-Voting in the European Elections of June 1989', *European Journal of Political Research*, 19: 31–54; Van der Eijk, C., Franklin, M.N. *et al.* (1996) *Choosing Europe*, Ann Arbor: Michigan University Press; Blondel, J., Sinnott, R. and Svenson, P. (1998) *People and Parliament in the European Union*, Oxford: Oxford University Press.

10 See Marsh, M. (1998) 'Testing the Second-Order Election Model after Four European Elections', *British Journal of Political Science*, 28: 591–607.

11 See Schmitt, H. and Thomassen, J. (eds) (1999) *Political Representation and Legitimacy in the European Union*, Oxford: Oxford University Press; Schmitt, H. and Thomassen, J. (2000) 'Dynamic Representation: the Case of European Integration', *European Union Politics*, 1: 319–40.

12 Reif and Schmitt, op. cit., suggested that voters in European Parliament elections would find it easier to vote 'with the heart', while 'voting with the head' would be the more frequent pattern in first-order elections. In another terminology, this same phenomenon is referred to as sincere vs. strategic (or tactical) voting. See e.g. Alvarez, R.M. and Nagler, J. (2000) 'A New Approach for Modelling Strategic Voting in Multiparty Elections', *British Journal of Political Science*, 30: 57–75.

13 See Reif (1985b), op. cit.

14 See e.g. Wessels and Schmitt, op. cit.; Franklin, M.N. (2001) 'How Structural Factors Cause Turnout Variations at European Parliament Elections', *European Union Politics*, 2: 309–28.

15 Schmitt and Mannheimer, op. cit., p. 50.

16 See Franklin, M.N., van der Eijk, C. and Oppenhuis, E. (1996) 'The Institutional Context: Turnout', in C. van der Eijk and M.N. Franklin (eds) *Choosing Europe*, Ann Arbor: The University of Michigan Press.

17 Sinnott, R. (2000) 'European Parliament Elections: Institutions, Attitudes and Participation', in H. Angé, C. van der Eijk, B. Laffan, B. Lejon, P. Norris, H. Schmitt and R. Sinnott (eds) *Citizen Participation in European Politics*, Stockholm: Statens Offentliga Utredningar, p. 70, summarising Blondel *et al.*, op. cit., 222–36.

18 See e.g. J. Smith who notes that 'Franklin, van der Eijk and Oppenhuis have challenged the sort of claims made in this section' and contends without further

empirical evidence or argument that 'Despite their scepticism it seems that attitudes do have a part to play in explaining behaviour in EP elections' (Smith, J. (1999) *Europe's Elected Parliament*, Sheffield: Sheffield Academic Press, p. 123, footnote 10).

19 See Blondel *et al.*, op. cit., p. 50.

20 Alvarez and Nagler, op. cit., p. 61, reviewing the strategic voting literature, cast doubt on the validity of data gathered with the *self-reporting intentions methodology*: 'Unfortunately, researchers using these survey questions do not appear to have seriously considered the quality of the survey responses obtained for questions asking for justifications of reported political behaviour.'

21 Sex, age, education, marital status, union membership and church attendance are used mainly as indicators of social integration and resource attribution.

22 Political involvement is measured by interest in politics (4-point scale from 'not at all' to 'very') and party attachment (4-point scale from 'not close to any party' to 'very close to a particular party').

23 Support for Europe and the EU is measured by two indicators. One is asking for respondents' support for European unification (in 1989 and 1994 on a 4-point scale from 'very much against' to 'very much in favour'; in 1999 on a 10-point scale from 'has already gone too far' to 'should be pushed further'). The other is the familiar membership 'trend' question from the Eurobarometers which establishes whether one's country's membership of the EC/EU, according to the respondent, is a good thing, neither good nor bad, or a bad thing.

24 Due to a lack of social integration; see e.g. Lipset, S.M. (1959) *Political Man*, New York: Doubleday & Co.; Tingsten, H. (1963) *Political Behavior*, New York: Bedminster Press (first printing 1937); Lancelot, A. (1968) *L'Abstentionisme électoral en France*, Paris: Colin; Wolfinger, R. and Rosenstone, S. (1980) *Who Votes?*, New Haven and London: Yale University Press.

25 Due to a lack of political involvement; see e.g. Lazarsfeld, P.F., Berelson, B. and Gaudet, H. (1944) *The People's Choice*, New York: Duell Sloan and Pierce; Berelson, B., Lazarsfeld, P.F. and McPhee, W.N. (1954) *Voting*, Chicago: University of Chicago Press; Campbell, A. (1962) 'The passive citizen', *Acta Sociologica*, 6: 9–21.

26 The pseudo R^2 indicates how the model performs. The Nagelkerke R^2 value is reported as it corrects the Cox and Snell value so that it can theoretically achieve a value of 1. Note that these pseudo R^2 measures confound goodness of fit and explanatory power of the model.

27 At the occasion of the French presidential election in spring 2002 and the German parliamentary election in the autumn of 2002 representative mass surveys were conducted by telephone shortly after election day which carried the same question about channels of pre-electoral information seeking as the European Election Study 1999 did.

28 One reason for this modest association might be that the young, while finding it easier to use the web, are at the same time more distant to politics than older citizens.

29 This is not only due to the fact that electoral participation and the use of the internet as a source of pre-electoral information are both caused, or influenced, by some of the same factors: education and political skills more generally are certainly among them, as is political involvement. However, it is even debatable what direction the causal arrow takes between information and participation: do people inform themselves because they intend to participate, or do they participate because they are well informed? We cannot pursue these questions any further here.

Part II
Legal considerations

5 Fundamental and political rights in electronic elections

Pierre Garrone *

Introduction

Voting is one of the key elements of democracy. For that reason, every major change in the voting system must be assessed in a very thorough manner. Such an assessment is necessary in order to respect the rule of law and, in particular, any relevant constitutional provisions and international treaties. But it is also important in order to retain the confidence of the voters who could react in an emotional way to such a fundamental change in their habits as the introduction of electronic voting.

Voting is also an aspect of present life that, like all others, is influenced by changes in the surrounding world. Computerisation has become a main feature of contemporary society and the exercise of political rights will not be immune to such processes. First it affected vote counting, commencing with the aggregation of results and moving on to the electronic reading of the voting ballots. The introduction of e-voting, that is the use of computers for the voting act itself, would, however, be a much more important innovation.

The question of the legal principles applicable to e-voting could have appeared a few years ago as a combination of science-fiction and the well-known penchant for lawyers to look for problems which never arise in real life – at least concerning e-voting outside polling stations. Now, it has become a topical matter and is being addressed at the international level. The Council of Europe, for instance, has set up a group of specialists on legal, operational and technical standards for e-enabled voting, which is due to prepare a draft recommendation to be submitted to the Committee of Ministers in 2004.

The scope of this chapter is not to make a choice between narrow-minded conservatism and naive openness to every innovation. On the contrary, it aims to analyse whether doubts expressed about the introduction of e-voting are founded from a legal point of view. It will then discuss the compatibility of electronic voting with the principles of the European electoral heritage and, more specifically, identify the risk of violating such principles, which could arise from the introduction of this new technology.

It will also examine how to eliminate, or at least reduce, such risks, without entering into the technical details.

The introduction of electronic voting would, of course, constitute a grand innovation but this does not mean that the problems associated with its introduction would be completely new, especially from a legal point of view. The present text will therefore show which questions arising from the innovation are novel and which are not new.

The *five main principles of the European electoral heritage* – or constitutional principles of electoral law – are universal, equal, free, secret and direct suffrage. They are enshrined, explicitly or implicitly, in international instruments like the Additional Protocol to the European Convention on Human Rights[1] or the International Covenant on Civil and Political Rights.[2] The content of these principles is detailed in the Code of Good Practice in Electoral Matters, adopted by the European Commission for Democracy through Law (Venice Commission) of the Council of Europe, and approved by the Parliamentary Assembly and the Congress of Local and Regional Authorities of Europe.[3]

This chapter will examine, in turn, the five principles and their implications for electronic voting. A final section will deal with the other fundamental rights linked to political activity as well as with the other framework conditions of free and fair elections.

Before getting to the heart of the matter, it may be useful to define a few technical expressions related to electronic voting:

- '*Poll site internet voting* refers to the casting of ballots at public sites where election officials control the voting platform.' In practice, it means that e-voting is taking place in polling stations.
- *Kiosk voting* means that terminals 'are located in convenient places like malls, post offices, or schools, but remain under the control of election officials'.
- '*Remote internet voting* refers to the casting of ballots at private sites (e.g. home, school, office) where the voter or a third party controls the voting client.'[4]

Direct suffrage

Direct suffrage means that the lower house of Parliament, as well as other legislative bodies, such as the parliaments of federated states[5] and the European Parliament,[6] and local assemblies, are to be elected directly by the people. Contrary to the other principles of the European electoral heritage this one would remain unaffected by the introduction of e-voting.

Universal suffrage

Universal suffrage means that, in principle, everybody is entitled to the right to vote and the right to be elected; however, political rights may be subject to conditions of age, nationality or residence; voters may be deprived of their voting rights only in exceptional cases (for example, mental illness, criminal conviction).

Since universal access to private computers is unlikely ever to be achieved, the introduction of remote e-voting as the *only modality* of voting would run counter to the principle of universal suffrage.[7] It is not a secret that many people, even in the most developed societies, are not familiar with new technologies and some have never used a computer.[8] They would, in practice, be excluded from voting if no alternative to e-voting (especially of the remote variety) were offered.[9] Providing all voters with access to computers (poll site or kiosk e-voting) could limit the risks of exclusion, but the procedure should be simple and explained to the voters sufficiently in advance of the voting day in order to prevent problems. This aspect of the problem will be addressed in greater detail in the section that follows on equal suffrage.[10]

Universal suffrage may be affected by the use of e-voting if such a type of voting is not secure or reliable. 'Whereas security refers to the resistance of a system to deliberate, intelligent, or interactive attack, reliability focuses on the questions of a system's ability to perform as intended, in spite of apparently random hardware and software failures.'[11] Such problems may make the expression of the vote impossible and, de facto, disenfranchise the voter. Poll site voting is much less susceptible to these problems than remote voting.[12] However, the introduction of e-voting only at the polling stations would strongly limit the reach of the innovation and would then not raise much interest. 'Kiosk' voting would allow us to avoid such drawbacks while making the access to the new voting procedure easier. The question of equal access to e-voting and the risk of unduly casting a vote in the name of another voter will be dealt with below.

Equal suffrage

A number of questions arise concerning the compatibility of e-voting, or at least of its modalities, with equal suffrage. Some are quite specific to this type of voting, whereas others are more traditional.

There are several aspects to equal suffrage;[13] the first one is *equal voting rights*, which is, in general, considered as its most straightforward element: every voter is entitled to one vote – and to one vote only.

Nevertheless, in the field of e-voting, this question is more complicated than it would seem at first glance. As soon as several people have access to the computer from which to e-vote, there is a risk of multiple voting by the same voter and/or voting by non-voters. This is not a new problem, since it may also happen with postal voting, when it is anonymous.[14] In order to avoid such kinds of fraud, e-voting, like postal voting, must not be anonymous, in the sense that a control of who actually voted has to be possible.[15]

Another question is *accessibility* of the voting procedure. In itself, this question is not new, but has to be addressed in quite a different manner for e-voting than for the traditional ways of voting. It must first be underlined that, as soon as e-voting is not conceived as the only modality of voting, it is aimed at making voting more accessible. The real point is whether such an access is offered equally to all voters.

Accessibility includes various aspects, which can be divided into two categories: practical aspects and aspects linked to knowledge.

From a *practical point of view*, equal vote in polling stations implies, for example, that such stations are at a reasonable distance from each voter's place of residence. Postal voting has to be avoided – and is generally avoided – in countries where the postal service is unsatisfactory. Likewise, effective e-voting should be made available to every voter. This means that it should not be limited to those who have access to a computer at home and/or at their workplace. Access to computers for e-voting should be made possible to the other voters at a reasonable distance from their place of residence (similar to the distance to the polling station). Moreover, the time when such computers are available should be, as much as possible, as long as the time for e-voting from the home or the workplace. It would, of course, be unreasonable to ask for availability 24 hours a day, but the days when voting is possible from personal computers and from special e-voting computers should be the same as for postal voting, and they should be accessible for a certain time outside the normal working hours. e-Voting could even be extended up to the closure of the polling stations (whereas, due to the time necessary for mail dispatching, postal voting may not take place so late). Needless to say, even if this is not required by constitutional principles, the time for e-voting should be longer than the opening of the polling stations, otherwise many of the expected benefits of the innovation would be limited.[16] Moreover, if remote e-voting is allowed, it should be secure from all computers, and not only from the most technically sophisticated ones.[17]

The question of *knowledge* is probably, alongside that of secrecy of the vote, the most important obstacle to the introduction of e-voting. The proportions of 'learned' and 'ignorant' may gradually become inverted, but the problem is not to be evaded. Once again, this is not a completely novel problem. Voting by ballot papers was introduced when illiteracy was still rather high. Solutions had to be found in order to allow illiterates to vote, and to remove obstacles like making handwriting of the names of the candidates by the voter himself compulsory. For example, symbols of the parties were introduced on the ballots.

From a purely legal point of view, making e-voting possible is not contrary to equal suffrage as long as non-initiated voters are given a similar possibility to express their choice. This means that if e-voting is conducted over several days voters who do not wish to use this new technology must be allowed to vote by post or at the polling station, during the same period.

As soon as a comparatively easy access is given to all voters, the expected increase in the participation of the initiated ones by the introduction of e-voting should not be considered as unequal from a legal (constitutional) point of view.

It may also be envisaged that voters who are not familiar with e-voting may go to an e-voting centre and be instructed about how to vote. Such a possibility is problematic from the point of view of free suffrage and will be discussed in the free suffrage section below.

e-Voting, like voting by mail or by proxy, could be limited only to those voters who are not able to go to the polling station. This would not be contrary to equal suffrage, since it would be justified by a difference of situations, but would strongly reduce the interest of the innovation.

Nevertheless, it must be underlined that e-voting could be very useful for voters who leave their normal place of residence for a certain time. If voting were possible from all computers, the voting material sent (electronically) to their residence could be made available to them in a much easier manner than when it is sent by normal post. This should not be considered as contrary to the principle of equality as long as it is possible for a voter to obtain the voting material in the same places by post and to send it back by the same way. On the contrary, if postal voting is allowed only from within the country – at least for those who are not resident abroad – e-voting from abroad should be excluded, because it would be the only modality of voting for some voters, and we have already seen that this is contrary to the principle of universal suffrage.[18]

This section would not be complete if it did not deal with the question of a possible indirect *discrimination based on age or gender*, since it is generally admitted that the use of the internet decreases with age and is more frequent among men than among women. Our opinion is that the solution of such a problem is not different from what was already stated. It is true that, in many legal orders (including that of the Community), discrimination based on gender is submitted to stricter scrutiny than discrimination on other grounds. However, in the field of political rights and, in particular, voting rights, inequalities are to be banned in general and should then be submitted to strict scrutiny, whatever the criterion used as a distinction. The same applies to the objection concerning more difficult access for poor people or members of minorities.[19] The solutions proposed above (access to postal voting in similar conditions as to e-voting) should eliminate legal inequalities.[20]

Free suffrage

Freedom of voters includes two aspects: freedom of voters to form their opinion and free expression of the voters' opinion.[21]

Freedom of voters to form their opinion is violated when the State does not respect its duty of neutrality, particularly in the matter of media access.

Of course, this is also true for the official websites of the authorities. In general, the internet should, nevertheless, increase the freedom of voters to form their opinion, since the availability of abundant sources of information weakens the effect of biased propaganda.[22] In particular, the effect of dissemination of untruthful electioneering material by private individuals or organisations should be reduced.

The development of information by internet actually has no direct link with e-voting. However, as soon as remote e-voting is introduced, the voters should be provided with official information on the vote not only by post, but also by e-mail. Official information provided to the voter via the internet should be the same as that provided through traditional channels, in order to avoid any inequality. This would be only a first step, and it would be advisable to make use of the advantages offered by the internet in order to make access to internet political sites easier. When sending the voting material, the authorities could refer to an official site, which could, in its turn, provide links with other sites. In that case, of course, the question of neutrality arises; the State should then provide links to all sites in direct relation with the voting, without any distinction. In the case of an election, these would be the sites of the parties and/or candidates standing for election.[23]

More questions arise about *freedom of voters to express their opinion*[24] through e-voting. Most of them are classical from a legal point of view, since they may also be raised for postal voting.

The most serious violation of freedom of voters to express their opinion would, of course, be one voter voting instead of another. This risk has already been discussed above and should be avoided by the prohibition of anonymous e-voting.[25]

Another problem is so-called 'family voting'. In some countries this phenomenon takes place regularly with voting at the ballot box. It inevitably becomes much easier to accomplish in the case of voting at home via the internet.

Once again, the problem raised is not new; postal voting is subject to the same type of fraud.[26] The introduction of remote voting – postal mail as well as e-voting – should, therefore, be avoided in the countries where the problem already arises at the polling station.[27] e-Voting could, however, slightly worsen the risk in the relationship between genders in comparison with postal voting, since men are in general more used to the internet than women. On the contrary, in the relationships between generations, e-voting could help to reduce the influence of parents, but could also make it easier to deprive the elderly of their free choice. In general, it may be asserted that the risk of large-scale fraud, like vote selling or trading, would be somewhat increased in comparison with paper absentee ballots.[28] As Auer puts it:

> the choice between different available technical devices and solutions is never a final one and is of a more political than technical nature:

> How much security can and must be guaranteed at a given moment
> in a given context without threatening or even sacrificing the essential
> advantages of e-voting?[29]

Of course, 'collective' voting is not possible only at home. For that reason, I would not be in favour of allowing e-voting at the workplace, where undue pressures are always possible. Furthermore, system administrators could also monitor or record the activity of the other dependants.[30]

Free expression of the voters' choice could also be endangered if the innovation were introduced just before the vote, without giving enough time for the election officials, as well as the voters, to be acquainted with the new proceedings.

Another aspect of the freedom of voters to express their wishes is the *accurate recording of the outcome of the ballot*, which means that the State must ensure that votes are counted properly.[31] Such a principle will be violated if security and reliability of the vote are not ensured,[32] and it must be admitted that, unfortunately, the internet creates the risk of automated fraud, which does not exist under the traditional voting methods.[33] To assess whether such violations may be avoided is a task for technologists. Another problem is that the tallying process is not transparent; this question will be considered later.[34]

In sum, problems concerning freedom of vote, and especially freedom to express one's vote, may arise with e-voting. Except for technical problems linked to security or reliability, this is nothing fundamentally new vis-à-vis the present situation in countries where voting outside the polling station, in particular postal voting, is broadly allowed. On the contrary, where voting outside the polling station is prohibited or exceptional, the introduction of remote e-voting could introduce or increase problems linked to remote voting. But let us not forget that e-voting, unlike postal voting, would not be very useful if it were limited to elderly, disabled or sick people.

Secret voting

Last but not least: the question of secret voting. It is actually not a separate principle but, rather, an aspect of voter freedom,[35] its purpose being to shield voters from pressures they might face if others learned how they had voted.

This point is one of the most delicate ones from a technical point of view. Scepticism is the rule in this field; the innovation will be fought not only from a political point of view, but also from a legal one, as long as real security and reliability are not ensured.[36] However, here again, there is nothing very original from a conceptual or legal point of view. Postal voting, also, as soon as it is not anonymous – and it must not be anonymous[37] – is subject to similar types of fraud. Opening of the (outer) envelope with the voting card has to be separated from opening the (inner) envelope with the ballot, in order to ensure the respect of secret suffrage. The same should apply, *mutatis mutandis*, to e-voting: the two operations, checking who voted and counting the vote, should be independent. How to make this possible is the task of the technical experts, as it is how to ensure that the voters are not able to prove how they voted.[38]

Furthermore, the risk of the voters having their voting act controlled by a member of their household, or by other people, is the same as in the case of postal voting and was already tackled in the previous section, in particular concerning so-called family voting.[39]

The creation of special 'e-voting stations' ('kiosks') could imply the possibility for the voter to ask for explanations by the officials responsible for the station. This would even be appropriate since, as straightforward as it may be, the voting procedure would not be self-evident. However, there is a risk of a violation of secrecy if the same computers are used for demonstration and for voting.[40] A computer would then have to be installed in every station for demonstration only. The 'voting computers' would be put into kinds of polling booths and access to them would be allowed only for voting and to one person at a time.

Other fundamental rights and framework conditions of free and fair elections

Proclaiming the principles of Europe's electoral heritage, and even spelling them out in detailed regulations, are not enough to guarantee their implementation. Three *general conditions* must also be fulfilled:[41]

- First, there can be no true democracy unless *fundamental rights* – and particularly freedom of expression, assembly and association – are respected.
- Second, there must be *procedural guarantees* to ensure that the principles are impartially applied.
- Third, electoral law must have certain *stability*, protecting it against party political manipulation.

The protection of *fundamental rights* other than the main principles of the European electoral heritage, including freedom of expression, assembly and association in political matters, would not be affected by the introduction of e-voting.

The *procedural guarantees* include the organisation of the vote by an impartial body, an effective appeal system and, more generally, respect of all rules, including the technical ones, applicable to the vote.[42] Due to the increased possibility of fraud (problems of security of e-voting), as well as to the technical complexity of the process, it would be more than appropriate either to create a specialised impartial control authority[43] or to include computer specialists in the existing electoral commissions or bodies responsible for the supervision of elections.

However, the problem is not only technical. As has already been pointed out, the tallying process is not transparent in the case of e-voting: '[w]ith electronic voting systems, public confidence in the election relies on trust in technical experts instead of a transparent process'.[44] According to the often-quoted dictum, 'justice must not only be done; it must also be seen to be done'.[45] Also, regularity of elections must not only be affirmed by specialists but, also, confirmed in a way that generates public confidence. In my opinion, this implies first the need to involve computer specialists/ technicians in the counting, and second to introduce an effective control of this counting by a superior body, preferably involving representatives of political parties who understand the main technical questions.

The last point, *stability of electoral law*, of course, does not mean immobility and opposition to innovation. It aims at avoiding manipulations in the interest of a political party, in particular by too frequent or last minute modifications of the electoral system per se or of the composition of electoral commissions. Changing the voting modalities is, in principle, less sensitive to manipulations, especially if the innovation were not compulsory, but only optional, as would be the case with e-voting. It goes without saying that any such innovations would have to be adopted sufficiently in advance of the first electoral contest to which they were applied in order to give the bodies responsible for organising the vote and the voters enough time to get acquainted with the new procedure. Otherwise, there would be a risk of irregularities, which could even lead to the invalidation of the vote.[46]

Conclusion

The introduction of e-voting and, in particular, of remote e-voting, would be a major innovation. It could even be considered by the public as the most important advance since vote by a show of hands was replaced by the use of paper ballots.

It is true that remote e-voting would be something completely new in the field of elections from a technical point of view: making it affordable, sure and reliable is a true challenge to specialists of computer engineering. The innovation would also imply the revision of a number of legal provisions. The present text focused, however, on the principles of the European electoral heritage and the risk of them being violated by e-voting: its scope was not to examine in detail what technical provisions should be reconsidered if the innovation were introduced; this will of course depend on technical choices inside every legal order.

It is indisputable that the problems of reliability and security of e-voting are the most serious obstacles to the organisation of free and fair e-voting, and that they have to be settled before e-voting is introduced, in order to ensure universal as well as free and secret voting. Nevertheless, from a conceptual and legal point of view, these problems are not completely new. It does not mean that truly new questions, like the introduction of specialists in computer engineering to the impartial body organising the vote, will not have to be settled. On the contrary, such problems as the risk of family voting from home, are no more serious than in the case of postal voting. Finally, it should be possible to set aside most fears arising from the so-called digital divide – and the risk of violation of universal and equal suffrage – through opening the access to postal voting as broadly as to e-voting.

This conclusion – and, more generally, the content of this chapter – could seem rather pessimistic, since it has underlined many of the difficulties and few of the positive points. Therefore, it must not be forgotten that this chapter is aimed at identifying the possible violations of the principles of the European electoral heritage, which could arise from the introduction of e-voting, and not the advantages of such a new technique. It must also be highlighted that many innovations, in their early stages, bring more difficulties than joys. This is true from a technical point of view, but also from a financial one, to say nothing about the time necessary to make the innovation completely operational. Law, and constitutional law in particular, does not escape such a rule: every innovation provides much work for lawyers, as well as for all other parties involved. The same was the case with the introduction of free and democratic elections. Now, the whole process seems easy and natural, at least in old democracies, whereas in other countries citizens still have to get accustomed to what is considered a strange novelty. In a few decades, or even in a few years, we shall, perhaps, wonder how it was practically possible to organise elections without e-voting, and remember how complicated it was, and the extent to which the innovation has simplified our life.

Appendix

The aim of the synoptic table below is:

- to show in a simplified fashion which specific problems would arise from the introduction of e-voting, for each fundamental principle applying to electoral law (second column); and
- to underline which of these problems are new, from a legal point of view, in comparison with those arising from the application of the traditional voting methods; in particular, voting by paper ballots at the polling station or by post (third column).

Principle	Specific problem	Novelty (legal)
Direct suffrage	None	—
Universal suffrage	e-Voting as the only modality of voting: exclusion of voters without any knowledge of computers (non-initiated voters)	Mainly new
	Lack of reliability or security	Not really new
Equal suffrage: equal voting rights	Risk of multiple voting and similar problems	Not new, settled by the prohibition of anonymous voting
Equal suffrage: accessibility of the voting procedure	Making a computer available to every voter	Mainly new
	Access barred to non-initiated voters	Mainly new, but the extension of postal voting should avoid any legal inequality
Equal suffrage: no discrimination on the basis of gender, age, race or ethnic origin, social conditions	Access barred to non-initiated voters (indirect discrimination)	Mainly new, but the extension of postal voting should avoid any legal inequality
Equal suffrage: equality of opportunity	See next item	
Free suffrage: freedom of voters to form their opinion	Neutrality of official information provided to the voter through internet	Not new
	Neutrality of the links to other (political) internet sites	New
Free suffrage: freedom of voters to express their opinion	Family voting and other types of 'collective' voting	Not new, except for undue intervention of system administrators
Free suffrage: accurate recording of the outcomeof the ballot	Lack of security or reliability	Partially new (risk of automated fraud)
Secret voting	Lack of security or reliability	Not really new
	Undue intervention of election officials during the voting process	Partially new
Fundamental rights in general	None	—
Procedural guarantees: organisation of the vote by an impartial body	Need of control by specialists of e-voting	New
Procedural guarantees: other aspects	Need to respect all the rules applicable to an election, including the technical ones	New only to the extent that new technical provisions have to be adopted
Stability of electoral law	e-Voting as a major innovation	New, but no legal problem if the innovation is introduced early enough before the vote

Notes

* This contribution reflects the opinion of the author and may not be considered the official position of the Council of Europe and the Venice Commission.

1 Article 3 of the Additional Protocol to the European Convention on Human Rights.
2 Article 25b.
3 CDL-AD (2002) 23 rev. (www.venice.coe.int); Resolution 1320 (2003) and Recommendation 1595 (2003) of the Parliamentary Assembly; Resolution 148 (2003) and Recommendation 124 (2003) of the Congress of Local and Regional Authorities of the Council of Europe. On the European electoral heritage, see also Garrone, P. (2001) 'Le patrimoine électoral européen – Une décennie d'ex-périence de la Commission de Venise dans le domaine électoral', *Revue du droit public et de la science politique en France et à l'étranger (RDP)*, 1417–54. A slightly revised version of this article has been published, in French and in English, as a document of the Venice Commission, CDL (2002) 7 rev.
4 Internet Policy Institute: Report of the National Workshop on Internet Voting: Issues and Research Agenda, March 2001, pp. 6–7.
5 See European Court of Human Rights, *Mathieu-Mohin and Clerfayt* v. *Belgium* judgment of 2 March 1987, Series A. No. 113, p. 23; European Commission of Human Rights, No. 27311/95, dec. 11.9.97, *Timke* v. *Germany*, D.R. 82, p. 15; No. 7008/75, dec. 12.7.76, *X.* v. *Austria*, D.R. 6, p. 120.
6 Cf. European Court of Human Rights, *Matthews* v. *United Kingdom*, judgment of 18 February 1999, ECHR 1999-I, paras. 36 ff.
7 Auer, A. and Trechsel A.H. (eds) (2001) *Voter par internet ? Le projet e-voting dans le canton de Genève dans une perspective socio-politique et juridique*, Basle, Geneva, Munich: Helbing & Lichtenhahn, p. 104.
8 For a detailed account of the cognitive capacity of users and the implementa-tion of e-voting systems see the chapter by Pratchett *et al.* in this volume.
9 On the same line, see Auer and Mendez in this volume.
10 See section on equal suffrage, this volume, pp. 113–15.
11 Internet Policy Institute, op. cit., p. 17.
12 Internet Policy Institute, op. cit., p. 14 ff. and p. 46.
13 For more developments, see e.g. the Code of Good Practice in Electoral Matters, CDL (2002) 23 rev., ch. I.2; CDL (2002) 7 rev., II.B.2.
14 Auer and Trechsel, op. cit., p. 95.
15 On the specific problem of (multiple) e-voting by EU citizens living in a member state other than their own – and dual nationals – see Auer, op. cit., pp. 9–10.
16 See Auer and Trechsel , op. cit., p. 21 ff.
17 Internet Policy Institute, op. cit., p. 16 and p. 26. See also the chapter by Pratchett *et al.* in this volume.
18 See section on universal suffrage, this volume, pp. 115–17.
19 On the so-called digital divide and its implications, see e.g. Auer and Trechsel, op. cit., pp. 27–8, p. 32, p. 38 ff., pp. 54–6 and p. 110, and references; Internet Policy Institute, op. cit., p. 26.
20 See Auer and Trechsel, op. cit., pp. 105–6.
21 For more details, see CDL (2002) 23 rev., ch. I.3; CDL (2002) 7 rev., II.B.3.
22 Issues related to opinion formation are dealt with in the chapter by Kies and Kriesi in this volume.
23 On information that could be provided to the voter through the internet, see Auer and Trechsel, op. cit., p. 58 ff.
24 On this question, see Auer and Trechsel, op. cit., p. 92; Auer, op. cit., pp. 12–13.

25 See section on universal suffrage, this volume, pp. 112–13.

26 Internet Policy Institute, op. cit., p. 22.

27 However, see Auer and Trechsel, op. cit., pp. 46–7, who consider that the risk is not much bigger in the case of remote voting than in the case of voting at the ballot box.

28 Auer and Trechsel, op. cit.

29 Auer and Mendez in this volume (p. 134).

30 See Internet Policy Institute, op. cit., p. 22.

31 CDL (2002) 7 rev., 27; Auer and Trechsel, op. cit., p. 101.

32 On security and reliability, see section on universal suffrage, this volume, pp. 112–13.

33 Internet Policy Institute, op. cit., pp. 31–2.

34 Internet Policy Institute, op. cit., p. 27; see section on other fundamental rights and framework conditions of free and fair elections (discussion of procedural guarantees), this volume, pp. 118–19.

35 CDL-AD (2002) 23 rev., par. 52.

36 See section on universal suffrage, this volume, pp. 112–13.

37 See section on equal suffrage, this volume, pp. 113–15.

38 See Internet Policy Institute, op. cit., p. 11.

39 See also Auer and Trechsel, op. cit., p. 94.

40 See Auer and Trechsel, op. cit., p. 38.

41 CDL-AD (2002) 23 rev., ch. II.

42 CDL (2002) 7 rev., 13 ff.

43 See Auer and Trechsel, op. cit., p. 94.

44 Internet Policy Institute, op. cit., p. 27.

45 See, for example, European Court of Human Rights, *Delcourt* v. *Belgium*, judgment of 17 January 1970, Series A, no. 11, point 31; *de Cubber* v. *Belgium*, judgment of 26 October 1984, Series A, no. 86, point 26.

46 See section on free suffrage, this volume, pp. 115–17.

6 Introducing e-voting for the European Parliament elections

The constitutional problems

Andreas Auer and Mario Mendez

Introduction

This chapter is divided into two sections that address, respectively, what may be called the two basic constitutional problems associated with the introduction of e-voting for the European Parliament (EP) elections. That is, first, the framing of an adequate legal basis and, second, ensuring the respect of fundamental and political rights.

The first part of this chapter explores not only the possibility of employing an existing legal basis, but also either amending it or creating a new one in order to ensure a tighter nexus between any Community legislative action in the e-voting sphere and the legal basis from which it stems. Resolving this dilemma should prove all the more vital in this new era of heightened sensitivity to the constitutional boundaries of Community action. The possibility of e-voting being pursued solely at the domestic level is also raised for consideration, with recent developments in the UK, toying with this option, being indicative of its promising potential. The conclusion is drawn that while the legal basis for e-voting is a matter worthy of serious deliberation, it is ultimately not at this hurdle that the e-voting agenda will encounter problems.

The second part of this chapter examines the potential impact that fundamental rights can have on this debate. It touches upon the complicated relationship between the Community legal order and the European Convention on Human Rights (ECHR) which is likely to rear its head if e-voting is introduced via Community legislative action. Recent jurisprudence from the Strasbourg-based court, shedding light both on this relationship, and the relevance of ECHR norms to EP elections, is also brought into the equation. Some specific aspects of the fundamental rights critique are then outlined, the most potent being the alleged incompatibility with a secret ballot. The position advanced is that with sufficient *ex ante* and *ex post* controls in place, fundamental rights objections should not pose a serious obstacle to e-voting. In sum, political will rather than competence and fundamental rights issues will determine the trajectory of e-voting.

Establishing a legal basis for the introduction of e-voting

It is axiomatic that in order to put into operation the basic political rights granted by constitutions or treaties, a panoply of implementing laws and regulations needs to be adopted. Electoral laws regularly deal not only with substantive elements related to elections and referendums, but also with vital procedural matters, such as the establishment of polling stations, configuration of the ballot, time and manner of voting, procedures for legal review, etc. The existence of a detailed body of rules relating to the electoral process taken as a whole is both a prerequisite and a consequence of the rule of law, upon which the European Union (EU) as well as the Member States are founded.[1] It follows that this new dawn of e-voting is a process that would need to be strictly defined, organised and put into operation, by law.

This begs the question of which law? EU law? The law of the Member States? A combination of the two? The analysis that follows is divided into two sections that address both the prospects under Community law and those under national law.

e-Voting in EP elections according to EU legislation

The principle of attributed competencies is a basic tenet of the Community legal order enshrined in the Treaty.[2] That is to say, the Community only has the competence to act in those areas in which the Treaty has granted it the specific competence to do so.[3] Much doubt has existed as to the seriousness with which the constitutional limits of Community action are policed, it being well documented that the EU had pursued an ambitious consumer and environmental policy agenda well before having been granted the explicit Treaty competence to do so.[4] To be sure, this might appear testimony to the very nature of a European project where, provided the political will can be found, any legal obstacles are likely to prove surmountable – not least because a legal basis can always be created.

That said, the European Court of Justice (ECJ) has recently endeavoured to demonstrate that these constitutionally enshrined competence boundaries are to be taken seriously. In its *Tobacco Advertising* judgment the ECJ invalidated, for the first time, a legislative measure for lack of competence.[5] Essentially, the case prevented the Community institutions from hijacking the internal market harmonisation provision of Article 95 for the purposes of adopting a health policy harmonisation measure, a competence that had been explicitly excluded by Article 152(4). The details of the case need not be delved into for present purposes,[6] suffice it to say that it reinforces the attributed competence personality of the Community, thus further underlining the need for legislative measures to be grounded in an appropriate legal basis.

At first glance, this might not seem especially problematic with respect to the subject-matter at hand. Article 190(4) ECT, since its amendment by the Treaty of Amsterdam (TOA), provides that '[t]he European Parliament shall draw up a proposal for elections by direct universal suffrage in accordance with a uniform procedure in all Member States or in accordance with principles common to all Member States'. This would appear to leave the EP with two pegs on which to hang an e-voting agenda. However, both raise problems.

In relation to the second of the two options, it would be an ambitious argument, indeed, that e-voting is a principle common to all Member States. Although, at the time of writing, one Member State is actively toying with the idea of e-voting for the 2004 EP elections, having already conducted various pilot projects on the matter.[7] Moving from this to a principle common to all Member States is a giant leap. It may not be beyond the realms of possibility that a future state of affairs could exist in which e-voting were a common principle, but at best this is some way off and, at worst, a flight of fancy.

Tellingly, the use to which this second formulation has already been put, since its introduction by the TOA, is not to push forward a radical new voting agenda but, rather, to break the deadlock that had existed as a product of the exacting requirements of the uniform procedure formulation. It takes the form of a Council Decision, the common principles included providing for, *inter alia*, members of the EP to be elected on the basis of proportional representation (Article 1(2)) and for the incompatibility of the office of member of the EP with that of member of a national parliament (Article 1(7)(b)).[8]

Even if e-voting were established in many Member States, thereby entitling it to a greater claim to the coveted status of a common principle, it clearly lacks the political salience of issues, such as dual-mandates and the type of electoral system, that have been tackled in the aforementioned Council Decision. Accordingly, though without rejecting its viability for the future, it is submitted that, as conditions currently stand, the second formulation under Article 190(4) does not provide a practical or fitting legal basis in which to attempt to ground e-voting for the EP elections.

A more optimistic assessment could be offered of the first option under Article 190(4). Drawing up a proposal for a uniform electoral procedure is undoubtedly a laborious task, the EP being unable to make any headway under this option despite repeated attempts.[9] The requirement of Council unanimity, combined with the assent of the EP by an absolute majority, and adoption by the Member States in accordance with their respective constitutional requirements is, to say the least, an imposing standard.[10] Clearly, a great deal of political energy, evidently found wanting hitherto, would need to be expended to generate support for anything resembling a uniform electoral procedure. It is with this in mind, and after many an attempt in vain, that the TOA introduced the alternative option based on principles common to all Member States.[11] In spite of this, and putting political practicalities to the side, one could still argue that the first option in Article 190(4) might provide a suitable opening on which to hang the e-voting agenda.

A conceivable argument could run that in order to have a truly uniform electoral procedure, as envisaged in Article 190(4), the different modalities of voting for EP elections should also be uniform. Put simply, EU citizens should have the same voting methods available to them, including but not exhausted by e-voting, across the EU. On this reasoning, one could tentatively conclude that e-voting could fall squarely within the parameters of the first option under Article 190(4).

Inevitably, arguments could be made the other way, to the effect that the first option in Article 190(4) does not envisage intricate harmonisation such that it encapsulates the voting modalities on offer, and that this would be to foist e-voting on EU citizens through an illegitimate back door. In a time of heightened focus on the appropriate delimitation of powers between the Community and its members, prudence would not be misplaced. From this point of view, and given that Article 190(4) has a procedural threshold tantamount to that required for Treaty amendment, one might suggest that the Member States would be better advised to move into this new era of e-voting with the precision and clarity that a Treaty amendment could specifically provide.

However, bringing the political practicalities back in for a moment, the Council's (*read Member States'*) intransigence that had been the main stumbling block to a uniform electoral procedure in the first place, is unlikely to mysteriously vanish as a result of the conviction of the wonders to be offered by e-voting. The salience of e-voting does not appear such that the political will could be generated for its EU-wide adoption any time soon, whether it be through anchoring it in the first option of Article 190(4), though the adequacy of this provision might be subject to contestation, or through Treaty amendment in a forthcoming intergovernmental conference. This is to underline, axiomatic though it may seem, that the real barrier for e-voting for the EP elections is not going to be at the competence level.

Not unrelated to the political practicalities issue is the draft Treaty establishing a Constitution for Europe (draft Constitution), which essentially reproduces Article 190(4).[12] The twin approaches of Article 190(4), as amended by the TOA, have been maintained with the same high thresholds in place. Consequently, the analysis outlined above would appear equally applicable. One substantive change relates to the type of measure that can be used to pursue the goals in what is currently Article 190(4) and what will become Article III:232(1) of the European Constitution, if negotiations on its adoption can be brought back on track. While Article 190(4) is framed in terms of the Council laying down the appropriate provisions which it shall recommend to the Member States for adoption, Article III:232(1) refers specifically to a European law or framework law of the Council of Ministers.[13] This would seem to give Article III:232(1) more bite, though without giving any cause to reconsider the analysis proffered.

If the draft Constitution is adopted with Article III:232(1) in place, and neither of the formulations therein, identical as they are to Article 190(4), are considered presently adequate for e-voting, it does not bode well for the likelihood of a firmer legal basis being created. Having just gone through the taxing process of drafting a European Constitution, it is unrealistic to expect that it will be opened up to address the finer points of voting techniques for the EP elections. Not least since the breadth of the first formulation in Article 190(4) has been preserved, suggesting that the latter provides sufficient room for manoeuvre, political will permitting, for any future ventures. The point to stress, in any event, is that whichever route is adopted will require substantial political capital and herein lies the major obstacle.

Finally, it is worth highlighting that whichever legal basis were to pave the way for e-voting for the EP elections, we should be under no illusions as to the feasibility of a truly uniform system of e-voting across the EU. For the search for complete uniformity is largely a chimera. In the same way that polling stations, ballot boxes and sundry other practicalities of voting are run and managed by regional or local Member State agents, e-voting would also have to be administered in a decentralised fashion.[14] Member State agents would be expected to operate within the restricting confines of an overarching European law, but fleshing out the details would be supplementary state rules and practices with all the scope for differentiation that this entails. Essentially, this means that each Member State is likely to have its own particular e-voting scheme tested, implemented and worked out at the national level.

The vision being sketched here of a multiplicity of diverse e-voting schemes operating across the EU, as the Member States get to grips with the practicalities of the task bestowed upon them, is theoretically no bad thing. With experimentation aplenty, there would be considerable scope for the mutual learning that lies at the heart of the much-hyped Open Method of Co-ordination (OMC).[15] The principles underpinning the operation of the OMC – the use of benchmarking, the identification of best practices and the like – could certainly be put to good use in ensuring as smooth a transition as possible for e-voting.

e-Voting in EP elections according to national legislation

Article 7(2) of the 1976 Act concerning the election of the representatives of the European Parliament by direct universal suffrage (1976 EP Act), provides that '[p]ending the entry into force of a uniform electoral procedure . . . the electoral procedure shall be governed in each Member State by its national provisions'.[16] The 2002 Council Decision amending the 1976 EP Act maintains in force the essence of this rule.[17] The effect is that in those areas that have not been addressed by common rule-making in the 1976 Act, or the amendments that have followed, the Member States remain competent to enact such legislation as they see fit. Voting techniques for EP elections not having been the subject of common rule-making leaves the Member States free to put in place those modalities, e-voting included, deemed appropriate. Though national initiatives do not require any form of approval at the EU level, there being no oversight in this regard, they must satisfy their own domestic constitutional requirements.[18]

Of the Member States, the UK has been the most pioneering in this area. It has conducted wide-ranging e-voting pilot schemes and has pushed strongly the possibility of introducing such pilots for the 2004 EP elections.[19] This is further evidence that an e-enabled future for EP elections is not the pipe dream some might suspect it to be.[20] Different Member States can, and likely will, experiment at their leisure providing fertile ground for innovative developments. To start with, an e-voting future that took place in this manner would not possess even the faintest semblance of uniformity. It would develop outside the remit of an overarching European law and in a wholly piecemeal fashion. Over time, however, it could lead to something a great deal more concrete with Member States co-ordinating their activities, and an OMC type approach could be incorporated, therefore helping to bring about a better designed and secure e-voting system in those Member States that opt for it.

For the time being it is this kind of strategy that remains the most realistic prospect for e-voting to take hold, and Community law poses no obstacles for this to thrive. Furthermore, the EU does not have to be an actor sidelined in this process but could, instead, have a complementary function. It has tools at its disposal to favour and to promote e-voting for EP elections. Action could be taken to provide financial assistance and technical support to those Member States taking these ambitious steps. Given existing political and practical constraints, the power of the purse could have a prominent role to play in solidifying the e-voting objective. Moreover, the Community could be well served by contributing financially and technically to a project that has the potential to enfranchise disillusioned voters, thus bolstering, if only negligibly, the legitimacy claims of the EU.[21] For their part, those Member States embarking on this might well consider such recompense a deserved quid pro quo for the bold steps they are taking.

To tie back in with the analysis in the previous section, though somewhat more optimistically, this approach might also lay the foundations for resort to the second option in Article 190(4). The more progress that is made with the e-voting agenda for the EP elections at the domestic level, the closer it comes to becoming a principle common to all Member States, and the easier it would be to rely on the second formulation in Article 190(4). More importantly, a future in which e-voting were pervasive would break down the political barriers to its adoption at the Community level. The added benefit would be that if an EU-wide e-voting law were adopted in such a context, it would be able to draw on the most promising aspects of the developments that had taken place domestically. To be sure, it is a long-term perspective that is being envisioned but it also happens to be the most feasible.

The content of e-voting regulations

As for the actual content of e-voting regulations, under Article 19(2) ECT every citizen of an EU Member State has the right to vote and to stand as a candidate in elections to the EP. Thus, the only direct political right that is granted to European citizens, and which is directly related to the EU institutional framework, is the right to participate and to be a candidate in EP elections. e-Voting within the EU, therefore, refers exclusively to this particular and basic democratic institution. Yet, the rules and regulations that are necessary for implementing and organising popular elections have a pronounced political impact and happen to be, mainly for this reason, quite important, complex and detailed. It follows that State legislation organising e-voting for the EP elections will have to deal with all those important, complicated and detailed rules, too. Moreover, most of these rules, as we have seen, are specific to each one of the Member States: constituencies, type of proportional representation, voting period, polling stations, election registers, authentication procedures, security checks, vote counting, etc. There will not be, in other words, much by way of comparison between the different legislations, even though they all have the purpose of dealing with the same democratic institution – popular election – and with the same voting technique, i.e. e-voting.

Yet, at the same time, it should be pointed out that e-voting is a technology that need not be restricted to EP elections. Were, for example, a European referendum to come into existence as a means to enlarge the political rights of EU citizens, one could not exclude the possibility of e-voting being extended to such institutional innovations.[22] And on this note, an argument not devoid of merit is that the practical feasibility of e-voting in a referendum would be much greater than that for an election. Voting Yes or No on a proposition, in a manner that the Swiss, for instance, have been long accustomed to, is an easier operation by far to conduct online than voting for one of many possible candidates on lists presented within several electoral constituencies. It could even be expected that, in contrast to the prognosis for e-voting for the EP elections, procedural rules for a European referendum could entail a large degree of uniformity and perhaps even be centrally assessed. While e-voting would, no doubt, be much easier to implement and handle in the context of an EU-wide referendum it is, until institutional reforms are made in this direction, far from becoming a reality.

e-Voting and fundamental rights

The preceding analysis has provided some tentative thoughts about where we might look for a suitable legal basis for e-voting. It tells us nothing, however, about the second constitutional problem pertinent to e-voting, that of its compatibility with fundamental rights.[23] The need to abide by the fundamental rights granted to European citizens is essential whether the introduction of e-voting is pursued within the EU framework or in a more patchwork fashion at the domestic level.

The analysis in this section is divided as follows. A few preliminary observations are provided concerning the various different sources from which such rights can be derived, the complicated interrelationship between them, and the importance of a recent decision by the European Court of Human Rights (ECtHR). The latter is a precursor to a brief assessment of some of the specific conflicts that might be foreseen between e-voting and fundamental rights.

Fundamental rights: the Community and the ECHR

The EU legal order itself has, from the most inauspicious beginnings, made significant inroads into the development of a comprehensive human rights agenda.[24] Pertinent fundamental rights are also enshrined in international instruments such as the European Convention on Human Rights (ECHR) and the International Covenant on Civil and Political Rights (ICCPR), to say nothing of national constitutions and the protection afforded therein to fundamental rights.

The relationship between all the aforementioned sources of rights is, however, a complex and multifaceted one. It is well known that the initial development of fundamental rights protection in the Community was a result of the ECJ's desire to see off a potential revolt by national constitutional courts, alarmed at the prospect of Community law infringing constitutionally protected rights at the domestic level.[25] Since those early days developments have continued apace, with the ECJ trying to tread a fine line between maintaining the independent nature of the fundamental rights it protects while ensuring more than just mere lip-service to international instruments and national constitutional provisions.[26]

This is of the utmost importance because it is partly from this base, that is, international instruments such as the ECHR and national constitutional provisions, that the ECJ is likely to derive the kind of political rights that are implicated by a move to e-voting. It also raises an issue fraught with tension and over which much ink has been spilt, namely the relationship between the ECHR and the Community legal order.[27] It is a relationship to which further complications have been added as a result of provisions of the Charter of Fundamental Rights which ostensibly purport to minimise potential conflict.[28] The intricacies of these developments are beyond the scope of this chapter, though a salient recent development in ECHR jurisprudence merits consideration in so far as it elucidates exactly why the ECHR can have an important role to play in this debate, independently of the status accorded to it by Community law.

In the *Matthews* case a complaint was brought against the UK for its failure to allow residents of Gibraltar to vote in EP elections.[29] At issue was Article 3 of the First Protocol (henceforth Article 3) of the ECHR, which provides: 'The High Contracting Parties undertake to hold free elections at reasonable intervals by secret ballot, under conditions which will ensure the free expression of the opinion of the people in the choice of the legislature.'

This provision raises the initial question of what exactly is meant by 'the legislature'. Notwithstanding the EP's central and burgeoning role in the Community legislative process,[30] the UK sought to exploit any uncertainty by controversially arguing that the EP was not a legislature within the meaning of Article 3. While, to the surprise of many, this argument had carried the day before the European Commission of Human Rights (ECommHR), the ECtHR, in a characteristically nuanced analysis, brought the EP within the meaning of the legislature in Article 3.[31]

The UK's argument that it should not be held responsible given that it did not have effective control over the act complained of, it being attributable to the 1976 EP Act which did not include Gibraltar as part of the UK for European elections, fared equally badly. The Strasbourg-based court famously responded that the ECHR 'does not preclude the transfer of competencies to international organisations provided that Convention rights continue to be "secured". Member States' responsibility therefore continues even after such a transfer.'[32] The ECtHR went on to find the UK in violation of Article 3, the applicant being directly affected by the legislation emanating from the Community and the very essence of her right to vote being denied.[33]

Two points germane to the e-voting agenda are established incontrovertibly by this case. First, elections to the EP do fall within the remit of Article 3. Second, the Member States are responsible for securing the rights in Article 3 even when the alleged complaints are the product of competencies exercised at the Community level. Taking only the first point, Article 3 is applicable if e-voting for EP elections is introduced solely at the domestic level, the possibility currently being floated in the UK. Taking the two points together, it is difficult to escape the conclusion that any e-voting legislation for the EP elections adopted by the Community institutions could be subject to evaluation vis-à-vis the benchmark of Article 3.

One vote only

Equal suffrage, not to be confused with universal suffrage,[34] is a principle that lies at the heart of modern democracies. There are several components to it, the core being the principle 'one person, one vote'.[35] Though it is not expressly mentioned in Article 3 of the ECHR,[36] it is enshrined explicitly in the Universal Declaration of Human Rights,[37] the ICCPR[38] and various constitutions of the Member States of the EU.[39]

Curiously, neither the EC Treaty nor the draft Constitution incorporating the Charter of Rights makes any mention of equal suffrage. And the Council, in the 2002 Decision to which we have already referred, rejected the proposal of the EP to include a reference to an 'equal ... ballot'.[40] Its status, however, in relevant international treaties and domestic constitutions indicate its potential to be a principle from which the ECJ would draw in its fundamental rights jurisprudence were the matter to arise.

In any event, not much turns on this point as Article 8 of the 1976 EP Act states that '[n]o one may vote more than once in any election of representatives to the European Parliament'.[41] The need to ensure respect for this provision would manifestly be applicable whether we are dealing with a European-wide e-voting law or Member State initiatives. Yet, even absent the complications likely to arise were e-voting introduced, Member States have had trouble ensuring full implementation of the principle 'one vote only'. We can only expect this to be compounded if e-voting became a reality although national mechanisms to effectively prevent double voting would, undoubtedly, have to become far more sophisticated.

As remote e-voting can take place anywhere, even outside the EU, provided that the necessary keys and codes are available, violations of the 'one vote only' rule are much more prone to going unnoticed and, accordingly, unsanctioned. The problem is rendered all the more complex as e-voting schemes will almost certainly rely on different and possibly incompatible programs, standards and authentication procedures in every Member State.

For example, in the case of those EU citizens exercising their freedom of movement and residing in Member States of which they are not nationals, the opportunity to breach the one vote only principle could be enhanced. Measures would have to be in place preventing them from voting twice, once in their state of residence and once in their state of nationality. How would the courts and administrations of the Member State of residence ensure that resident EU citizens have not already, or will not subsequently, attempt to exercise on-line voting rights, were they to exist, in accordance with the procedure in their state of nationality? The same problem arises for the courts and administration in the state of nationality for their residents abroad.

A deceptively easy answer would be for either Community e-voting legislation, or, as the case may be, for individual Member State legislation to limit the right to vote on-line to Member State nationals. Such an approach, however, would not escape unscathed from the scrutiny of the non-discrimination principle laid down for such purposes in Article 19(2) ECT. The latter provides that:

> every citizen of the Union residing in a Member State of which he is not a national shall have the right to vote and to stand as a candidate in elections to the European Parliament in the Member State in which he resides, under the same conditions as nationals of that State.

A 1993 Directive lays down detailed arrangements for the exercise of this right.[42] It gives all EU citizens the opportunity to choose whether to participate in elections to the EP in their home state or their state of residence within the EU, if these are not the same, on equal conditions in the state of residence as apply to nationals of that state. Clearly, any distinctions drawn between nationals and resident non-nationals for e-voting purposes are likely to fall foul of the rights accorded EU citizens by Article 19(2), as interpreted by the 1993 Directive. A more suitable response would be to put into operation a system in which co-ordinated interaction occurs between the Member States as a means of resolving such conflicts, the tools of the OMC could also be harnessed to this end. Different political, administrative and judicial bodies, as well as technical teams of varying capacity across the EU could be enrolled in a collaborative endeavour of mutual learning that curtails the hazards of e-voting.

At root what is needed is a secure e-voting system to minimise many of the foreseeable tensions with fundamental rights, over and above the one vote only issue. But the importance of technical considerations should not be overstated. For one finding seems to be quite indisputable: there is probably no 100 per cent safe solution to the undoubtedly complex security problems raised by e-voting. The question, therefore, cannot be to look for absolute security under any circumstances and to drop the idea of e-voting if maximum-level security cannot, for any reason, be guaranteed. Constitutional requirements by any means do not and cannot ask that much. The question is to find optimal security standards under given circumstances, which are necessarily subject to change. Even traditional voting procedures are no stranger to occasional mishaps and errors and, as such, to expect or, indeed, require perfection from e-voting is to be too exacting.[43]

The choice between different available technical devices and solutions is never a final one and is of a more political than technical nature: how much security can and must be guaranteed at a given moment in a given context without threatening or even sacrificing the essential advantages of e-voting? There are no easy solutions to such conundrums and the inherent value choices involved. The most that can be expected is that *ex ante* and *ex post* controls are in place to diminish the problems of fraud, voter authentication and the like, that will inevitably be posed to a greater extent by e-voting than at present in the off-line world of voting. This would go some way to placating the fundamental rights concerns of the e-voting sceptics.

Equality

The most acute challenge from a fundamental rights perspective is the strain under which the secrecy of the ballot is placed by e-voting. However, before proceeding to the issue of ballot secrecy, it should be noted that there is another guise in which the equality issue presents itself, to which technical solutions will be of no avail. Three aspects of it are worth flagging, and although none raise decisive legal obstacles their political ramifications could be considerable.

The first is the well-known 'digital divide', which refers to differences in access between the information haves and have-nots.[44] If e-voting were introduced as, or if it were to become, the only possibility of voting in EP elections it would clash with the principle of universal suffrage given that not everyone can be expected to have access to the internet or the necessary skills for its use.[45] The academic niceties of this point need not trouble us here, for e-voting has never been seriously contemplated in this exclusionary fashion; rather, its proponents envisage it playing the role of an additional mechanism on which voters may, but need not, rely.

The second aspect of the equality issue would be raised by the coexistence of different Member State responses to the challenges posed by e-voting, with some pushing forward on this front and others, unconvinced of its benefits or otherwise, remaining wedded to the more traditional voting techniques. The alternative of e-voting being an obligation imposed by Community law, notwithstanding the diversity that this still entails, elicits no such equality concerns. But the question that needs to be asked is whether it is acceptable for EP elections to be held in some Member States with the additional aid of e-voting, while recourse to this technology is excluded in others. We have already seen that existing Community law on this point is categorical, that which is not within the span of the amended 1976 EP Act remains to be governed by the domestic provisions of the Member States.[46] Differences in electoral matters for the EP elections are, therefore, unsurprisingly rife, and would be further accentuated with the staggered introduction of e-voting. On the positive side it has already been suggested in the first part of this chapter that this need not be looked at in a negative light, taking account of the conducive environment it provides for e-voting to foster at the domestic level. And it is difficult to see from which legal angle such differentiation between Member States could realistically be challenged. Federal states have a long history of dealing with such alleged inequalities whenever their constitution leaves a matter to be entirely or partially regulated by the decentralised entities,[47] and one can hardly expect the minutiae of such divisions of competence to be a subject for close inspection by judicial organs such as the ECtHR.

The third facet of the equality issue could crop up whether e-voting is pursued at the domestic or at the Community level. It can be dubbed the 'double-standards problem' and would arise in the event that a Member State introduced e-voting for EP elections, whether of its own initiative or at the behest of Community law, but then decided not to extend the latter to national elections. Solely from the perspective of the EU, such differential treatment of European and national elections would be of no consequence. The 1976 EP Act has nothing to say on this point and, in general, the Community order has not been averse to the acceptance of double-standards in other areas.[48] This does not preclude the issue being of significance under the domestic constitutional standards of a Member State. Nor does it detract from the frustration that would surely be felt by the electorate were such manifest double-standards in place. It would take some persuading to convince the electorate of why they should be entitled to vote from the comfort of their home in matters European but not so in the case of national elections. This predicament would be exacerbated were national and European elections to be held on the same day, as is practised in some Member States, under otherwise identical procedures.

While this scenario might seem far-fetched, it should be emphasised that the pilot projects in which the UK is engaging are for the EP and local elections alone. e-Voting for the EP elections could certainly be viewed from an experimental optic, the much-touted benefits of which, if substantiated, could then be extended to the national level. That is to say, the European elections can be seen as a convenient laboratory in which practical experience is generated that can lead to a more trouble-free application for national elections, undeniably the politically more sensitive of the two. Such an approach, however, does nothing to dispel the existing tendency to regard EP elections as 'second-order events'.[49] From the point of view of enhancing the democratic legitimacy of the EU this tendency is to be regretted. But envisioning the possibility of e-voting for the EP elections providing the impetus for its extension to national elections, rather than the other way round, should not be viewed as an argument against its introduction. For it would not be the first time that developments have taken place at the European level before the spill-over to the national level has occurred.[50]

The secret ballot: a real fundamental rights problem?

It is with secrecy of the ballot that the greatest tension between e-voting and fundamental rights arises.[51] It is a right that is enshrined in various international provisions,[52] including Article 3 of the First Protocol of the ECHR, and various national constitutions of the Member States.[53] It is not, however, explicitly articulated in any existing Community law in force. It seems a surprising oversight, though its status as one of the main principles of the European electoral tradition would indicate that the ECJ would not be hard pressed to treat it accordingly. And recent developments, apparently recognising this oversight, have sought to give it an explicit grounding in Community law. In the first place Article 39(2) of the Charter of Fundamental Rights provides 'Members of the European Parliament shall be elected by direct universal suffrage in a free and secret ballot'. Notwithstanding that the explanatory memorandum to the Charter states that Article 39(2) corresponds to Article 190(1) ECT, the latter, in fact, makes no mention of either a free or secret ballot, this is the first explicit articulation in Community law of the core electoral principles of a free and secret ballot. It has been reinforced by also gaining a place in Article 19(2) of the draft Constitution. Further, Council Decision 2002/772/EC also introduces a reference to free and secret elections.[54] It seems straightforward then that even pending the entry into force of the Council decision, or possible agreement on the draft Constitution, the ECJ would have more than adequate grounds on which to found the need for a secret ballot for EP elections.

But the fact that we can identify secrecy of the ballot as a norm by which e-voting legislation could be measured tells us nothing about the standard of secrecy required. One looks in vain to European law for even an inkling of what this might entail. The ECJ could be expected to look to ECHR jurisprudence, were the need to arise, but then there is no such jurisprudence on this point either. Interestingly, the explanatory memorandum to the Charter does not identify Article 39(2) as corresponding to that in Article 3 of the First Protocol, indicating that even if there were ECHR jurisprudence on the secrecy point it could still be subjected to the gloss of the European judiciary.[55]

There is a complicated relationship between the various conflict avoidance provisions of the Charter which are not explored here; the aim is simply to bring forth the possibility that different standards of secrecy could be applicable. Why should this matter? We simply need remind ourselves of the significance of the *Matthews* decision, which 'is unequivocally the strongest affirmation to date of Member State responsibility for Community acts under the Convention'.[56] Put starkly, the Member States cannot shirk their obligations under Article 3 of the First Protocol of the ECHR simply by virtue of the fact that action is taken at the European level.[57] And, a fortiori, Member States cannot shirk that responsibility if action is taken only domestically.

Having raised the spectre of different standards, the question that needs to be asked is whether it could seriously be contended that e-voting is precluded by the strictures of the ECHR or European law. Do we really expect the ECtHR, or the ECJ for that matter, to be so unbending as to put a brake on such innovations? In relation to the standards in the ECHR, one author at least seems persuaded that remote voting from the home is likely to be incompatible with a secret ballot as enshrined in Article 3 of the First Protocol.[58] This seems unlikely. Absolute adherence to the principle of a secret ballot is a slippery slope to go down. Where would it leave postal voting, a practice under which the state can also no longer ensure the preservation of secrecy in the act of voting? Are we to expect that voting modalities must forever remain anchored firmly in the past? With current levels of voter apathy[59] should modernisation, to use a somewhat loaded term, be rejected out of hand? The ECtHR has been at pains to stress that 'the Convention is a living instrument which must be interpreted in the light of present-day conditions'.[60] It would be odd if the Strasbourg court were then to remain uncompromising in the light of technological, social and cultural advances.

It is promising to note that the ECtHR has thus far exhibited flexibility in its approach to Article 3; this was evident in the short shrift given to the UK's argument in *Matthews* that the EP lacked the attributes of a legislature. It was also evident in the manner in which the Strasbourg Court, endorsing the stance of the ECommHR, has read universal suffrage into the provision.[61] In doing so the ECtHR underlined that such rights, the right to vote and stand for elections, 'are not absolute . . . there is room for implied limitations'. While not directly on point,[62] it may give some cause for optimism as to the type of analysis that would ensue were the issue of secret ballot to come before the Court. We can expect further light to be cast on this matter in the forthcoming Council of Europe e-voting guidelines.[63] For the moment it seems fair to say that the case against the introduction of e-voting from a fundamental rights perspective has yet to be made.

Conclusion

e-Voting seems to be, at first glance, a mere procedural device. Citizens are allowed to cast their vote not only at the traditional polling stations or by correspondence (postal voting) but also on-line. According to common continental European legal heritage, procedure is, of course, supposed to be secondary. What ought to prevail is the substantial law or right which the procedural rule merely helps to enforce. From this perspective, elections and referendums – as the major institutions of political democracy – are primary. What matters is who can vote, for whom he or she can vote and, in the case of referendums, on what proposition he or she can vote. The question of how one votes, by what means he or she may cast their ballot, seems to be of minor importance.

Yet e-voting is different. The possibility for the voter to use his or her computer for electing the people's representatives in parliament and for voting on propositions submitted to a referendum has acquired a considerable political and scientific salience. The main reason for this quite unusual attention given to a simple procedural device is not technical. It is not legal either. Neither is it of a political nature. It probably has something to do with deeply entrenched voting cultures. In many respects voting is intimately linked to a series of ritual expressions and acts which can be serious obstacles when considering supplementary or alternative voting modalities, such as postal voting or e-voting. Usually, voters have no choice regarding the modality of casting their vote[64]: They have to walk (or drive) to the official polling station in order to fill out the official ballot and, finally, to place it in the official ballot box, which the officer (at least in France) officially attests by pronouncing the solemn formula '*a voté*'. Seen from this lens e-voting could appear to constitute a serious threat to certain long-established and much cherished 'voting cultures'. Moreover, these potential pockets of 'cultural' resistance, being deeply anchored in history and tradition are less open to rational discussions about efficiency gains or enhanced convenience.

Democracy is, without doubt, one of the most cherished and valued goods of contemporary state and society. Few dare to even question its justification. At the same time, the new information and communication technologies have become irreplaceable tools of our daily social, economic and personal life. Yet, to juxtapose democracy and computer technology, on the input and not only on the output side of the electoral contest, seems to generate unusually strong passions. The true efficiency of the latter, some contend, depends on its availability to the former. The very legitimacy of the former, others respond, is challenged by the latter.

It is possible that the legitimacy of online democracy techniques might well become one of the major constitutional (and not only political or moral) problems of implementing e-voting at the EU level.[65] e-Voting can only be recognised as a valid alternative voting modality if it does not threaten the strong legitimacy that is attached to the democratic process itself. As democracy is weak and still controversial at the EU level, its ideological ties and strings are quite loose and exposed to various pressures. e-Voting should not by any means be introduced for European Parliamentary elections if it has the effect of weakening those ties. But does it really? There is a case – maybe not a strong one but a case at any rate – that e-voting, especially if accompanied by other institutional innovations such as referendums, might well be a means by which the EU could endeavour to enhance the credibility and democratic character of its institutions and policies.

Notes

1 See, for example, Article 6(1) TEU ('[t]he Union is founded on the principles of liberty, democracy, respect for human rights and fundamental freedoms, and the rule of law, principles which are common to the member states').
2 Article 5 ECT provides '[t]he Community shall act within the limits of the powers conferred upon it by this Treaty and of the objectives assigned to it therein'.

3 There is a residual role for Article 308 ECT for the purposes of adopting measures necessary to attain the objectives of the Community where the Treaty has not provided the necessary powers.

4 See, for example, Weatherill, S. (1999) 'Consumer Law', in P. Craig and G. de Búrca (eds) *The Evolution of EU Law*, Oxford: Oxford University Press; on environmental policy see, for example, Scott, J. (1998) *EC Environmental Law*, New York: Longman.

5 Case C-376/98 *Germany* v. *Parliament and Council* [2000] ECR I- 8419.

6 For an informative discussion of the judgment see Wyatt, D. (2001) 'Constitutional Significance of the Tobacco Advertising Judgment of the European Court of Justice', in *The ECJ's Tobacco Advertising Judgment*, Cambridge: University of Cambridge, Centre for European Legal Studies, Occasional Paper No. 5; de Búrca, G. (2001) 'The Tobacco Judgment: Political Will versus Constitutional Limits', in *The ECJ's Tobacco Advertising Judgment*, Cambridge: University of Cambridge, Centre for European Legal Studies, Occasional Paper No. 5.

7 See the UK's Electoral Commission's Recommendation, December 2003, for the electoral pilots at the June 2004 elections. Available at: www.electoralcommission.gov.uk.

8 Council Decision 2002/772/EC amending the 1976 Act concerning the election of the representatives of the European Parliament by direct universal suffrage [2002] OJ L283/1. The Decision is yet to be adopted by the Member States in accordance with their respective constitutional requirements and takes effect the month after they have adopted it, accordingly all citations are to the Council Decision and not the Act as amended.

9 For example, the three adopted parliamentary resolutions of 1991, 1992 and 1993, on a uniform electoral procedure, were not considered proposals within the meaning of Article 190 by the Council.

10 See Article 190(4) ECT.

11 Subject, however, to the same procedural thresholds.

12 See Article III:232(1) of the draft Treaty establishing a Constitution for Europe.

13 Defined in Article 32 as follows:

> [a] European law shall be a legislative act of general application. It shall be binding in its entirety and directly applicable in all Member States. A European framework law shall be a legislative act binding, as to the result to be achieved, on the Member States to which it is addressed, but leaving the national authorities entirely free to choose the form and means of achieving that result.

14 Decentralised enforcement lies at the very heart of the Community system and though it does not come cost-free it allows the Community to operate with the minimum of resources. On a related point see Weatherill, S. (2002) 'Pre-emption, Harmonisation and the Distribution of Competence to Regulate the Internal Market', in C. Barnard and J. Scott (eds) *The Law of the Single European Market: Unpacking the Premises*, Oxford: Hart Publishing, who investigates the constitutional implications of the building of a market in which rules agreed at the transnational level are implemented and enforced by national legal and administrative institutions.

15 For a recent overview looking at many of the strengths and weaknesses of this new form of governance see de Búrca, G. (2003) 'The Constitutional Challenge of New Governance in the European Union', *European Law Review*, 28: 814.

16 Annexed to Council Decision 76/787 [1976] OJ L278/1.

17 See Council Decision 2002/772/EC, op. cit., Article 1(8). If the Decision is adopted by the Member States in accordance with their constitutional require- ments the relevant part of the new Article 7 of the 1976 EP Act will read, '[s]ubject to the provisions of this Act, the electoral procedure shall be governed in each Member State by its national provisions'.

18 For a report in the UK context providing an assessment of the legal changes needed for the implementation of various forms of electronic voting, see Watt, B. (2001) 'Implementing Electronic Voting', at: www.local-regions.odpm.gov.uk/ egov/e-voting/01/index.htm.

19 For an assessment of the implications of such developments see the UK's Electoral Commission's Recommendation, December 2003, for the Electoral pilots at the June 2004 elections. Available at: www.electoralcommission.gov.uk.

20 However, the Electoral Commission (ibid.) has come down against the intro- duction of such pilots for the 2004 elections on the basis that 'no region is ready for such innovation at this stage in the development of the electoral modern- ization programme' (p. 28).

21 From a democratic theory perspective it is not merely a matter of increasing the 'quantity' of the vote but, rather, the 'quality' of the vote. For a related discus- sion on enhancing the 'quality' of the vote via e-voting and other ICT measures see the chapter by Kies and Kriesi and the chapter by Schmitter in this volume.

22 Auer, A. and Flauss, J.-F. (eds) (1997) *Le référendum européen*, Bruxelles: Bruylant. See both the chapters by Ladeur and Schmitter in this volume for further insights concerning the introduction of e-referendums. See also Kaufmann, B., Lamassoure, A. and Meyer, J. (eds) (2003) *Transnational Democracy in the Making*, Amsterdam: Initiative & Referendum Institute Europe.

23 This issue is also explored in the chapter by Garrone in this volume, however, the analysis proffered here takes a different angle and any overlap has been kept to the minimum. See also Kley, A. and Rütsche, B. (2002) 'eVoting aus der Sicht der Wahl- und Abstimmungsfreiheit – Verfassungsrechtliche Bedeutung einer neuen Technik', in Th. Koller and H. Muralt-Müller (eds) (2002) *Nationale und internationale Bezüge des E-Commerce – Auswirkungen von E-Democracy auf den Rechtsstaat*, Bern: Stämpfli, pp. 255–78.

24 For a balanced and lucid overview of such developments see Craig, P. and de Búrca, G. (2003) *EU Law*, Oxford: Oxford University Press (3rd edition), pp. 317–69.

25 Craig and de Búrca, op. cit., pp. 319–23.

26 Craig and de Búrca, op. cit., pp. 323–7.

27 See the discussion in Craig and de Búrca, op. cit., and references therein to the vast literature spawned.

28 Since its proclamation the Charter has been incorporated into the draft Constitution, though its legal status remains unresolved given the recent failure to agree to the European Constitution.

29 App. 24833/94, *Matthews* v. *United Kingdom*, judgment of 18 February 1999; (1999) 28 EHRR 361.

30 See, for example, Maurer, A. (2003) 'The Legislative Powers and Impact of the European Parliament', *Journal of Common Market Studies*, 41: 227.

31 See App. 24833/94, *Matthews* v. *United Kingdom*, op. cit., paragraphs 33–54.

32 See App. 24833/94, *Matthews* v. *United Kingdom*, op. cit., paragraph 32.

33 See App. 24833/94, *Matthews* v. *United Kingdom*, op. cit., paragraphs 64–5.

34 The latter referring to all people, subject to certain conditions, being entitled to exercise the right to vote and stand for election. See, further, the chapter by Garrone in this volume.

35 Self-evident though the principle may seem, even great thinkers have advocated a plurality of the vote, most notably Mill, J.S. (1998) 'Considerations on Representative Government', in J. Gray (ed.) *J.S. Mill: On Liberty and Other Essays*, Oxford: Oxford University Press.

36 Neither is universal suffrage which the ECtHR has, however, recognised as implicit in the provision. For discussion see Jacobs, F. and White, R. (2002) *The European Convention on Human Rights*, Oxford: Oxford University Press (3rd edition), pp. 334–5.

37 Article 21(3).

38 Article 25(b).

39 For example, in Article 28 of the German Basic Law and Article 117 of the Austrian Constitution.

40 The EP had proposed '[e]lection shall be by direct universal suffrage through an equal, free and secret ballot'. The final version (see Council Decision 2002/772/EC, op. cit., Article 1(3)), reads '[e]lections shall be by direct universal suffrage and shall be free and secret'.

41 See Council Decision 76/787, op. cit.

42 Directive 93/109/EC [1993] OJ L329/34.

43 This issue is explored in greater detail in the chapter by Pratchett *et al.* in this volume.

44 See the chapters by Gibson and Norris in this volume.

45 See the discussion in the chapter by Garrone in this volume.

46 Recent confirmation of this point has come in the aftermath of the *Matthews* saga. The UK's implementing legislation, the European Parliament Representation Act 2003, extended the franchise to Gibraltar through including non-EU citizens who qualify as Commonwealth citizens. In response to a complaint by Spain, the Commission has recently advanced the position that because the 1976 EP Act does not address the issue of franchise, the national provisions are applicable, entitling the UK to act according to its national electoral system which enfranchises Commonwealth citizens.

47 For the Swiss case see Auer, A., Malinverni, G. and Hottelier, M. (2000) *Droit constitutionnel suisse. Volume I L'Etat*, Bern: Stämpfli, paragraph 881, p. 299.

48 For example, Community law in the field of free movement is notorious in its acceptance of reverse discrimination, see Weatherill, S. and Beaumont, P. (1999) *EU Law*, London: Penguin Books (3rd edition), pp. 606–7.

49 See the chapter by Schmitt in this volume for a detailed discussion of EP elections as 'second-order elections'.

50 For an illuminating example in the UK public law context see Craig, P. (2003) *Administrative Law*, London: Sweet & Maxwell (5th edition), p. 324 and pp. 875–7 (noting how there are instances where Community law has a 'spillover' effect for the resolution of analogous problems of a purely domestic nature and giving the example of the infamous *Factortame* litigation which resulted in interim injunctive relief having to be made available against the Crown in the EC law context, thereby providing the catalyst for the rethinking of this issue within purely domestic law).

51 For the purposes of this discussion the secrecy of the ballot is discussed separately though it should be noted that it is considered an aspect of free suffrage. On this see the chapter by Garrone in this volume and the 2002 Guidelines on Elections adopted by the Venice Commission, at: www.venice.coe.into/docs/2002/CDL-AD(2002)O13-e.html.

52 Article 25(b) ICCPR and Article 21(3) UN Declaration of Human Rights.

53 For example, in Article 113 of the Portuguese Constitution, Article 28 of the German Basic Law and Article 117(2) of the Austrian Constitution.

54 See Council Decision 2002/772/EC, op. cit., Article 1(3): '[e]lections shall be by direct universal suffrage and shall be free and secret.'

55 See the notes to Article 39(2) and Article 52 of the Charter.

56 Harmsen, R. (2001) 'National Responsibility for European Community Acts Under the European Convention on Human Rights: Recasting the Accession Debate', *European Public Law*, 7: pp. 625–49, p. 633.

57 Further light was expected to be shed on the issue of Member State responsibility in the *Senator Lines* case (App. 56672/00). An action was brought against the 15 member states, the EC itself not being a party to the ECHR, in order to trigger their collective responsibility for alleged breaches of the ECHR by the European Commission. The potential conflict brewing in this case was defused as a result of a CFI decision setting aside the fines that had been imposed by the Commission under its competition powers (Joined Cases T-191/98 and T-212/98-T-214/98, *Atlantic Container Line and Others* v. *Commission*, judgment of 30 September 2003, nyr.). The President of the Strasbourg court responded accordingly by cancelling the hearing, see press release issued by the Registrar 16.10.2003 at: www.echr.coe.int/Eng/Press/2003/oct/SenatorLinescancelled.htm.

58 Watt, op. cit., pointing, in support, to the lack of an explicit derogation clause in Article 3, unlike other provisions of the ECHR. See, however, the view espoused by the authors of a leading text on the ECHR, that '[f]rom the fact that Protocol No. 1 does not contain a reference to Article 15(2) of the Convention it follows that . . . Article 3 . . . does not belong to the provisions which are non-derogable'. (See van Dijk, P. and van Hoof, G. (eds) (1998) *Theory and Practice of the European Convention on Human Rights*, The Hague: Kluwer (3rd edition), p. 665.)

59 To put this in perspective, notwithstanding the escalating importance of the EU, turnout for EP elections has dropped 13 per cent between 1979 and 1999 (from 62 per cent in 1979 to just under 50 per cent in 1999). See also the chapter by Schmitt in this volume. The EP is not alone, the figures for national elections in some of the Member States are as follows: 16.6 per cent drop in the UK between 1979 and 2001; 16.5 per cent drop in Portugal between 1979 and 1999; 14.8 per cent drop in the Netherlands between 1977 and 1998; 13.3 per cent drop in France between 1973 and 1997; 12.9 per cent in West Germany between 1976 and 1990; 11.8 per cent drop in Austria between 1986 and 1999; 10.2 per cent drop in Ireland between 1977 and 1997; 10 per cent drop in Finland between 1979 and 1999. See further: www.europa.eu.int/futurum/documents/other/oth010203_en.htm.

60 See App. 24833/94, *Matthews* v. *United Kingdom*, op. cit., paragraph 39 with citations to further relevant cases.

61 *Matthieu-Mohin and Clerfayt* v. *Belgium*, judgment of 2 March 1987, Series A, No. 113; (1988) 10 EHRR 1.

62 For brief discussion of the case see Jacobs and White, op. cit., pp. 334–8.

63 For ongoing works on the topic of e-voting within the Council of Europe see the relevant integrated project 'Making democratic institutions work', at: www.coe.int/t/e/Integrated_Projects/democracy/.

64 For a short *résumé* of the different voting procedures see Rideau, J. (ed.) (1997) *Les Etats membres de l'Union européenne: adaptations – mutations – résistances*, Paris: LGDJ.

65 See Auer, A. and von Arx, N. (2002) 'La légitimité des procédures de vote – les défis du e-voting', *Pratique juridique actuelle*, 11(5), pp. 491–9.

Part III
Designing e-voting

7 Internet voting and opinion formation

The potential impact of a pre-voting sphere

Raphaël Kies and Hanspeter Kriesi

Introduction

The growing literature on internet voting has until now focused on the question of the technical/legal feasibility and the impact it could have on electoral turnout. Surprisingly, no research has focused on the impact that i-voting could have on electoral opinion formation. We believe this to be a fundamental issue that should not be ignored, since, as some critics have already pointed out, a limited introduction of i-voting could, by accelerating, simplifying and individualising the act of voting, have a negative impact on opinion formation. If so, should i-voting still be promoted? Should public administrations, in other words, promote a new 'technology of democracy'[1] that could increase the quantity of participation at the expense of the quality of participation? We argue that the introduction of i-voting, if implemented with what we call a 'pre-voting sphere', could not only increase electoral turnout but also improve the quality of electoral opinion formation.

According to the way we propose to use the term, the 'pre-voting sphere' corresponds to all the possibilities of vote-related information and communication (forums, chat-rooms) provided by the voting site. The presentation of information and the access to communication spaces at the voting site have the potential to contribute to the quality of citizens' opinion formation. The discussion of this potential will be the object of the first part of this chapter. Whether this potential will actually be realised depends to a great extent on the design of the website which will serve as the portal to electronic voting. Questions of design will be dealt with in the second part of this chapter.

In order to put the discussion of the potential contribution of a pre-voting sphere to the process of opinion formation into perspective, we would like to briefly introduce the reader to the results of recent research on public opinion formation. Following the models from the psychology of attitudes, we can distinguish between two qualitatively different paths of individual opinion formation:[2] a heuristic and a systematic path. The distinction between these two fundamentally different ways of opinion formation is based on the role played by arguments. *Systematic* opinion formation is essentially *argument based*, while *heuristic* opinion formation is essentially based on *shortcuts*, which do not make any reference to substantive arguments. Whether, and to what extent, individuals use systematic arguments as opposed to heuristic cues in their opinion formation is generally determined by their *motivation* and their *competence*. Thus, the key hypothesis of the 'elaboration-likelihood' model of attitude formation presupposes that argumentative strategies are used, when individual and contextual characteristics guarantee a high degree of motivation and competence.

There may be elections and direct-democratic votes which provide strong incentives for the voters to participate and to form their opinion in a systematic way, but we cannot generally assume that high motivation and competence are guaranteed among voters. If motivation and competence are low, as is likely to be the case for many voters, individuals tend to rely on heuristic forms of opinion formation, i.e. on various *simplifying strategies*.[3] Confronted with a decision-making problem people behave as 'cognitive minimalists', i.e. they try to limit the cognitive investment and they are satisfied with acceptable (not optimal) strategies.[4]

The required heuristic cues for the voters are provided by the *political elites*, the media, experts and opinion leaders of all sorts. According to Zaller's influential theory,[5] the political elites constitute the driving force in the process of opinion formation: it is precisely because they are badly informed that citizens have to rely on the cues and recommendations supplied by the political elites. In particular, the quality of the individual citizens' opinion formation largely depends on the strategies of the elites, especially on the quality[6] and the intensity[7] of the campaign they organise for the election or vote in question.

The pre-voting sphere could constitute a crucial site for providing the relevant heuristic cues to voters who want to decide in a 'quick and dirty' way. By providing additional, more detailed information and the possibility to communicate with other voters and/or opinion leaders, the pre-voting sphere could also cater to the needs of citizens who wish to choose in a more systematic way. Indeed, a well-designed pre-voting sphere could even motivate some citizens to make a more elaborate choice than they originally intended.

The potential impact on electoral opinion formation

The ability of the pre-voting sphere to improve electoral opinion formation depends on two complementary aspects – the attitudes and evaluations of the political actors involved, and the inherent characteristics of this new form of opinion formation. As far as the relevant actors are concerned, we can distinguish between three groups:

- the *political parties and candidates* who would mainly be concerned with presenting and discussing their electoral program;
- the *'netcitizens'* who would use it for getting electoral information and for participating in online electoral discussions; and
- the *public authorities* who would have the delicate role of deciding whether a pre-voting public sphere should be created at all, and if yes, how it should be designed and controlled.

A brief presentation of the way these key actors perceive and use the internet should help us to get a first idea of the democratic potential of the pre-voting sphere and of the format it is likely to acquire.

Political parties and candidates

As to the *political parties* and *candidates*, it is generally considered that they do not stimulate deliberative processes online but that, rather, they perceive the internet as a 'showcase' and as a platform for internal communication.[8] Norris,[9] who has analysed the online campaigns of political parties and candidates, indicates that 'most campaigns by mainstream parties and candidates have proved relatively conservative in design, acting more like electronic "top-down" electronic pamphlets than as a radically new forum for interactive "bottom up" participation'. This result is confirmed by a recent empirical survey covering the websites of 144 political parties in the 25 EU countries. The survey shows that the most important feature of the internet for national and European political parties is the possibility to provide information, while the aspect of multilateral interactivity has proven to be much less important for them.[10] Such results are not surprising, when we keep in mind that the principal goal of parties and candidates is to gain electoral support by presenting an attractive and coherent public image of themselves. Now, can we expect the pre-voting sphere to change anything in the attitudes of the parties' members and candidates on the net? Can we expect politicians to become more deliberative and interactive in the pre-voting context? If this seems unlikely on the basis of the empirical evidence so far, it may well be that the specific context of a pre-voting sphere might encourage political parties and individual politicians to adopt a more interactive stance. Whether and to what extent they will take a pre-voting sphere seriously will, however, depend on the attitudes and the behaviour of the second group of actors – the citizens.

Citizens

With regard to the *citizens*, electoral studies for the 2000 US presidential campaign show that more and more citizens get politically informed on the internet: 'Overall only one in ten voters reported getting most of their news from the internet, but almost one-third (30 per cent) got at least some news about the political campaign.'[11] The way they used the web was quite conservative since people tended to consult journalistic sources with established reputation and credible authority.[12] It is equally interesting to note that among the citizens who used the internet to get information about the presidential election 2000, roughly one-third (35 per cent) used the web to participate in online polls and to get information about a candidate's voting record (30 per cent), while there has been a sharp decline in the participation in online discussions: the latter dropped from 36 per cent in 1996 to only 8 per cent in 2000.[13] Similarly, a study carried out in Pennsylvania based on a representative sample[14] indicates that, on average, people discuss politics online eight times a year, compared to a rate of discussing politics both on- and offline of 84 times per year. This is to say that online discussions about politics correspond to only roughly 10 per cent of all political discussion – 'a small but perhaps not negligible amount'.[15]

The question is, of course, whether a relevant number of *citizens* would be willing to use a pre-voting sphere instead of, or in addition to, traditional sources of information and communication. Can we expect citizens to take advantage of the new opportunity provided by a pre-voting sphere? A recent survey among internet users in the context of an ongoing i-voting project in the canton of Geneva gives us a first idea of the desirability of such a site for potential users of internet voting facilities. Users who had tested the prototype online voting system answered, when asked about future improvements of the voting site, that the latter should contain more tools for information and interaction between the citizens and the State as well as among the citizens themselves.[16] This study attests to the desirability of a well developed pre-voting site. Of course, this does not prove that the latter will be used and that it will have a positive impact on opinion formation, once it is available. This result does, however, tell us that there is some *demand* on the part of the users of internet voting for a pre-voting sphere.

Another indicator of citizens' demand for such a site comes from a recent American report produced by the Pew Research Center,[17] which shows that American internet users increasingly use official websites for public/political purposes. For instance, 62 per cent of internet users said that they have used an official website to seek information on public issues; 34 per cent sent comments about an issue to a government official; 21 per cent used it to get information that helped them to decide how to vote in an election; and 19 per cent have used the official site as part of a concerted lobbying campaign. Hence, we have reason to expect the i-voting site – by definition an official site – to be frequented by similar numbers of users.

Of course, i-voting will not have the same appeal to all groups of citizens. It might, however, bring the campaign preceding the vote to the attention of some groups, who otherwise would not have taken notice of it, because they are heavy users of the internet, while they ignore other media such as the press or direct mail. We are primarily thinking of the *younger generations*, who have a particularly low interest in politics and a correspondingly low participation rate in elections and direct-democratic votes.[18] Moreover, the gap with respect to the interest in following public affairs between the younger generation ('Generation X') and the generations of their parents and grandparents is growing – at least in the US.[19] In his well-known analysis of the decline of the American community, Putnam[20] attributes about half of the overall decline in social capital and civic engagement in the US to generational change, which is, in turn, shaped by changes in social habits and values.

A recent survey among voters in the canton of Geneva adds some evidence to the possibility of a participation effect of the introduction of i-voting, especially among the young[21]: Asked about their voting intentions in the case of the introduction of the new voting procedure, a third of the irregular voters and abstentionists declared that they would vote more regularly if they had the possibility to vote on the Web. The corresponding share reached up to 50 per cent in the age categories below 40, while it was negligible among the age groups over 60.

We believe that the pre-voting sphere will be particularly appealing for the younger generation, since it is adapted to the peculiar characteristics of the newsgathering approaches of the new generation. Citing Zukin,[22] Graber[23] mentions five such distinctive characteristics:

- this generation as a whole is far more visually oriented than previous ones and superbly adept at extracting the central meaning conveyed by pictures;
- its members like diversity in their information supply, they are perpetual surfers who move quickly from program to program to find what catches their fancy;
- they like to participate in shaping their information menu;
- they prize interactivity;
- they are niche viewers, i.e. they skip stories that they do not like and get more information about preferred stories as long as they are readily available at the push of a button or the click of a mouse.

The internet provides the technical means for accommodating these characteristics. It allows for the predominance of visual formats, the proliferation of venues, the ending of time-clock tyranny, the weakening of gate-keeper control, the growth of interactivity and the emergence of niche programming.[24] Given the opportunities the internet provides and the trends in news-seeking behaviour of the younger generation, an optimistic interpretation of the current situation can be made.[25] However, as we shall argue later on, one should not adapt the pre-voting sphere exclusively to the needs and preference of the younger generations. To put it bluntly, we should avoid transforming it into a political televisual/videogame just for the sake of attracting the younger generation. Such a strategy could be detrimental to the quality of opinion formation in general and for the participation of other categories of the population who do not appreciate the same characteristics. A virtuous compromise has to be found.

By and large the behaviour of citizens with respect to a possible pre-voting sphere will depend on the way this site will be designed, and this, in turn, heavily depends on the attitudes and decisions of public authorities, the third type of actor involved here.

Public authorities

With regard to *public authorities* studies show that while they are generally keen to develop their administrative efficiency through programmes of e-government,[26] they are much less ready to implement e-democratic tools such as providing pluralistic information, forums for discussion or systems of e-consultation. As a Slovenian study based on governmental sites suggests:

> The central decision-making in Slovenian policy perceives the internet potential simply as an opportunity for improving information ... [it] focuses on presenting its work, ideas, and different proposals to the interested public. The aim therefore is not to discuss the issues or dilemmas, not even to open new questions.[27]

Given the public authorities' reluctance with regard to e-democracy – an attitude which is also reflected in the way they have implemented their parliamentary websites[28] – can we expect them to introduce an i-voting system containing a pre-voting sphere? This question can be divided into two parts: the first is whether we can expect public authorities to introduce i-voting in the first place. This seems to be likely. The spread of i-voting feasibility studies and the diffusion of i-voting pilot projects worldwide are indicative of the public authorities' interest in i-voting procedures. This interest in the implementation of i-voting facilities is in line with the efficiency philosophy behind the introduction of programmes of e-government: indeed, i-voting can facilitate electoral procedures such as voter registration, the counting of votes and the act of voting itself. In addition, from the *politicians'* perspective, being at the forefront of the development of an innovative e-democratic tool constitutes an international publicity stunt for the political authorities who are responsible for moving ahead.

The second part of the question refers to whether we can expect i-voting, if it is introduced, to be complemented by the introduction of a pre-voting sphere. This seems to be much less obvious. The pilot project and the one existing binding official i-election we are aware of – a local election in the UK and the referendum in the commune of Anières (Switzerland) –

did not introduce such a space and the reports as well as the studies commissioned by the various States on the question of i-voting tend to be silent on this issue.[29] This does not mean, however, that public authorities oppose such an option, but it simply means that this question has not (yet) become the object of a public debate. We hope to contribute to the public authorities' awareness of the importance of the issue at stake.

The inherent characteristics of the pre-voting sphere

A functioning pre-voting sphere has some inherent characteristics that contribute to its potential for improving the process of opinion formation and to its attractiveness for all groups of actors involved. First of all, the pre-voting sphere is likely to generate a high rate of interest among the voters and the parties/candidates alike, since it will become a highly visible public sphere. The simple fact that all those who vote by internet will automatically enter the pre-voting space *just before voting* implies that it will become a space of 'prime time visibility' where individual citizens and political organisations (political parties and their candidates, interest associations, social movement organisations) will be highly motivated to provide their cues and to express their opinions. In particular, as Norris[30] points out for digital politics more generally, the pre-voting sphere 'has the potential to amplify the voice of smaller and less well-resourced insurgents and challengers, whether parties, groups, or agencies, which have difficulty being heard through the conventional channels'.

Second, by centralising all the information concerning elections in an easily accessible and efficient way and by offering a space for public deliberation – the pre-voting sphere has the potential to become *the site of reference* for all netcitizens seeking relevant information on the election. Why search elsewhere if the most accurate and complete electoral information is to be found at the voting site itself? This reasoning is particularly valid for the large number of citizens who wait until the last moment to get information for voting. The experience with the ballot pamphlet sent by the government to all Swiss voters before a direct-democratic vote provides some grounds for an optimistic assessment of such a site. This pamphlet constitutes the printed equivalent – the 'poor parent' if you will – of an electronic pre-voting sphere. It typically presents a brief introduction to the issues on the ballot, stating the government's point of view as well as, more briefly, the opponents' position. This pamphlet is not only widely used (up to 50 per cent of the voters used it in the early 1990s), it also has a significant effect on the issue-specific level of information of the voters.[31] By pushing the analogy one step further, we could say that the pre-voting sphere corresponds to a new *genre* of pamphlet that is more informative, more pluralistic, more tailor-made for the particular needs of a given citizen and, in addition, it is interactive. In other words, it constitutes a 'cyber-pamphlet'.

Third, the pre-voting sphere has the potential for contributing to enhanced systematic opinion formation, because it allows for the presentation of a plurality of diverse and conflicting opinions and because it opens the possibility for each individual to participate in public debates.

To summarise our argument up to this point, we have argued that the pre-voting site has the potential to improve the quality of democratic choices by raising the quality of citizens' opinion formation. In particular, we have argued that its openness, visibility, appeal and convenience make it likely that it will be widely used – both by citizens looking for relevant information and by political parties and candidates offering the relevant information. However, these are just potentialities. Whether these potential advantages will become true or not, depends a lot on how the pre-voting sphere will be implemented, i.e. on how it will be technically organised and administratively regulated. As Lessig[32] puts it, on the internet 'code is law'. Which means that the technological architecture that will be adopted (code) for this pre-voting sphere will automatically define the freedom of expression of its users (law).

Design and control of the pre-voting site

We now propose to define which *code* should be adopted for the pre-voting sphere in order to take full advantage of its potentialities. From a normative point of view, the pre-voting sphere should be constructed with the following four objectives in mind. It should:

* be easy to use;
* allow for a plurality of points of view;
* be adapted to both heuristic and systematic paths of opinion-formation;
* encourage the heuristically inclined to adopt a more systematic approach.

Only if these criteria are followed can we expect the pre-voting sphere to have a maximum impact on the electoral opinion formation. We propose to put these normative criteria into practice by focusing on three aspects that are fundamental in the construction of the site. The first concerns technical solutions that guarantee maximum accessibility of the site. Next, we discuss how the plurality and the quality of the information provided could be secured and promoted. Finally, we deal with online interaction and speculate about the format and the rules to be adopted in order to maximise the civic potential of the pre-voting sphere.

Accessibility of the site

The accessibility of the site is an essential pre-condition for the full realisation of its potential for improving citizens' opinion formation. Not only should the i-voting site be open to all citizens interested, but measures should be taken in order to encourage the passive and active use of the pre-voting sphere.

A first measure designed to promote accessibility is a measure to overcome the digital divide due to lack of access to the internet. This would consist in placing computers connected to the voting sites in public places during the electoral period. Such a measure would offer citizens who are not connected but who nevertheless would like to i-vote – not only the possibility to cast their vote online, but also to get politically informed and active online through the pre-voting sphere. This measure could be complemented by the presence of a specialised staff who would be available to assist voters.

A second measure to increase the openness of the pre-voting sphere would be to increase its visibility. Indeed, visibility on the internet is one of the sought after features because of the wide availability of information and competing websites. As a site of public utility, the official website should aim at maximum visibility. One provocative proposition would be to introduce a public icon on the operating system and/or the web browser that would provide direct access to the relevant voting site. Such a measure could dramatically enhance its visibility.

Pre-electoral information

How should information be organised and presented within the pre-voting sphere? The pre-electoral information should be adapted to the needs of both the heuristic and systematic decision-makers and should encourage the minimalist citizens to adopt a more argument-based decision mode. To provide heuristic cues, we could take inspiration from NGOs such as Democracy Network,[33] Debate America[34] or Vote Smart,[35] which have developed easily accessible information systems.[36] Of particular interest is the 'issue grid' developed by D-net:

> DNet's 'issue grid' allowed voters to read each candidate's position on a wide range of issues. Each row of this grid represented an individual candidate for the respective office ... each column represented a particular issue. A cell was checked if the candidate provided a position statement on the specific issue identified by the respective column. Clicking on the checked boxes led the user to the candidate's statement. ... The issues were arranged alphabetically in an attempt to treat all issues equally and to avoid editorial decisions. ... Candidates could ask for issues to be included in the grid. Other candidates could then submit their opinions on these topics. Namely, a candidate's name would be moved on the top of the candidate list whenever that contender provided new information. Inattention could lead a candidate to move further and further down the issue grid, creating an incentive to address new issues and update their issue positions.[37]

Examples of other, less elaborate tools for presenting concise information cues, tools more centred on the citizens' immediate needs, are provided
by the experiments that took place during the most recent elections in the
Netherlands, Finland and Switzerland. These interactive techniques allow
website visitors to answer *a series of multiple-choice questions on current issues*,
which are subsequently compared with the information provided by the
candidates and political parties. As a result of this process the e-technique
identifies the candidates and parties that are closest and furthest from
the visitor's political preference and proposes a list of suitable choices
to the voter.[38]

The issue grid as well as the 'political matching machine' are just some
examples among many that could provide a system of information that
is adapted to the needs of the minimalist citizens, but which also has the
potential to incite them to adopt a more systematic path of opinion formation. Such tools would offer them easy, user-friendly and rapid access to
the essential information about the key issues and the candidates. The implementation of such tools in a visible context such as the pre-voting sphere
could lead to a certain equalisation of party competition, since all candidates
and political parties would have the same opportunity to be heard.[39]

In the same vein, the pre-voting sphere could also provide more *auditive
and visual information*. It could, for instance, provide an audio-video archive
of the speeches not only of the politicians but also of personalities (jour-
nalist, academics, interest groups etc.) who have opinions related to the election campaigns and the candidates and issues at stake. Indeed, as argued
above, visual information is likely to better correspond to the expectations
and needs of the younger generation. Visual elements could also provide
complementary information for those citizens who would like to have a
more 'sensorial contact' with their electoral choice.

In addition, systematic, argument-based information should also be provided. An interesting possibility would be to facilitate retrospective voting,
which is so essential for the functioning of representative government,[40] by
presenting the *voting record of incumbents* for the previous legislative period. For
new candidates one could enter a *quasi-voting record* – how they would have
voted, had they been in the legislature during the previous period. This
quasi-record would have to be collected by interviewing the new candidates
prior the campaign. For *direct-democratic votes*, one could provide the arguments in favour and against the issue in question in more or less detail. In
addition to such richer information, the i-voting portal could also provide
links to websites of the political parties in the case of elections, and of the
political parties and other political organisations, which have expressed an
opinion on the issue at stake, in the case of direct-democratic votes. Such
additional and more elaborate sources of information would correspond to
the information-related expectations of the citizens who make their choices
in a systematic way and, possibly, invite the heuristically deciding citizens
to become more systematic.

Pre-electoral interaction

Some sort of online interaction should also be introduced in the pre-voting sphere, because it could enhance the political involvement and the political competence of its users by both offering the possibility to make comments and by providing the opportunity to read about the opinions of politicians and other citizens. This competence-enhancing potential is, as we argued above, a particularly noteworthy aspect of the pre-voting sphere.

While it is obvious that an interactive system should be introduced in the pre-voting sphere, it is much less clear how it should be implemented. In order to discuss this question we shall begin by adopting the same criteria that we identified above for discussing the provision of information. In particular, the system should be adapted to both heuristic and systematic paths of opinion-formation and it should encourage the heuristically inclined citizens to adopt a more systematic approach. In addition, it should be compatible with the general requirements of the normative communicative ethic of Habermas, which offers some more precise guidelines for how such forums of discussion should be designed. In a nutshell, Habermas[41] maintains that a democratic society should be grounded in a multiplicity of public spheres the internal dynamics of which should approach an 'ideal speech situation', i.e. a discursive context characterised by: (1) its *freedom, openness* and *discursive equality*, i.e. everybody capable of speech and action should be equally entitled to enter the public sphere and to take part in the debate without being subject to any type of restriction; and (2) the *discursive attitudes* of the participants, i.e. the participants should be rational, sincere, respectful, comprehensible and motivated to reach an agreement or consensus.

Turning now to the concrete implementation of this ideal, we can distinguish between two general aspects which the architects of the discussion forum should take into account in their attempts to implement such a discursive space: *the electronic system of exchange* and the *human system of exchange*. On the internet, various technical systems of exchange exist that can be more or less adapted to the discursive requirements. These systems can be distinguished according to the following criteria:

- written versus audio-visual exchanges (teleconference);
- synchronous (chats) versus asynchronous exchanges (forum).

We believe that the discursive ideals will best be served by a system of written/asynchronous exchange, the so-called *forum of discussion*, not only because this type of system is technically adapted to most computers, which guarantees a greater openness, but also because it would encourage a systematic process of opinion formation. Indeed, a forum of discussion would promote a greater reflexivity on the part of the participants, since it would encourage them to *write* their opinions. In addition, such a context of interaction would encourage those citizens who in other types of discursive context (face-to-face, television, radio, etc.) would remain silent, to express their opinion. This does not preclude the possibility to envision systems of interaction that are better adapted to the minimalist citizens who may not be willing to enter a process of deliberation. In particular, as we proposed with respect to information, there could be a more visual system of interaction that may be better suited to the needs and expectations of such citizens.

In addition to its technical architecture, the internet also involves other rules that regulate exchange, what we might call a *human system of exchange*. There is no *magic formula* to tell us which rules a discussion forum should adopt and the empirical research on the question is almost non-existent.[42] But it is essential to find a suitable formula. Such a formula will depend on many factors including national political cultures, the saliency of the vote and the level of internet penetration of the country. It will also depend on the type of the vote (election and/or referendum). The major issues concern, above all, the type of control at the entrance of the forum, the identification of online users and whether or not there should be a system of moderation. We are aware that this is by no means an exhaustive list of the issues at stake, but we are convinced that these issues are particularly important at the early stage of the debate.

Who should be allowed to participate in the pre-electoral forums? Should everybody (citizens, politicians, minors, foreigners, etc.) be allowed to leave comments or should there be certain restrictions at the entrance? The answer to this question may seem obvious if one applies our normative principles literally: any restriction of entry would impose limits on the plurality of opinions. However, such a point of view does not take into consideration the technical and social limits of the public sphere. We expect very large numbers of people to participate in the pre-voting forum. Therefore, if all the opinions are expressed in a single forum the result is likely to be disorder and confusion within the forum, which means that, as a consequence, the discursive ideals would be subverted.

We face, in other words, the following dilemma: on the one hand, by opting for a total openness of the forums the regulator would, in the likely case of high levels of participation, annihilate any possibility of realising an ordered, systematic and discursive deliberation in the pre-voting sphere. On the other hand, by limiting, on the basis of certain rules, the expression of opinions in the forums of discussion the regulators of the pre-voting forum can promote a small, intimate and civic space of interaction that could provide the appropriate arena for an ordered and competence-enhancing debate that would favour a discussion based on arguments. But such a solution presents a double risk: it would exclude some citizens from the possibility of expressing their opinion, which is difficult to accept in a democratic society, and it would limit the expression of a plurality of opinions, which is essential for a systematic opinion formation.

A virtuous compromise should aim to keep the forum as open as possible while at the same time allowing it to be as discursive as possible. Such a compromise could, first, imply the constitution of a *multiplicity of forums*, in such a way that the flux of opinions would be channelled into different sites. One could think of random devices directing citizens to different sites; one could also think of solutions, where the citizens self-select themselves into various discussion groups on the basis of a menu of selection criteria which the pre-voting site would offer them at the entrance. While randomisation guarantees that every citizen is confronted with a plurality of opinions, self-selection might lead to a situation where a voter only encounters like-minded citizens in the discussion forum. In other words, self-selection could foster the phenomenon of 'balkanisation', which Sunstein[43] and others[44] are so afraid of. Second, one could introduce a system of *synthesising the debates* that would help users to follow the debates and participate in them, even if they joined them at a later stage and even if the forums are highly frequented. Another option to promote the deliberative quality of the forums would be to adopt a *decentralised rating system*, such as the one used by some commercial (*eBay*) and discussion sites (*Slashdot*). The aim of this technique is to promote the transparency of the forum by rendering more visible the comments that are considered more interesting or relevant by the participants. The major drawback of such a system, however, is that minor opinions run the risk of being ignored.

Should the participants at the forums be identified? Again, two contrary positions can be distinguished: on the one hand, one could argue that there should be no monitoring of identities, because such a request could undermine the freedom of interaction and the potential egalitarian character of the exchange derived from a lack of the social cues. On the other hand, it may also be argued that 'politics is too important to be debated by unidentified persons'.[45] Non-identified participants could participate in an irresponsible and uncivic away. Indeed, some authors argue 'that anonymity not only encourages disruptive behaviour in discussions, but may also lead to fraud in the promotion of unsupported viewpoints and the libel of individuals (troll)'.[46] Faced with this dilemma, we propose to adopt the following compromise: participants should be allowed to hide their real identity – for example, by using nicknames – but their identity should be known to the administrative authority so that in the event of a violation of rules (e.g. trolling, racist and xenophobic views) the perpetrator could be identified. In other words, the users should just be *identifiable*. Such a solution would have the advantage of 'responsabilising' them, while at the same time maintaining the increased freedom allowed for by written forums.

The last issue we would like to raise is whether the pre-voting forum should be moderated. We believe it should be. In fact, the pre-voting public forum is, as we have seen, a site that is likely to be visited very frequently and to foster intensive debates around electoral issues. Therefore, it constitutes a site that is particularly sensitive to certain threats such as confusion, personal attacks, racist and sexist comments, commercial spamming, excessive volume of postings. As numerous examples show, such types of behaviour strongly undermine the discursive potential of the forums and discourage participation in the first place. It is therefore essential to construct a system of controls that protects the public forum from such threats. To this end we propose to create a team of supervisors. Its role would be to protect the forum from acts that could seriously damage the deliberation and to promote the transparency of the forums. In order to protect the forum from anti-discursive threats, the supervisors should be entitled to a set of progressively dissuasive sanctions, such as *informative warning*, *cancel command* and the *kill command* for exceptional cases. Obviously, the use of these tools would have to be regulated and possibly controlled by an independent body.

Other democratic possibilities

Before concluding we would like to point out some complementary democratic possibilities that support the introduction of a pre-voting sphere. In particular, the pre-voting sphere constitutes a protective device against the danger of 'push-button democracy'. Moreover, it could contribute to an increase in participation and to a homogenisation of the national (and maybe also European) public sphere.

If i-voting were to be introduced without any pre-voting sphere, this could have a negative impact on the process of electoral opinion formtion. The facilitation of the act of voting could encourage certain categories of the population to vote without being properly informed. The categories of particular concern would be those groups of citizens who usually do not vote at all, but who could be encouraged to vote because of the introduction of i-voting procedures. For this reason, we are also quite sceptical about extending the voting procedures to portable phones connected to the internet, since the latter offer very limited possibilities for getting informed and for deliberation.[47]

In turn, we think it is possible that the introduction of a pre-voting sphere could encourage greater participation among citizens given that the site would offer them tailored information and relevant knowledge to facilitate their choice. As Levine[48] puts it:

> What keeps citizens from voting is not the inconvenience of casting ballot. Even if we allowed citizens to vote instantaneously from home, most would not be able to choose a candidate, either because they would lack relevant knowledge or because the choice would be unappealing.

Finally, why should the pre-voting sphere encourage the *homogenisation* of the public sphere? As mentioned above many authors argue that the internet has just the opposite effect. They maintain that it contributes to the 'balkanisation' of the society since online public spaces are mainly visited by like-minded people with similar opinions. They are concerned about its 'filtering' effect and about the personalising technology, which allows people to define in advance exactly the information they do – and do not – want to see. The more efficient the filter, the smaller the chance that a citizen would be exposed to a healthy surprise or share experiences with the rest of society. People tend to filter, because they team up with others whom they like, because they defend themselves against information overload and, because of the availability of so many options, they will simply opt for some options and not for others. The implication would be a new type of fragmentation and polarisation of society.[49]

We believe that, far from contributing to the further fragmentation of the public sphere the pre-voting sphere may, in fact, contribute to its (partial) homogenisation. If appropriately designed, it may encourage citizens to read plural information and to participate in debates that contradict their political convictions. Moreover, it has the potential to enhance mutual perception and understanding among citizens visiting the site. We count on the appropriate designs for discussion forums (e.g. randomisation of assignment to groups), on the curiosity of the citizens and on a key feature of the web – its linking capacity, which facilitates unexpected encounters: you never quite end up where you intended to when surfing on the web.

Conclusion

Summing up our argument, we have maintained that the implementation of i-voting should be accompanied by the introduction of a 'pre-voting sphere', i.e. the voting portal should provide information and possibilities for interaction concerning the election or the direct-democratic vote. As we have pointed out, the pre-voting sphere has the potential for increasing the quality of electoral opinion formation since it is likely to be pluralistically organised and intensely used. We have also underlined that the pre-voting sphere presents some additional important opportunities for improving the quality of a democratic vote:

- it could reduce the dangers of 'push-button democracy' that are often associated with the introduction of i-voting;
- it could increase turnout by offering information tailored to the citizens' needs;
- it could contribute to the fairness of party competition by increasing the visibility of minor/marginal parties; and
- it could contribute to a partial re-homogenisation of the public sphere.

However, such favourable outcomes are neither automatic nor straightforward. For them to be realised, we have proposed a series of theoretically grounded measures concerning the design and the control of the pre-voting sphere. These measures are intended, on the one hand, to achieve maximum visibility of the voting portal and, on the other hand, to offer a system of information as well as interaction opportunities suited to the needs of the different categories of voters, helping them to be better informed and encouraging them to get involved.

It goes without saying that the implementation of such measures will require extra public resources that, for smaller political entities (small countries, regions, municipalities), may be particularly difficult to raise. However, the democratic consequences are so important that the implied costs are largely justified. From a normative perspective, it is the only way to proceed if the introduction of i-voting is intended to increase not only the *quantity* of participation but also its *quality*.

Notes

1 See Trechsel, A., Kies, R., Mendez, F. and Schmitter, P. (2003) *Evaluation of the Use of New Technologies in Order to Facilitate Democracy in Europe: E-democratizing the Parliaments and Parties in Europe*, European Parliament, STOA (Scientific and Technological Option Assessment) Report, Directorate-General for Research.

2 Eagly, A. and Chaiken, S. (1993) *Psychology of Attitudes*, New York: Harcourt Brace Jovanovich, p. 306.

3 This idea goes back to Simon's pioneering work on 'satisficing' and 'bounded rationality', see Simon, H.A. (1959) 'Theories of decision-making in economics and behavioral sciences', *American Economic Review*, 49: 253–83 and to Tversky and Kahneman's 'cognitive heuristics', see Tversky, A. and Kahneman, D. (1974) 'Judgment under uncertainty: heuristics and biases', *Science*, 195: 1124–31.

4 Downs had already applied this insight to the choices in representative democracies: he had argued that citizens simplify their choices by using cognitive shortcuts and by delegating the search for information or even the decisions to other actors, whom they trust and believe to be competent. It is very likely that voters will use similar strategies in direct-democratic procedures. See Downs, A. (1957) *An Economic Theory of Democracy*, New York: Harper Collins, p. 230 ff.

5 Zaller, J.R. (1992) *The Nature and Origins of Mass Opinion*, Cambridge: Cambridge University Press.

6 As Kuklinski *et al.* suggest, 'the much lamented limitations of citizen competence are less inherent in the capabilities and dispositions that individuals bring to politics and more a consequence of deficiencies in the political environment than scholars and practitioners often suppose'. See Kuklinski, J.H., Quirk, P.J., Jerit, J. and Rich, R. (2001) 'The Political Environment and citizens competence', *American Journal of Political Science*, 45: 423.

7 By lowering the information and motivation hurdles for the citizens, intensive campaigns diminish the difference between the cognitive strategies of informed and uninformed citizens. This could not only be observed for elections to the American senate, see Kahn, K. and Kenney, P.J. (1999) *The Spectacle of U.S. Senate Campaigns*, Princeton: Princeton University Press, but also for direct-democratic campaigns in the US, see Bowler, S. and Donovan, T. (1998) *Demanding Choices. Opinion, Voting, and Direct Democracy*, Ann Arbor: The University of Michigan Press, chapter 8.

8 Nixon, P. and Johansson, H. (1999) 'Transparency through technology: the internet and political parties', in B.N. Hague and B.D. Loader (eds) *Digital Democracy*, London: Routledge.

9 Norris, P. (2002) 'Revolution, what revolution? The internet and U.S. elections, 1992–2000', in E.C. Kamarck and J.S. Nye Jr (eds) *Governance.com*, Washington: Brookings Institution Press.

10 See Trechsel *et al.*, op. cit., pp. 29–30.

11 For details, see Norris, op. cit., p. 64.

12 When asked where the internet users went more often for news about the 2000 elections:

> almost half of news consumers (47 per cent) said they frequented the websites of major news organizations such as CNN and the *New York Times*, and in contrast few often visited candidate websites (7 per cent) or issue oriented websites (4 per cent).

See Norris, op. cit., p. 65.

13 For details, see Norris, op. cit., p. 69.

14 Data were obtained from 524 respondents, with a response rate of 65 per cent. According to Muhlberger the sample was sufficiently representative. See Muhlberger, P. (2000) *Access, Skill, and Motivation in Online Political Discussion: The Democratic Digital Divide*, Draft Document, Institute for the Study of Information Technologies and Society, Heinz School of Public Policy, Carnegie Mellon University. Available at: www.communityconnections.heinz.cmu.edu/papers/AgencyPublicSphere.doc.

15 Muhlberger, op. cit., p. 1.

16 With regard to information, while the official information concerning the object of the referendum was present and widely used (76 per cent), 32 per cent of the respondents asked for more official information, 54 per cent would like to have direct links to political parties' websites, 44 per cent to media websites and 43 per cent to other political actors' websites. With regard to interaction, 67 per cent of the respondents indicated they would like to have the possibility to contact through e-mail the political authorities and 55 per cent said they would like to see discussion forums being proposed on the official website and 36 per cent showed an interest in having 'chat'. See Christin, T. and Muller, R. (2002) *Analyse quantitative du test Alpha Ter: Analyse par Questionnaire du système du vote par Internet*, Geneva: University of Geneva. www.ge.ch/chancellerie/e-government/doc/rapport_alphater_e-voting.pdf.

17 Pew Research Center (2002) *Rise of the E-Citizen*, at: www.pewinternet.org/reports/toc.asp?Report=57.

18 A huge amount of literature suggests that political involvement increases with age, see, for example, Milbrath, L.W. and Goel, M.L. (1977) *Political Participation: How and Why do People Get Involved in Politics*, Chicago: Rand McNally, pp. 114–16; Wernli, B. (2001) *Contraintes institutionnelles, influences contextuelles et participation aux élections fédérales en Suisse*, Bern: Haupt, pp. 87–104. For direct-democratic participation, in particular see Mottier, V. (1993) 'La structuration sociale de la participation aux votations fédérales', in H. Kriesi *et al.* (eds) *Citoyenneté et démocratie directe*, Zurich: Seismo, pp. 123–44.

19 Graber, D.A. (2001) 'Adapting political news to the needs of twenty-first century Americans', in W.L. Bennett and R.M. Entman (eds) *Mediated Politics. Communication in the Future of Democracy*, Cambridge: Cambridge University Press, p. 435.

20 Putnam, R. (2000) *Bowling Alone. The Collapse and Revival of American Community*, New York: Simon and Schuster, p. 266.

21 Kies, R. and Trechsel, A.H. (2001) 'Le contexte socio-politique', in A. Auer and A.H. Trechsel (eds) *Voter par internet? Le projet e-voting dans le canton de Genève dans une perspective socio-politique et juridique*, Geneva, Basle, Munich: Helbing & Lichtenhahn, p. 53 ff., at: www.ge.ch/chancellerie/e-government/doc/Voter_par_Internet.pdf.

22 Zukin, C. (1997) *Generation X and the News*, Washington, DC: Radio and Television News Directors Foundation.

23 For details see Graber, op. cit., p. 435.

24 For details see Graber, op. cit., p. 438.

25 For details see Graber, op. cit., p. 447.

26 For a review and evaluation of e-government initiatives worldwide refer to West, M.D. (2002) 'Global e-Government 2002', Brown Policy Report, at: www.brown.cdu/Administration/News_Bureau/2002–03/02–022.html.

27 Oblak, T. 'Boundaries of interactive public engagement: Political institutions and citizens in new spaces of political actions', paper presented at the Euricom Colloquium: Computer Network and Democratic Engagement, University of Nijmegen, 2002, p. 12.

28 The already quoted study indicates that very few parliaments in Europe have introduced e-democratic tools such as the e-forums, e-consultation, e-feedback. On the other hand, most of them offered the possibility to contact the MPs through e-mail, but as the study shows this does not constitute a guaranty of reply. See Trechsel *et al.*, op. cit.

29 A notable exception, however not a public one, are the i-voting binding experiences of the Italian 'Partito Radicale' for electing a part of its executive board every year. For these elections an elaborate pre-voting sphere was set up: each candidate could present their CV; people could deliberate on the election among themselves and with the candidates; an elaborate system of questioning the candidates was proposed etc. For more information on this avant-gardiste experience see the case study by Kies on the e-democracy strategy of the Partito Radicale in Trechsel, A. *et al.*, op. cit.

30 For details see Norris, op. cit., p. 239.

31 See Kriesi, H. (1994a) 'Le défi à la démocratie directe posé par les transformations de l'espace public', in Y. Papadopoulos (ed.) *Présent et avenir de la démocratie directe*, Geneva: Georg; Kriesi, H. (1994b) 'Akteure-Medien-Publikum. Die Herausforderung direkter Demokratie durch die Transformation der Öffentlichkeit', in F. Neidhardt (ed.) *Öffentlichkeit, öffentliche Meinung, soziale Bewegungen*, Opladen: Westdeutscher Verlag.

32 Lessig, L. (1999) *Code and Other Laws of Cyberspace*, New York: Basic Books.

33 See www.dnet.org.

34 See www.debateamerica.org.

35 See www.vote-smart.org.

36 For a presentation of these different independent web-based campaign organisations see Levine, P. (2003) 'Online, in D.M. Anderson and M. Cornfield (eds) *The Civic Web*, Maryland: Rowman & Littlefield Publishers.

37 Elberse, A., Hale, M.L. and Dutton, W.H. (2000) 'Guiding voters through the net: the democracy Network in a California Primary Election', in K.H. Hacker and J. van Dijk (eds) *Digital Democracy: Issue of Theory and Practise*, London: Sage Publication, p. 135.

38 For details, see Trechsel *et al.*, op. cit.

39 However, a study about how citizens consult an independent civic site aiming at increasing the electoral civic competence showed a limited equalising effect: 'the statements of the four major candidates were viewed more often than statements provided by other candidates', see Elberse *et al.*, op. cit., p. 144. This

is not surprising, since people are, above all, interested in candidates whom they know and who have the best chances to be elected. Nevertheless, this does not mean that such sites will have no impact at all. We still believe that the introduction of such tools could encourage citizens to consult electoral information that they otherwise would have ignored.

40 Manin, B. (1995) *Principes du gouvernement représentatif*, Paris: Flammarion, p. 228.
41 Habermas, J. (1989) *The Structural Transformation of the Public Sphere*, Cambridge: Polity.
42 Theoretically grounded empirical analysis allowing us to define the appropriate format for online forums for promoting the civic competence of the citizens are largely lacking. As Lupia puts it:

> A problem with many claims made by advocates of deliberation and other competence-generating proposals is that they are disconnected from empirical work on belief change in the social and cognitive sciences. They do not attend to discoveries regarding aspects of perception, attention, and retention that affect how people process new information. By ignoring this literature, many advocates cannot articulate what conditions are necessary and/or sufficient for their proposal to cause any particular belief or behavior change. It is, therefore not surprising that the returns to investment in competence-generating proposals are so poorly understood.

See Lupia, A. (2002) 'Deliberation disconnect: what it takes to improve civic competence', *Law and Contemporary Problems*, 65: p. 23, at: www-personal.umich. edu/~lupia/deliberation.pdf.
43 Sunstein, C. (2001) *Republic.com*, Princeton: Princeton University Press.
44 See, for example, Shapiro, A. (1999) *The Control Revolution*, New York: Public affairs; Davis, R. (1999) *The Web of Politics*, Oxford: Oxford University Press; Wilhelm, A.G. (2000) *Democracy in the Digital Age: Challenges to Political Life in Cyberspace*, New York: Routledge.
45 Maldonado, T. (1997) *Critica della ragione informatica*, Milano: Feltrinelli, p. 58.
46 Dahlberg, L. (2001) 'The internet and democratic discourse', *Information, Communication & Society*, 4: 615–33.
47 For details see Kies and Trechsel, op. cit., p. 23 f.
48 Levine, op. cit., p. 123.
49 This view, however, has two problems, as Fallows points out, 'one involves the Internet, the other involves the non electronic ways in which citizens interact'. Compared to the past and present balkanisation involved by social cleavages based on religion, ethnicity, region or class – remember the construction of class- and confession-specific sub-societies (pillarisation) in the early twentieth century, the internet seems a trivial source of the problem at hand. Moreover, and quite contrary to the assertions of Sunstein, the internet actually functions less as a filtering device, than as the general interest intermediaries that Sunstein thinks are so important. As Fallows observes, 'if you start looking up information on Web sites, you almost never end up where you expected'. See Fallows, J. (2002) 'He's Got Mail', *The New York Review of Books*, 14 March: pp. 4–7.

8 Balancing security and simplicity in e-voting

Towards an effective compromise?

Lawrence Pratchett, Melvin Wingfield,
N. Ben Fairweather and Simon Rogerson

Introduction

Achieving system security while, at the same time, enhancing simplicity and convenience of use, is one of the fundamental problems facing the development of electronic voting (e-voting). One of the primary reasons for wanting some form of electronically mediated voting process is to enhance voter convenience and flexibility.[1] Rapidly declining turnout rates at national and local elections have prompted many to seek technological fixes to the problem, suggesting that recent declines might be halted, or even reversed, by the implementation of e-voting systems. Research for the Electoral Commission immediately after the UK General Election of 2001 suggested that two-thirds of non-voters (in other words, 27 per cent of the total electorate) would have been more likely to have voted if they could have done so through various electronic means[2] and this ignores the added convenience that current voters might find with e-voting. A consultation paper from the Office of the e-Envoy on electronic democracy also makes the case for voter convenience as a primary justification for the implementation of e-voting.[3] While many of the assumptions on which enhanced turnout through e-voting are based are essentially contestable,[4] the argument that any implementation of e-voting must make it easier, not harder, for people to vote is difficult to resist. For e-voting to enhance the electoral process it must correspond with the way other day-to-day activities are undertaken and be more, not less, convenient than the current system of voting.

At the same time, however, it is widely recognised that the security of e-voting systems is a major barrier to their widespread implementation. A range of reports on the implementation of various e-voting systems, from the California Internet Voting Task Force[5] through to the UK Hansard Society's Independent Commission on Alternative Voting Methods[6] have identified security as a major concern with such implementation. The security risks vary, from problems of authenticating the right of individuals to vote through to protecting the integrity of the overall electoral system from attack.[7] The problem is that such security is best achieved by 'increasing the complexity and the burden on the user of the system'.[8] This problem creates a widely recognised dichotomy:

> While a main argument in support of internet voting is the potential increase in convenience, the primary arguments against internet voting are security concerns. There is a fundamental trade off between security and convenience at a given level of technology.[9]

> The democratic process warrants an extremely high level of security, but the security measures cannot be so cumbersome to voters that the new process would prevent participation. An appropriate balance between security, accessibility and ease of use must be achieved before internet voting systems should be deployed.[10]

> The responsibility of the Government is two-fold: to protect the democratic exercise of the franchise and to combat abuse at the poll. Any measure intended to prevent electoral fraud must be set against the effect it will have on legitimate voters. It is not the Government's intention to cause inconvenience to anyone except those intent upon fraud.[11]

In other words, there is a fundamental trade-off between system security and user convenience in e-voting systems.

The trade-off between security and convenience is the focus of this chapter. The chapter argues that e-voting cannot be successfully introduced unless an effective compromise is reached that satisfies the demands of both security and simplicity. However, unlike most accounts of this supposed dilemma, the chapter does not argue that the solution lies in more sophisticated technological applications which tighten security and prevent electoral abuse. Instead, this chapter argues that many of the security problems that are inherent in e-voting systems are a feature of social and political behaviour rather than the technology through which e-voting might be implemented. While more robust and secure technological platforms are desirable, many of the solutions lie in conventional electoral practice. In particular, the chapter argues that in designing e-voting systems there is too much attention paid to preventing electoral abuse. While such prevention is laudable, an equally appropriate solution might be to pay as much attention to *post hoc* detection and penalisation of electoral abuse. Central to this argument is a belief that it is the integrity of the electoral system and citizens' confidence in it, that is most important, rather than the behaviour of individuals within that system. Elections are supposed to return the people's preferred candidates to political office. Integrity, in this context, means that citizens must be confident that e-voting systems have achieved this aim. While electoral abuse needs to be prevented wherever possible, it is not critical to the election process provided that such abuse does not substantively affect the overall outcome of the election (i.e. it does not influence who is returned to office) and does not undermine citizen confidence that the will of the people has been represented. In this respect, developing the perfectly secure system is probably not necessary, provided subsequent independent audit can verify the integrity of the outcome. Indeed, such independent audit may do more to provide citizen confidence in the integrity of the outcome than supposedly failsafe secure systems, not least because it would be able to highlight the extent of abuse and confirm that it had not had an affect upon the overall outcome. Of course, where the overall outcome has been affected, then alternatives, such as re-running the election, may have to be considered.

This argument does not seek to deny the value of secure electronic voting systems. Where possible, electoral abuse such as personation, multiple voting and so on, should be prevented. Similarly, the broader risks to the electoral system that seek to prevent people from voting (such as spoofing or denial of service attacks) also need to be guarded against. However, the argument is one of striking the right balance. Audit and verification, coupled with an appropriate penalisation regime, may be an equally good way of dealing with many of the security concerns of e-voting. Consequently, the argument is one in which technological solutions should be reserved for technological problems.

To pursue this argument the chapter draws upon recent research into the implementation of e-voting in the UK.[12] Consequently, much of the analysis draws upon UK electoral experience and the ways in which implementation is being planned in the UK. However, many of the technological problems that are raised and, indeed, the potential solutions to them, are generalisable to e-voting as it is being developed elsewhere, especially in the EU. To develop the argument, three sections follow. The first section focuses upon the technologies that e-voting in the UK is likely to be built upon and the threats to security that they introduce into the electoral system. Central to this section is a distinction between those threats that are inherent in the technology and those that are simply highlighted or exaggerated by electronically mediated voting. The second section concentrates upon the issues of simplicity and convenience in e-voting, and examines the inherent conflict that appears to exist between security and simplicity of use. At the heart of this analysis is a concern with inclusive system design and the dangers of social and political alienation that might arise if insufficient attention is paid to how voters would really use e-voting. Finally, a third section examines the alternatives to the technological fix that is often expected to resolve the problems of system security. In particular, this concluding section examines the extent to which a proper balance can be struck between security and simplicity that provides for inclusiveness while safeguarding the integrity of elections.

Technological challenges

From the outset it is important to distinguish the broad concept of e-voting from the much narrower concept of internet voting. Electronic voting (or e-voting) is a generic term that captures a wide range of different methods of voting, from the electronic counting of manually cast ballots, the use of touch screen or other technologies in polling stations, through to remote voting via the internet, telephone, interactive digital television (iDTV) or any other appropriate technology that might emerge. While all of these introduce technological challenges into the voting process, it is those that facilitate remote voting that offer the most potential advantages to voters but also present the most significant challenges in terms of security. It is these technologies that this chapter will focus upon.

While the ways by which remote voting by electronic means might be achieved are numerous,[13] there are four major technologies that are currently under investigation in the UK as having the greatest potential for implementation and which are the subject of further testing and experimentation:[14]

- *Telephone voting* using touch tone telephones to register a vote. This type of system may operate either through fixed (land) line telephone systems or cellular (mobile or portable) telephones. Within the UK such voting systems have been used for advisory referendums in some local authorities (Milton Keynes, Bristol and Croydon) and were tested in local government elections during the 2002 and 2003 electoral pilots.[15]
- *SMS text voting* using the Short Message Service (SMS) facility on mobile telephones to cast a ballot. Examples of this type of process were tested in local government elections during the 2002 and 2003 electoral pilots. This is distinct from telephone voting in so far as it requires voters to compose a single message including voter identification, password and candidate identity and send it to a specified address. Within policy circles this method of voting is expected to appeal particularly to younger voters.
- *Internet voting* using designated websites to allow citizens to vote from any location that has an internet connection, provided they have their voter identification and password available. There have been some overseas experiments with this technology (for example, the Arizona Democratic Primaries). In addition, several authorities included internet voting in the 2002 and 2003 electoral pilots. All of these, to date, have used commercial companies to supply the website and manage the election.
- *Interactive Digital Television voting* (iDTV) using the interactive capacity of evolving facilities to enable voters to cast their ballots via their televisions. This was trialled in the UK in four separate, distinct localities

in the 2003 electoral pilots. Penetration of digital TV across the UK will grow (currently 41 per cent of UK households as the threatened switch-off of the analogue signal in 2010 approaches).[16]

These technological platforms, alongside a retention of polling station-based voting (some involving e-voting machines) are beginning to form the basis of e-voting implementation in the UK. In principle, this diverse range of platforms allows flexibility and choice in the way that citizens choose to vote. However, they also raise a number of technological challenges. For analytical purposes, the threats to security can be considered along two main dimensions: the adversaries (those who would seek to challenge the system); the vulnerabilities (the limits to system security).

This section will consider each of these threats in turn. Throughout the analysis that follows, the focus is particularly upon identifying the extent to which new technologies create, magnify or, more simply, help identify potential threats to the integrity of elections.

The adversaries

The security threat most commonly considered in relation to computerised systems comes from hackers. However, in the context of e-voting, the threat could come from a range of sources and not just hackers. Understanding from whom the potential threats may come is the first step to analysing the risk and taking appropriate measures to protect the system against such threats. There are five groups of potential adversaries, all of whom generate different types of threat.

Hackers and publicity seekers

Hacking is a well-known phenomenon around electronic systems. Consequently, it is likely that hackers or publicity seekers would see a major election in a western democracy conducted largely by electronic means as a worthwhile target. Attacks on prominent websites are routine. The first major democracy to use extensive online electronic voting is liable to be attacked simply because it is the first. Moreover, even if electronic voting had already become routine, a successful attack on a major election could be expected to generate considerable publicity for the attackers. To generate such extensive publicity, serious doubt would have to be cast on the validity of the results in several constituencies, at least, or inconvenience or annoyance caused to tens of thousands of voters. Attacks that can generate limited publicity, at most, can also be expected, including from those whose interest is the technical challenge, rather than publicity. However, the greater the disruption that it is possible to cause, the greater the publicity that could be gained and, thus, the more likely an attack, *ceteris paribus.* Consequently, hacking is a serious threat to system security, especially for elections in major European countries.

Hackers are a uniquely technological problem in so far as it is the technological challenge that creates the interest rather than the election itself. Unlike many commercial systems, there is no financial transaction at stake in e-voting systems and, consequently, no financial gain to be made from hacking. Most hackers, except under commission from a third party, would not be seeking to effect a particular outcome. Rather, hackers are likely to want to test system security simply for the challenge.

Hostile regimes and terrorists

Certain states that are ideologically opposed to particular countries are likely to have significant technical ability, facilities and resources at their disposal, should they choose to attempt to disrupt an election. While the probability of such attacks is lower than for attacks from hackers/ publicity seekers, the resources at the disposal of such regimes are much greater, so they would be able to mount a very wide range of attacks. These adversaries may have specific reasons for wanting to effect a particular outcome.

Partisans

Electronic voting systems may increase the probability of political parties seeking to manipulate votes cast in their favour. Despite their claims to being corruption free, UK elections have been plagued by accusations of 'granny farming' and the creation of 'ghosts' in certain elections, especially when they have been closely contested.[17] While these incidents are rare, it does seem possible that certain parties, or activists within them, would seek to use e-voting as another tool by which to manipulate an election outcome in their favour. In particular, telephone voting might lead to many greater instances of 'granny farming', as activists knock on doors and offer to 'help' the technologically illiterate to vote by using the mobile phone that they have with them. Indeed, in the telephone voting system experimented with by Swindon Borough Council in its 2002 elections, one party did exactly this, although there is no evidence in this instance to suggest that they actually behaved improperly by casting the vote for the voter themselves or by directing the citizen to vote in a particular way. In these and similar circumstances, e-voting exaggerates an existing threat to vote security rather than creates a new one. A significant part of this threat comes from the improper actions of activists and external sympathisers of parties who might use techniques that the party leadership would not condone to secure a victory. However, it is also possible that extreme parties may use such techniques to gain power.

Opportunists within the system

Experience elsewhere in computer security suggests that systems are significantly vulnerable to insider attacks, with perhaps 70 per cent of attacks coming from insiders.[18] Unusually for an application of computer security, financial gain cannot be achieved by corrupt insiders without external backers. Simple opportunism within the system is less likely than with many other systems. While many with insider access are likely to have political views they might seek to promote, fewer will be prepared to risk their jobs and break the law to exploit opportunities that arise. By contrast, the likelihood of attacks using insider access is significant if such attacks are backed by financial inducements from a hostile regime, partisans, terrorists or dissident groups. Thus, while insider opportunism does not increase the probability of an attack to any great extent, it could increase the severity. It cannot always be assumed that insiders will be trustworthy. This could, particularly, be a problem if the same insider or small group of insiders have:

> direct access to individual ballots, vote totals, population statistics, registration information and pre-existing voting patterns. It is possible for employees of election companies who provide full service operations to have access to all of these databases simultaneously. This information could then be applied in order to shift tallies in swing precincts in subtle ways that would be hard to detect. This is extremely powerful, since many elections are won by small percentages.[19]

Indeed, there are growing concerns that the companies creating 'touch screen' voting machines for future US elections are too closely allied to the Republican Party.[20] Consequently, e-voting systems provide unique technological opportunities for insiders to corrupt the electoral process, often without being detected if they are sophisticated enough with the way in which they attack the system.

Disruption by strikes, commercial contract disputes and failures

Any electronic voting system is inevitably much more dependent on the commercial world than the current system is. Most alternatives would depend on a single supplier (of telecommunications, for example) for some part of the process for a highly significant number of voters. Both trade unions and commercial contractors may attempt to exploit the leverage this gives them to pursue their own ends.[21] Such threats are not unique to the technology. Rather, they are a feature of the political and economic context in which elections might take place and it is certainly feasible that key workers or companies might seek to disrupt non-electronic elections through other means. The technology simply provides another channel through which such disruption might take place.

The vulnerabilities

Given the range of potential adversaries, the vulnerabilities that electronic voting is exposed to are equally broad.[22] However, voting systems are generally exposed to three main vulnerabilities: attacks that seek to prevent citizens from voting; attacks that seek to steal or alter particular votes; and attacks that seek to undermine citizen or political confidence in the integrity of the election. Each of these can take a number of forms.

Preventing votes

Denial of service attacks are a favourite technique of hackers/publicity seekers, often attacking websites. Other adversaries may also choose to use these techniques. The favourite method for this type of attack is to over-load the server so that genuine users of the service cannot gain access. Such a denial of service can also occur unwittingly when a large number of users log on to the same server at the same time. For example, users of the UK's 1901 census data that was made available online in 2002 managed to lock the system up for several weeks in January 2002 because demand for access far outstripped the resource made available. Another alternative method would be to propagate a date-triggered virus that would disable computers on election day, thereby preventing e-votes from being cast. Denial of service attacks are a particular problem because elections are unusually time-critical. Elections only take place over a specified time period. If certain groups of voters are denied access to the voting system for a sustained period, this could have a significant effect upon the outcome of the election.

Stealing or altering votes

There are a variety of ways in which votes might be stolen from voters or be altered after they have been cast. The most obvious is the crime of personation, in which someone takes on another voter's identity in order to steal their vote. Personation is not unique to electronic systems and has been a longstanding problem with existing electoral processes. However, e-voting may increase the opportunity for personation if adequate voter authentication is not developed. Such authentication is an area where voting systems have tended to concentrate resources, although it still remains problematic.

Other challenges to security are more common in other electronic systems. Spoofing of websites[23] is a common problem for commercial organisations and is not limited to the internet – it is equally feasible to see how short-term spoofs of telephone sites could be created to collect votes from unsuspecting citizens. Alternatively, insiders or hackers may gain access to the main tabulation computer and alter votes cast for different candidates. Changing the votes or simply removing the anonymity of voters by invading the privacy of the vote may undermine an election. Finally, it is also possible to consider the threat that viruses or malware might introduce into an e-voting system. As Schneier has argued, 'not only is there no reasonable way to trust a client-side program in real usage, but there's no possible way to ever achieve that level of protection'.[24] Hackers and publicity seekers may well seek to exploit this route of attack by distributing a computer virus/worm/trojan horse infection that enables them to subvert the client-side programs for casting votes. Furthermore, it cannot be assumed that all of the software houses producing e-voting systems, the distributors of those systems and the relevant personnel within those organisations, will be benevolently neutral about the political situation in a given country. Because of the intimate relationship between such software and the computer on which it resides, such software, if so designed or manipulated, could interfere so that the apparent operation of the computer is normal, while, for some proportion of voters at least, votes are changed.

Confidence attacks

All of the threats identified above are potential ways to disrupt an election. Perhaps the most effective way of disrupting an electronic election, however, is not so much by achieving one or more of these attacks but in claiming that such an attack has taken place. Anecdotes of voters being unable to gain access to the system or of individuals gaining unauthorised access are likely to have a negative effect upon public perception, far in excess of the reality of the potential attacks. Dot.com companies have experienced this phenomenon with many people fearing the security that such companies offer their credit cards.[25] Anecdotes of this nature could easily be exploited by losing candidates or parties, especially where the election outcome is unexpected or particularly close. Such confidence attacks could do more damage to an election than an actual attack because they would undermine the credibility of the election and, ultimately, the legitimacy of those representatives elected in this way.

The need for security

What emerges from this brief analysis of security threats to e-voting is that there is a range of different adversaries, each of whom may draw upon a range of different methods for disrupting or undermining an election. Two broad issues underpin this analysis, however. First, there is the issue of how relevant new technology is to the creation of some of these threats. Some adversaries and the way in which they might threaten elections are clearly a product of the technology – hackers who seek to challenge a system because of its technological sophistication would clearly only be interested in disrupting an e-enabled election because of the challenge it might present and the publicity that they might gain from such disruption. Other threats, however, are only tangentially linked to the technology and are more a product of socio-economic or political circumstances. While e-voting technology might exacerbate the problems that these threats create, they are neither new nor unique to e-voting. Consequently, it seems plausible to argue that the solutions to such problems may not be wholly technological.

Second, there is an issue of scale. Some forms of attack appear to threaten the whole, or substantial proportion, of an election. Such attacks would be sufficient to undermine the election result. Others, however, appear only to have a small effect upon the election or to threaten a minority of voters. While such attacks are not to be condoned and need to be guarded against, their effect on the election needs to be kept in proportion. The lesson for systems design in this instance is to develop security that is commensurate with the level of the threat. Such design may require a different approach to security that focuses less upon preventing electoral abuse and more upon detecting and punishing such abuse.

The temptation in developing new systems is to seek complete security. Consequently, there is a temptation to build in complex modes of authentication, such as sophisticated voter IDs and passwords that cannot easily be replicated by unauthorised individuals. In some instances, even biometric devices have been suggested. Similarly, system designs are considered that build in firewalls and other security devices to prevent hacking and other unwanted intrusions into the system. In short, it is possible for system designers to conceive ever more complex structures that prevent all but the most determined of attackers from getting near the heart of the system. In so doing, e-voting pitches the best resources of the state against the resources of those who would seek to undermine it. Such security, however, is seldom achieved in electronic systems and has certainly never existed in conventional electoral systems. Despite the electoral abuses observed by Charles Dickens in the nineteenth century,[26] the UK election system still operates in much the same way as it did over 100 years ago – before the advent of universal suffrage. Electoral law is still based in nineteenth-century legislation, although there have been many amendments to it in order to slowly address aspects of fraud that have been perpetrated over many decades. Consequently, it is possible to conclude that there remain imperfections in the current system despite over a century of refinement. It seems almost ridiculous, therefore, to expect technology to fix all of the problems that over 100 years of electoral experience has been unable to resolve.

Simplicity and convenience

The trade-off between security and simplicity has already been emphasised. This section offers the corollary to system security by focusing upon how necessary it is to develop e-voting systems that are simple and convenient for all voters to use. Voting systems are different from most electronic systems in so far as they demand a principle of universality. If elections are to remain free and fair (notwithstanding extant problems with that concept) then systems should not be designed that support the skills and capacities of a minority, or even a majority, of citizens. Rather, e-voting must be available to all voters without the requirement for specialised skills or knowledge in order to use it. If this principle is sacrificed then voting systems run the risk of advantaging some groups over others.

Simplicity of the voting system is a combination of three main factors: the access that voters have to the technology for e-voting; the willingness of voters to use particular technologies; and the cognitive capacity of voters to use e-voting systems. It is only by understanding all three of these factors that the full demands of simplicity and convenience can be understood and balanced against the demands of system security. This section draws upon a range of data sources to investigate these factors. As well as a range of survey data, the section also draws upon focus group work undertaken by BMRB International as part of a broader investigation into the *Implementation of electronic voting in the UK*.[27] This work involved 12 focus groups in four UK cities, covering a range of age groups and differing voting behaviour. Consequently, it provides important insights into the way UK voters perceive issues around e-voting and the limits that they might impose upon its implementation.

Technological access

The significance of differential access to the technologies that might form the basis of e-voting is covered by other chapters in this book (see the chapter by Gibson) so the theme will not be greatly extended here. From a quantitative point of view it is worth noting the penetration of key technologies within the UK population:

- 93 per cent of UK households have fixed line telephones, with a further 6 per cent estimated to have a mobile telephone as an alternative.[28] In addition, 73 per cent of UK adults have a mobile phone, of which the majority (70 per cent) are pre-pay packages.
- 12 million UK households (48 per cent) have access to the internet from home while, in total, some 61 per cent of UK adults have accessed the internet at some time.[29] The distribution follows expected socioeconomic and demographic patterns with only 13 per cent of the lowest two deciles by income and 6 per cent of the over-65s having internet access from home, compared with 80 per cent of the highest two deciles and 73 per cent of 25–44 year olds.
- 41 per cent of UK households have digital television (the largest proportion in Europe) although only half of these use interactive

services. Interestingly, digital television is more commonly found in lower socio-economic groups in almost inverse proportion to the internet, although there is still only a low level of penetration among the over-65s.

Most of the arguments that can be made about this differential access are obvious and concern the extent to which some socio-economic or demographic groups will have greater advantages than others. However, an important supplementary point that emerges from these figures is the absence of experience that large sections of the UK population have in using these technologies. Given the low levels of experience of leading edge technologies among many sections of the population, it seems likely that many citizens would have difficulty in using e-voting systems if they were not made inherently simple. This is a theme that will be returned to later.

Willingness

Notwithstanding the differential access to the technologies that might underpin e-voting, the willingness of citizens to use various forms of e-voting has a bearing upon how many security hurdles they might be prepared to overcome in order to cast an electronic ballot. Stated simply, the more advantages that a citizen can see from e-voting and the keener they are to use it, the more prepared they will be to accept some barriers or delays in gaining access to the system. Conversely, those less keen to use e-voting will be unhappy with any security barriers that they deem as unnecessary and will be easily put off from voting if access is not easily or immediately gained. For example, repeated requests to key in or dial a mis-typed security number might lead to a less enthusiastic person giving up after only a few attempts. Given the fragile nature of turnout in most elections, erecting unnecessary barriers to electoral participation through complex security measures seems to militate against the desire to make voting more convenient and simple as part of a process of re-engaging citizens with politics. Willingness to use e-voting, therefore, is one of the indicators that need to be taken into consideration.

Various surveys have asked the public whether they would be willing to use the electronic methods to access a range of government services, among which voting is one of many. The KPMG Consulting e-government report for 2001 provides one such example.[30] Their survey asked respondents (1,964 face-to-face interviews conducted in February 2001) which activities, if any, they would be likely to do electronically. This definition of electronic interaction included 'the internet, digital TV or an electronic Post Office kiosk'. Overall, 29 per cent of their respondents would be prepared to vote electronically – the second most likely use of electronic services after renewing car tax. However, this figure increases substantially, when the question is restricted only to those with access to the technology.

Data from the BMRB International internet monitor (a panel survey of 1,000 internet users aged 15 or above) shows that around two-thirds of internet users would use the internet for voting in national or local elections.[31]

The BMRB internet monitor also shows some interesting patterns in relation to gender and age. Male internet users are marginally more likely to use it for voting (67 per cent) than their female counterparts (65 per cent), although this masks the fact that women are less likely to have internet access than men. More interestingly, however, the analysis between different age groups challenges some contemporary assumptions about younger people being more likely to use the internet for voting than older people. As Figure 8.1 shows, there is little variation between age groups, with those aged between 35 and 44 being those most willing to use the internet for voting (74 per cent) while those aged under 25 are the least likely. Indeed, those aged over 55 are more likely to want to use the internet for voting than those aged under 25.

The distribution by socio-economic status shows a more expected pattern. As Figure 8.2 demonstrates, internet users from social grade AB (the more affluent and generally better educated groups) are slightly more likely to use the internet for voting than users from lower social grades.

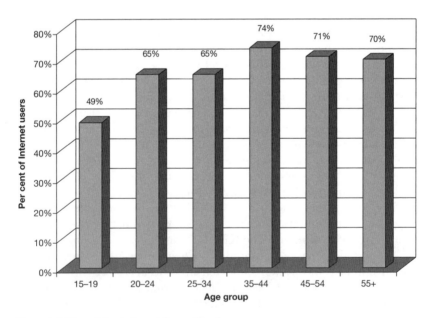

Figure 8.1 Use of the internet for voting, by age

Source: BMRP International Internet Monitor (2001) November 2001 base – All GB Internet users aged 15+ (1,001 respondents) *Which of these activities would use the Internet for?* Respondents answering 'Voting in General Elections'.

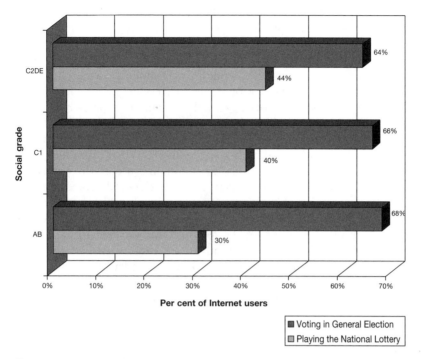

Figure 8.2 Use of the internet, by socio-economic status

Source: BMRB International Internet Monitor (2001) November 2001 base – All GB Internet users aged 15+ (1,001 respondents) *Which of these activities would use the Internet for?* Respondents answering 'Voting in General Elections' or 'Playing the National Lottery'.

Note: Social grades are as follows:

AB Higher and intermediate managerial/administrative/professional.
C1 Supervisory clerical/junior managerial/administrative/professional.
C2 Skilled manual workers.
D   Semi-skilled and unskilled manual workers.
E   On state benefit, unemployed or lowest-grade workers.

Interestingly, this is the exact opposite to the likelihood of the same respondents using the internet to play the National Lottery, suggesting that attitudes to internet use reflect more the respondents' opinion of voting and the National Lottery per se than they do their opinion of the role of the technology in affecting their engagement.

This data is interesting, because it holds access to the technology constant. All of the respondents to the survey are current internet users. Consequently, what emerges is a pattern of propensity to vote that mirrors conventional voting patterns. Two broad conclusions can be drawn. First, even among experienced internet users, a substantial minority would not want to use it for voting purposes. Second, those most resistant to e-voting among internet users are also likely to be from within those socio-economic and demographic groups that are, themselves, most resistant to voting generally. Consequently, on the basis of this data at least, willingness to use e-voting does not seem to be a factor of the technology as much as a factor of voting per se. Those who vote would generally be willing to use electronic methods (with some exceptions, undoubtedly), while those who do not normally vote would not be enticed by e-voting.

While the data reported above suggest that a significant proportion of the UK population would be willing to use e-voting, it is worth noting that there is no great demand for it. The 12 focus groups that formed part of the research reported here support this argument. When prompted at the beginning of the focus groups to discuss the main reasons why people did not vote, the convenience and modernity of the electoral process was low down on most respondents' priorities – political apathy and impotence and a mistrust of politicians and political institutions were much more signifi-cant. While most participants in the focus groups warmed to the idea of e-voting (especially those who currently vote), most suggested that they would only want e-voting if it made the process simpler and more conve-nient. In other words, systems that were complicated to use would not be welcome and would be a disincentive to use.

Cognitive capacity

For those who are familiar with new technologies it is easy to over-estimate the cognitive capacity of citizens and their ability to understand an e-voting process. Such an argument is not one of intellectual or cultural superiority – it is much simpler and more profound in its implications than that. Quite simply, those who have no experience of using a computer in their daily lives (and that is a relatively large proportion of the popula-tion, at least in the UK), find the implicit rules and norms embedded within computerised systems difficult, if not impossible to comprehend. This cognitive capacity, and the limitations it imposes upon universally available voting systems, was painfully exposed during the focus groups. As part of the discussion, participants were invited to log on to a mocked up voting system, enter a password and then cast a vote for a preferred candidate. While some had no difficulty in undertaking the task, others found it difficult, first of all, to log on to the system and, subsequently, to enter passwords. Some gave up after several repeat attempts in which the system refused to allow them to proceed because of errors in entering a number. Others were clearly embarrassed by their inability to make sense of what was required of them.

The problem of cognitive capacity appears to have little to do with the general aptitude of participants. Many of those who were unable to access the e-voting mock-up were otherwise strong contributors to the focus groups, demonstrating a good understanding of the broader issues under discussion and making valuable contributions where relevant.

Rather, cognitive capacity appears to have more to do with the general life experiences of the individual. In order to understand the rules of an e-voting system it is necessary to have had some prior experience of using the type of technologies on which it is based. Clicking a mouse-button or using tab and return keys on a keyboard are obvious requirements for those who use computer-based technologies every day. For those who have not had such opportunities, such functions are not obvious and need to be explained in some detail. Furthermore, even where detailed explanations are available, the confidence of individuals to perform the appropriate acts in sequence, especially where they give the appearance of being complex, is potentially limited.

The lessons of the focus groups for system design are those of simplicity. Even the most basic systems will confuse or alienate otherwise intelligent and engaged voters if they do not explain every step required in some detail. The arcane and potentially threatening language of computer systems is likely to discourage many of the non-computer literate from voting. More complex security systems that require logging on to several servers or entering lengthy identity and password combinations are also going to act as a barrier to electoral participation for many. As a result, the trade-off between simplicity and security appears to be more fundamental than ever, on the basis of this research.

Striking the balance

The combination of access, willingness and cognitive capacity means that without an inherently simple system, many voters will be dissuaded from participating in future e-enabled elections. At the same time, however, the earlier analysis of challenges to security demonstrated that there are a wide range of potential adversaries and a similarly wide range of methods that might be used to attack a future electronic election. The security risks of e-voting seem substantial and suggest the need for sophisticated security mechanisms to minimise such threats. Is it possible, therefore, to strike a compromise that meets the needs of both security and simplicity?

The starting point of reaching any such compromise is to recognise that the current electoral system, at least as it operates in the UK, is not completely failsafe. There have been numerous examples of electoral fraud committed in the UK and elsewhere in Europe. There are even examples of Presidents being elected on a minority of the votes actually cast. However, the voting systems that are in use are remarkably simple to understand and follow. Furthermore, in creating simplicity they create a degree of equity in the voting process, ensuring that everyone, from the poorest to the wealthiest and from the least to the best educated, votes through the same process. In developing the electoral process over the last century or so, the legal and operational framework for elections has gradually refined the process to reduce the opportunities for fraud while ensuring that no individual group of voters was unfairly discriminated against. In particular, it seems fair to argue that the extant system seeks to strike a balance between what Watt[32] describes as the *door-keeper* principle and the *verification, tally and audit* principles in elections.

Following Watt's definitions, the doorkeeper principle requires that 'each person wanting to vote must be personally and positively identified as an eligible voter and permitted to complete no more than the correct number of ballot papers'. In other words, this is the principle of voter authentication. It seems sensible that electronic systems should seek to preserve or enhance current levels of authentication. However, it is maybe expecting too much to require e-voting systems to provide a thorough door-keeping process when current systems do not.

The other end of voting security in contemporary systems comes through the verification, tally and audit process. As Watt puts it, 'there must be some mechanism to ensure that valid votes, and only valid votes, are received and counted. The system must be sufficiently open and transparent to allow scrutiny of the votes and subsequently the working of the political process'. In the UK, certainly, much more emphasis is currently given to this end of the election process than to the door-keeper or authentication process. Under current UK electoral law, anyone presenting themselves at the polling station as an eligible voter (i.e. on the electoral register) is entitled to a vote – the only check being the suspicions of the presiding officer that someone is not whom they claim to be. By contrast, the verification and tallying of ballots is keenly observed and appeals can ensure a thorough auditing of the process. Consequently, the current system seeks primarily to catch electoral fraud or wrongdoing after the event, rather than at the moment of the act. In terms of system integrity and voter confidence, this system seems to work well, with most citizens appearing content that UK elections are free and fair.

It seems strange, therefore, that many of the proponents of e-voting systems place such a strong emphasis upon the door-keeper principle and take the verification, tally and audit principle almost for granted. As the introduction to this chapter argued, while it is difficult to take issue with the desire to tighten up on authentication, system security should not be at the expense of simplicity of use and voter convenience. It would be far better to put in place effective verification, tally and audit procedures that confirm the free and fair nature of the election and identify any malpractice after the event.

Notes

1 See, for example, Internet Policy Institute (2001) *Report of the National Workshop on Internet Voting*, at: www.nsf.gov; Public Administration Select Committee (2001) *First Report 2001–2002*, London: HMSO.
2 See Electoral Commission (2001) *Election 2001: The Official Results*, London: Electoral Commission. Online. Available at: www.electoralcommission.org.uk/about-us/election01results.cfm (accessed 22 January 2004).

3 See Office of the e-Envoy (2000) *e-Government: A Strategic Framework for Public Services in the Information Age*, London: Stationery Office; Office of the e-Envoy (2002) *In the Service of Democracy: A Consultation Paper on a Policy for Electronic Democracy*, London: Cabinet Office. Online. Available at: www.edemocracy.gov.uk/downloads/e-Democracy.pdf (accessed 22 January 2004).

4 See, for example, Pratchett, L., Birch, S., Candy, S., Fairweather, B., Rogerson, S., Stone, V., Watt, B. and Wingfield, M. (2002) *The Implementation of Electronic Voting in the UK*, London: Local Government Association. Online. Available at: www.odpm.gov.uk/stellent/groups/odpm_localgov/documents/pdf/odpm_locgov_pdf_605188.pdf (accessed 22 January 2004); Clarke, H., Sanders, D., Stewart, M. and Whiteley, P. (2001) *Britain (not) at the Polls, 2001*. PDF available at: www.essex.ac.uk/bes/papers/pollsrev.doc; Whiteley, P. (2002) 'Stay at home citizens', *The Guardian* 1 May 2002, p. 15. www.guardian.co.uk/analysis/story/0,3604,707819,00.html.

5 See California Internet Voting Task Force (2000) *A Report on the Feasibility of Internet Voting*. PDF available at: www.ss.ca.gov.

6 See Coleman, S. (2002) *Elections in the 21st Century: from Paper Ballot to e-Voting*, London: Electoral Reform Society. PDF available at: www.electoral-reform.org.uk/publications/books/exec.pdf.

7 See, for example, Oudenhove, B. Van, Schoenmakers, B., Brunessaux, S., Laigneau, A., Schlichting, K. and Ohlin, T. (2001) Report on electronic democracy projects, legal issues of internet voting and users (i.e. voters and authorities representatives) requirements analysis, Volume 1, at: www.eucybervote.org/KUL-WP2-D4V1-v1.0.pdf.

8 See California Internet Voting Task Force, op. cit., p. 2.

9 Internet Policy Institute, op. cit., p. 16.

10 See California Internet Voting Task Force, op. cit., p. 2.

11 See Northern Ireland Office (2001) *Combating Electoral Fraud in Northern Ireland*, London: The Stationery Office (Cm 5080), paragraph 4.

12 For details see Pratchett *et al.*, op. cit.

13 See, for example, Fairweather, B. and Rogerson, S. (2002) *The Implementation of Electronic Voting in the UK: Technological Issues*. PDF available at: www.odpm.gov.uk/egov/e-voting.

14 Others that have already been discounted include the use of bank ATMs and the National Lottery network, both of which offer a potentially secure system for implementation but raise significant problems in respect of access and public acceptability.

15 See Electoral Commission (2002) *Modernising Elections: A Strategic Evaluation of the 2002 Electoral Pilot Schemes*, London: Electoral Commission. PDF available at: www.electoralcommission.org.uk/files/dms/Modernising_elections_6574-6170_E_N_S_W_.pdf; Electoral Commission (2003) *The Shape of Elections to Come: A Strategic Evaluation of the 2003 Electoral Pilot Schemes*, London: Electoral Commission. PDF available at: www.electoralcommission.org.uk/files/dms/The_shape_of_elections_to_come_final_10316–8346_E_N_S_W_.pdf.

16 See www.media.guardian.co.uk/broadcast/story/0,7493,959970,00.html.

17 'Granny farming' is the practice of collecting applications for postal votes in an elderly person's home (or other location where voters are unlikely to be active) and then rewriting them as applications for proxy votes, so that party workers can cast the votes themselves. 'Ghosts' are created when party workers invent names on the electoral register or preserve names that are no longer valid, so that they can vote on their behalf. See, for example, Davies, N. (2001) 'Vote Early, Vote Often', *The Guardian*, 9 May 2001. www.guardian.co.uk/g2/story/0,3604,487777,00.html; Select Committee on Home Affairs (1998) *Fourth report 1997/8*, London: The Stationery Office.

18 See Schneider, F.B. (ed.) (1999) *Trust in Cyberspace*, Washington, DC: National Academy Press. www.nap.edu/books/0309065585/html/index.html.
19 See Mercuri, R. (2001) *Electronic Vote Tabulation Checks and Balances*, Ph.D. Thesis: University of Pennsylvania. www.notablesoftware.com/Papers/thesdefabs.html, pp. 96–7.
20 See Gumble, A. (2003) 'All the President's Votes?', *The Independent Review*, Tuesday 14 October 2003, pp. 2–5.
21 See Harris, B. and Allen, D. (2003) *Black Box Voting: Ballot Tampering in the 21st Century*, High Point, NC: Plan Nine Publishing. www.blackboxvoting.com.
22 See Rubin, A. (2000) *Security Considerations for Remote Electronic Voting over the Internet*, Florham Park, NJ: AT&T Labs. PDF available at: www.avirubin.com/e-voting. security.pdf.
23 The practice of creating a false website that looks like the real thing and would garner votes from unsuspecting voters but would not pass them on to the real server or, even worse, might alter them before passing them on.
24 See Schneier, B. (2000) *Secrets and Lies: Digital Security in a Networked World*, Chichester: John Wiley, p. 310.
25 See Jones, R. (2003) 'More banks hit by email fraud', *The Guardian*, Tuesday 28 October 2003, at: www.guardian.co.uk/online/news/0,12597,1072478,00.html.
26 See, for example, Dickens, C. (1999) *The Pickwick Papers*, London: Penguin. Available at: www.online-literature.com/dickens/pickwick/.
27 See, for example, British Market Research Bureau (2002) *Public Attitudes Towards the Implementation of Electronic Voting: Qualitative Research Report*. PDF available at: www.odpm.gov.uk/egov/e-voting.
28 See Oftel (2001) *Market Information: Mobile Update*, London: Office of Telecommunications.
29 See Office of National Statistics (2003) www.statistics.gov.uk/STATBASE/ssdataset.asp?vlnk=6929.
30 KPMG (2001) 'e-Government For All', at: www.mori.com/polls/2001/kpmg.shtml.
31 For details see Pratchett *et al.*, op. cit.
32 Watt, B. (2002) *The Implementation of Electronic Voting in the UK: Legal Issues*, London: Local Government Association.

Part IV

Institutional visions

9 e-Voting, e-Democracy and EU-democracy

A thought experiment

Philippe C. Schmitter

Introduction

Neither e-democracy nor EU-democracy exists. Both are projects that have been imagined and advocated by theorists and practitioners, but have not been realised – yet. Moreover, their relationship to each other is ambiguous. To the extent that experiments in politicking are currently being made in Europe with the use of information and communication technologies (ICT) for voting in elections, expressing opinion, sharing information, recruiting members, organising protests, campaigning by candidates, soliciting funds and just plain 'interacting' among citizens, they have been confined largely to the local level. Extending them systematically to national democracies already seems risky, perhaps premature and definitely over-ambitious. The supra- or cross-national level, i.e. Europe as a whole with its diversity of languages, cultures, institutions and legal systems, must appear to most citizens as 'virtually' impossible to reach.[1] The European Union, *par contre*, has just undergone a unique experiment with its 'Convention on the Future of Europe'. The resulting draft constitution is utterly conventional in its approach to the mechanisms for governing a continental-sized democracy. There is no explicit mention of ICT and no obvious place for its utilisation. If the draft document were to be ratified as is by the Intergovernmental Commission, it would surely not advance the cause of e-democracy.

So, I am constrained to speculating about something that might happen – sometime and somehow. My conviction is that ICT is such a powerful force that it will have to affect the practices and, eventually, the values of democracy in Europe at all of its multiple levels. The firms that produce its 'soft' and 'hard' components are powerful enough to capture and hold the attention of politicians. The citizens who have learned to use it (especially young people) will find it increasingly anachronistic to employ traditional methods of voting, joining, contributing and petitioning. Finally, the (temporary) representatives and (permanent) officials within the polity will become increasingly dependent upon ICT in their day-to-day activities and may grow more confident about extending it to the crucial mechanisms of democratic accountability and responsiveness themselves.

First, what should we assume?

Let us begin with five hefty assumptions.[2] None of them is true at the present moment, but all of them could become true in the foreseeable future. What seems critical is some as yet unforeseeable convergence of trends and events – combined with the diffusion of (hopefully) successful experiments at the local level – that will compel actors within the 'multi-level' and 'poly-centric' polity that is the existing EU, to apply ICT in a systematic and comprehensive fashion to the task of democratising itself.

- All security problems potentially involved with using ICT, either from publicly provided kiosks, office machines or home computers, have been resolved and there is general public confidence that this is so.[3]
- The distribution of access to ICT is sufficiently broad and equal across all social categories that only modest supplementary efforts would be necessary so that every citizen would have the possibility of using ICT to vote for candidates or in referendums, communicate with representatives or officials, join virtual or real organisations, or contribute voluntarily or compulsorily to parties, associations or movements.[4]
- The member-states of the EU have unanimously made a strong commitment to democratise its institutions and are actively concerned to come up with the most appropriate set of mechanisms for this purpose.[5]
- All of the member-states also agree on the specific rules that should be applied when engaging in EU-politicking via ICT.[6]
- Finally, the EU effort in this domain should not be completely isolated, but co-ordinated with national and sub-national efforts in the same direction.[7]

We may be far from satisfying all of these prior assumptions, but we are moving in their direction – admittedly at very different speeds. Therefore, it is not a complete waste of time to try to imagine what advantages e-politicking via ICT could have for the eventual democratisation and legitimation of the European Union.

Second, why bother to do anything?

At least one distinguished academic has declared that democracy has no business in such an inter-governmental institution and that, anyway, the draft constitution produced by the Convention (if ratified) will be sufficient to produce its political 'maturity'.[8] So, why should the EU, which is not yet an old-fashioned democracy, think about becoming a new-fashioned one by committing itself to use ICT extensively in its politicking?

- The first answer is ironic: precisely because the EU is not yet democratic (and yet has most of the formal institutions of a democracy), there should be less resistance to the introduction of new norms and practices. The elected politicians in its Parliament and the selected officials in its Commission are aware that the familiar formal rules of liberal democracy are not producing its substance when transposed to the European level, largely because the intervening mechanisms of parties, associations and movements are not connecting individual citizens in their constituencies with the representatives and rulers who are supposed to act as their agents. That this has not yet reached the level of a manifest crisis of legitimacy or compliance is primarily a function of the low visibility of most EU policies and of their implementation indirectly through longstanding national institutions. But as the EU gets more and more involved in highly controversial matters such as policing, extradition, migration, asylum granting, subsidisation of industry, defence, foreign affairs and harmonisation of taxation, popular resistance is bound to increase, as will attention to the way in which such decisions are made.

- During this interval between European economic and European political integration, there just may be both a greater anticipation of difficulties to come and a greater willingness to resort to novel means for resolving them than in the better-established, archeo-democracies of its member-states. In other words, the EU is already 'in transition' and during this period of uncertainty of outcomes it may be easier to derive fair rules that both principals and agents will be willing to play by in the future.

- Certain properties of ICT make it very appealing as a means for overcoming precisely what are the strongest obstacles to the successful transposition of orthodox liberal democratic institutions to the EU, namely, the sheer *scale* of actors involved, the *distance* that separates them from each other and from their rulers, and the *diversity* of their cultures, languages and life-worlds. Electronic flows of information and communicative exchanges make it possible for a large number of persons to be involved in a transaction without regard for the physical distance between them. Granted that English has imposed itself as the dominant language of exchange on the internet, but it is a simplified form that is relatively easy to learn and is less and less the obvious expression of a hegemonic power. Moreover, virtually instantaneous translation into other languages seems to be within reach. Federalism and territorial representation were the last major political inventions designed to overcome these problems of scale, distance and diversity. No one doubts that something like federalism and multi-layered representation will characterise the future Euro-polity, but should these not be supplemented by a heavy reliance on ICT?[9]

- e-Democracy, for some of the reasons sketched above, also has the potentiality for creating something that almost everyone agrees does not yet exist on a regular basis and is particularly difficult to attain as long as Europe is not a nation and the EU is not a nation-state, namely, a distinctive and significant '*European public sphere*'. Leaving aside the somewhat abstruse discussion about different meanings that have been attached to this concept, at a minimum it implies that persons and organisations within a democratic unit should be capable, if they wish, of thinking about and discussing among themselves the same topic and, by so doing, not only discover each other's differences of opinion but also learn from them and even change their opinions. They may also find it easier to reach a consensus by engaging in such a process of deliberation – although that remains to be proven in such a large and diverse polity. Given the linguistic and physical barriers – not to mention the sheer numbers – it is impossible to imagine this occurring face-to-face in the Euro-polity. Granted that simultaneous media coverage can be helpful – more Europeans watch the Eurovision Song Contest and the European Football Cup Final than vote in European or even national elections – but in order to qualify as deliberation the exchange has to be more interactive and focused on specifically political issues.[10] The internet has proven that it can effectively (and even affectively) bring persons and organisations together to create more enduring (and, presumably, opinion transforming) political experiences.

• The decline in voting in EP elections has been almost inexorable, worse in some countries than in others, but widespread enough to be of general concern. If abstention in these elections follows established national patterns, the least likely citizens to vote in Euro-elections are young people. While the evidence on whether postal voting improves turn-out is controversial, it seems at least likely that electronic voting will prove especially appealing to youths – who, after all, use the web much more frequently than older people and who are more likely to have received formal instruction in its use.[11] What is even more appealing than a simple proportional rise in those voting is the potentially greater balance across age groups within the citizenry. As it now stands, the elderly not only vote more often but they are taken much more seriously in the calculations of politicians (who themselves seem to be getting older as they get more professional). The result is a systematic maldistribution across generations in the allocation of public funds (and benefits) with serious implications for the future legitimacy of democracy itself. The EU might just be able to correct for this by making a concerted effort to convince youths that this new polity is much more open to experimentation and to responding to new trends than are most of their respective national governments – and e-politicking would have to be part of such an image of rejuvenation of democracy.

• One of the definite advantages of electronic voting, when combined with a longer period of valid voting, is that it permits – even encourages – efforts to get more information from the voters themselves. They can vote for candidates for more offices (national, sub-national and supra-national where possible), for more issues (when combined with referendums or initiatives), for the distribution of vouchers (when linked to funding schemes for parties, associations or social movements) and even for just expressing their opinion on matters that concern them. In terms of democratic theory, it opens up the possibility of measuring not just 'numbers', but also 'intensities'. Citizens are usually given one vote to place on one candidate or party list and it is subsequently up to politicians and pundits to discern what this means in terms of governing priorities and popular resistances. If the voter can also express his or her opinion on specific issues, distribute funds to specific organisations, vote according to some sliding scale of approval for a specific candidate or candidates, or even declare that he or she wishes to vote for 'none of the above' as a protest, we could learn vastly more from the act of voting and this might just lead to more responsive policies and legitimate governments. At virtually no additional cost – even considerable economies of scale and scope – an ICT driven election could reveal lots more about citizen preferences than the present system – provided, of course, politicians are willing to take the chance of revealing these preferences publicly.

• In line with this 'more information' advantage, e-voting could even be used to identify not just the winning candidate, but also the winning constituency. It has long been presumed by liberal democratic theory that territory provides the 'natural' and only relevant unit in which citizens should vote and to which representatives should be held accountable. While there is a lot of variation in the size of these units and the number of candidates to be elected in each of them, there is no variation in their nature.[12] What if voters were given a choice between an established territorial constituency – in the European case it would make sense to use some relatively standardised system of sub-national 'regional' ones – and another constituency based on whatever category they prefer? Initially, the voters would choose one fixed and one variable constituency. The latter would only become available at the subsequent election five years later provided a minimal, fixed number of citizens had chosen it. For example, one of my Italian students might prefer – in addition to voting for a party list for, say, the Region of Tuscany – to be a member of a constituency of 'European Doctoral Students' (wherever they are located) or 'European Progressive Intellectuals' (whatever that might mean). If enough others across Europe picked the same 'ideologico-functional' constituency, he or she would be entitled to nominate a candidate for the EP five years later – and, based on a PR calculation across all of Europe, someone might actually get elected from one of these 'virtual' and cross-national consistencies. ICT makes it possible not only to build in such a flexibility (and thereby identify under-represented infra- and supra-national constituencies), but it also gives individuals the means to contact *ex ante* other potential members in order to build such unorthodox constituencies.

- Finally, an obvious point in favour. By adopting e-democracy (and especially by adopting it extensively before the national governments of its member-states), the EU would identify itself as an innovative and forward-regarding polity that is willing to take risks to bring itself closer to its citizens and to give them an enlarged voice in its deliberations. Even if it did not include all of the *bizarreries* that I have introduced above and were confined to the strictly passive 'Schumpeterian' act of choosing between alternative candidates nominated by national political parties with one set of the winners forming a governing elite for the EU, that would still be a major step toward democratisation (and considerably more than is contained in the 'constitution' drafted by the Convention). It would also place the Euro-polity firmly in the vanguard of politico-technological innovation and that might do something to counter its present reputation for exclusively economico-technocratic governance. And there could be another less obvious pay-off. If one believes, as I do, that the democratisation of the EU will require literally a re-invention of the mechanisms, processes and norms of democracy – something the founding fathers of the American republic very self-consciously did – then, by relying on ICT, the founding fathers of Euro-democracy would be sending the subtle message that it will also be different than what has been previously experienced at the national level and, therefore, its performance should not be judged exclusively by the norms and expectations generated at that level.

Third, what should we expect?

The simple answer is: 'Not too much right away'. ICT should be introduced very gradually and incrementally into EU-democracy, *au fur et à mesure* that public confidence develops in its reliability and security. In part, this will be a derived function of the course that experimentation takes at the local and national levels, although it should not be excluded that the EU might pioneer certain applications of it. For example, the neo-democracies in Eastern Europe seem already to be experimenting with more advanced uses of ICT than many of the archeo-democracies of Western Europe – perhaps, due to less constraining constitutional or legal norms; perhaps, due to a more concerted desire to 'catch up' to their elders. The EU might, therefore, begin in these new (and often smaller) member-states on some partial basis before tackling application to its more hide-bound (and larger) members.

Potentially, the range of application is enormous.[13] There is virtually not an act of democratic politicking that cannot somehow be performed directly, or affected indirectly, by ICT – which is not to say that it will always be performed better. As the sheer scale of political transactions increases and the likelihood of face-to-face exchanges decreases due to distance and cultural impediments, the value-added of ICT should become more evident to Euro-citizens – and, hopefully, more acceptable to them.

The crucial missing element, however, is whether ICT can revive 'citizen interest in politics'. There is considerable evidence of a decline in this property in contemporary democracies – whether from voter turn-out or in public opinion surveys – and, if this is a 'terminal condition', there may be nothing that can be done about it, least of all at the EU level where such interest was never high in the first place and where it has been a matter of deliberate strategy to keep it low as long as possible. Sara Bentivegna has put it well: 'the increase in information made possible by the sum of new technologies can be utterly irrelevant if citizens are not interested (in politics) and simply prefer to use (these technologies) to consume entertainment.'[14] And, so far, the entertainment value of the EU has been very low.

So, we have to make another leap of faith into the future and imagine that the various *demoi* that presently make up the merging Euro-polity have come to realise:

- that decisions by the EU have an increasing significance for their daily lives and welfare;
- that the political units with which they have traditionally identified are no longer sovereign and, hence, capable of providing them exclusively with the security they desire;
- that the process of European integration has irrevocably expanded from the strictly economic to the political realm;
- that the institutions of the EU are open to the collective expression of citizen interests and passions; and
- that these collective actions, whether expressed through electoral or other channels, can have a predictable and effective influence on EU-governance.

It is precisely that last point that has been at the heart of the weakness in EU-democracy. Elections for the Euro-Parliament have no direct effect on the formation of the Commission and most of the effective influence on specific policies has been obscured by the machinations of so-called 'comitology' (of which normal Euro-citizens have no knowledge and to which they would have no access even if they did know what was going on in these hundreds of advisory groups and drafting committees). The Convention's draft constitution does marginally improve the powers of the EP in this domain, but the formation of a pseudo-EU-government, i.e. the Commission, still lies firmly in the hands of the governments of the member-states. This calculated unwillingness to 'open up' EU-politicking to mass publics and to tie its policy orientation to the ebb and flow of partisan preference suggests (to me) that, even if it is ratified, the new constitutional treaty will do little to enhance 'citizen interest in politics' at that level. Certainly, the Convention itself did nothing to improve this situation.

So, with regard to expectations, we find a dilemma. If the EU introduces ICT *before* having made a credible commitment to democratising its institutions, the impact will be negligible. Alone, ICT is unlikely to stimulate greater citizen interest in politics. Only competition between significant policy choices and a predictable connection between the winners and the processes of government formation and intervention can do that. If the EU waits until *after* it has made that commitment, the subsequent introduction of ICT will become more difficult because EU institutions will have already been structured around more traditional forms of politicking and the politicians who have benefited from playing the (now more significant) 'game' that way will not wish to change the rules. Assuming that this dilemma in timing can be overcome, what applications can we expect within the EU?

e-Voting

This would probably be the 'cutting-edge' application of ICT at the EU-level. It is relatively simple (provided, I stress, that the 'hefty assumptions' noted at the beginning of this essay were satisfied). Elections for the Euro-parliament already exist and, given the scale of the constituencies involved, the usual arguments about the 'community effect' of direct polling are scarcely applicable. Since the UK changed its electoral system, all Euro-citizens (or, better, the diminishing number of them who take the trouble to vote) choose a closed party list either for the country as a whole or for some region of it. Being able to do this over a longer period (or even more than once) might allow for the progressive introduction of new features such as: (1) *preferential voting* (alterations in the rank-order of individual candidates); (2) *split-ticket voting* (allowing the voter to distribute his or her vote across more than one list); (3) *voting in primaries* (allowing some subset of voters, e.g. party members, to participate in the nomination process); (4) *multiple voting* (according parents the right to vote for their children from birth until the age of maturity); (5) *reversible voting* (permitting citizens to change their preferences at any time during the voting period as the result of intervening discussions or events); and (6) *negative voting* (allowing citizens to vote for 'none of the above' as an expression of disgust at the quality of existing candidates). Especially appealing given the complexities of representation in a polity 'beyond the nation-state' are the notions of *dual voting*, i.e. giving to each Euro-citizen the right to vote for a candidate or list running in another member-state as a way of indicating cross-national appeal, or of *parallel voting*, i.e. giving the right to vote in the usual fixed territorial constituency and also in a second, non-territorial, constituency of one's choice as a way of signalling the importance of emerging novel units of representation. Initially, both dual and parallel voting might be offered on an experimental basis – just to test for citizen interest – but they could become an iterative component of a more flexible way of ensuring some fit between citizens, their constituencies and their representatives. All of these 'unorthodox' additional features would contribute to a secondary goal, namely, that of calling the attention of Euro-citizens to the fact that elections on this scale are not mere replicas of those held at the usual national and sub-national levels.

e-Referendum

As mentioned above, one of the greatest advantages of 'protracted e-voting' is that it allows the extraction of more information from the voter – provided, of course, that he or she is willing to devote the time and effort to doing so. One way of bringing EU policy-making closer to the citizens of Europe – a frequently stated objective of EU rulers – would be to allow them to express their opinion *ex ante* on the desirability of specific policies via referendums.[15] What is absolutely essential, if this practice is to have any Euro-wide effect, is that such referendums should be held on the same day and, needless to say, on the same topic in all the member states.[16] Nothing is farther from present practice. At best, the national citizens of member-states are increasingly allowed *ex post* to ratify initial entry or subsequent treaty modifications – each on a date and in a manner chosen by the national government. Since there are many 'delicate ambiguities' involved in the actual mechanics of referendums: turn-out (usually lower, occasionally very high), frequency (a curvilinear relationship – very infrequent and no one turns out, very frequent and even less turn out), content (often manipulated by authorities), timing (separate or in conjunction with regular elections), and significance (binding or non-binding), it would seem best to enter this minefield at the European level gradually and prudently. ICT makes its marginal cost rather low – both to the voter and to the authorities – but its marginal benefit might even be lower. Hence, I have advocated that all Euro-referendums should be drafted and chosen by the European Parliament – at least, initially – and that there should only be one or two, concomitant with each election of its deputies.[17] Also, the results should be non-binding. The only catch is that such a 'bland' and 'inconsequential' design may so discourage participation that the entire idea will be permanently discredited! Later, one could envisage adding such more appealing attributes as 'citizen-initiated referendums', 'binding jurisdiction' and even 'mandatory convocation' with regard to changes in basic rules.

e-Vouchers

Vouchers fit well with ICT. They are a form of *ersatz*-money that can only be spent for pre-designated goods or services – and doing so by electronic means resolves all of the overhead costs of printing them out and diminishes the likelihood that they will be exchanged on some 'grey market' for other purposes. Moreover, ICT makes it possible for the voucher-giver to receive virtually free information about different providers (and can afford easy access to those who wish to complain about their performance). Their most obvious and democratic use within an eventual EU-democracy would be to provide a reformed system for providing citizens with an equal capacity for financing the channels of representation at the European level. To do this would require three, closely interrelated, reforms: (1) the establishment of a distinctive *semi-public status* for European parties, interest associations and social movements; (2) the financing of these associations through *compulsory contributions*; and (3) the distribution of these funds by means of *citizen vouchers*. Only organisations that were 'European' in nature, i.e. had members and some degree of presence in a minimal number of EU member-states could acquire the semi-public status. They would have to agree to obey a common set of norms and submit themselves potentially to the jurisdiction of the ECJ (as well as be prepared to operate within the legal norms of whatever member country they might find themselves in). The financing of these representative organisations would come from designated EU funds – much as present subsidies and contracts do[18] – and the voucher system would run in tandem with the holding of Euro-elections by ICT, alongside voting for MEPs and in eventual Euro-referendums. Such an arrangement would avoid the specification by EU authorities of any fixed or pre-existing category of representation based on class, status, sector, profession, partisanship or cause, but would leave the task of determining the level of support and organisational boundaries to the initiative of party officials and interest entrepreneurs, the self-determination of social and ideological groups, and the subsequent competition for vouchers. These specially designated, non-transferable units of account could only be assigned to European-level organisations with semi-public status and only in proportions chosen by individual Euro-citizens. For a variety of reasons, it would seem prudent to divide these organisations into two eligible 'pools' for funding, one for political parties and the other for interest associations and social movements.[19] The only cost involved for the citizen in spending them would be the individual's time and effort in getting acquainted with alternative recipients via files provided by ICT, plus the few moments it would take to check off boxes or fill in blanks. The benefits could be multiple:

• Such a scheme would permit a relatively free expression of the multiplicity of each Euro-citizen's preferences, rather than confine him or her to one party list as do most exclusively territorially based voting systems.

- It allows for an easy resolution of the 'intensity problem' that has long plagued democratic theory, since their proportional distribution by individuals across parties, associations and movements should reflect how strongly the citizenry 'really' feels about various interests and passions.[20]
- It equalises the amount and severs the decision to contribute from the disparate command over resources that individual citizens unavoidably have in an economic system based on the unequal distribution of income and property.
- It offers no rational motive for waste or corruption since the vouchers cannot provide a direct or tangible benefit to the donor and can only be spent by certified organisations for pre-designated public purposes with the EU.
- In fact, the distribution of vouchers should provide a very important incentive for reflection on the nature of one's interests/passions, thereby encouraging the opening up of a new public space at the level of Europe as a whole. Since they would be repeated over time, this distribution would present a virtually unique opportunity to evaluate the consequences of one's past choices.
- They would, therefore, become a powerful mechanism for enforcing the accountability of existing Euro-parties, associations and movements since, if the behaviour of their leaders differs too remarkably from the preferences of those who spent their vouchers on them, citizens could presumably transfer their vouchers elsewhere.
- Vouchers make it relatively easy, not just to switch among existing rival conceptions of one's interest, but also to bring into existence previously latent groups that presently cannot make it over the initial organisational threshold.
- Finally, they offer a means of extending the principle of Euro-citizenship and the competitive core of Euro-democracy that neither makes immediate and strong demands on individuals, nor directly threatens the entrenched position of *élites*.

e-Contacting

So far, one of the core premises of the application of ICT to EU-democracy is that it would be anonymous. Citizens would have to be reliably identified (and thereby prevented from voting or participating more than once), but their identity and other characteristics would be rigorously protected. But what if citizens wished their identities revealed – for example, to the parties, associations or movements to which they had assigned vouchers? What if they still wished to protect their personal identity, but consented to inform the public in general, and politicians in particular, about their age, occupation, location and other social characteristics? And, even more, what if they wanted to enter into some exchange with the politicians they had elected or the organisations they had funded – for example, to be notified when certain issues come up within the Commission or are referred to the Parliament? Now, this is the sort of intermediation that political representatives are supposed to engage in, but they often do so under misleading conditions or exaggerated stimuli. Public opinion polling is notoriously used (and misused) by politicians for this purpose. But what if there existed a more direct, differentiated and continuous method for doing this? The EU suffers particularly from the weakness of existing mechanisms for the revelation of preferences. The distances from Euro-citizen to Euro-deputy to Euro-commissioner are long (and expensive to overcome); the opinion polls are few and far-between (and have to rely on dubiously worded standard items); and the diversity of languages means that only the most salient and episodic of messages manage to get into that elusive 'European Public Sphere'. Might it not be possible – admittedly only in the distant future – for ICT, once it had been used habitually for the purposes outlined above, to provide a much more reliable mechanism for improving political communication? And is it completely utopian to imagine that by opening up such interactive channels between citizens, intermediaries and rulers, the quality of democracy itself could be improved?

Conclusion

e-Democracy is not and will not be a panacea for EU-democracy. Alone, it will not fill in the much decried (if rarely proven) democracy deficit of the European Union. Moreover, just reaching (unanimous) agreement on how and where to apply ICT will be a difficult proposition, given the diversity of interests and experiences of its 25 member-states. And, there is no reason at all to expect that its inexorable diffusion to individuals and firms will automatically bring about its application to political agents and agencies.

Nevertheless, as I have argued in this thought experiment, e-democracy does have several potentially interesting features for overcoming some of the most obvious difficulties if and when the EU does decide to democratise itself. If one believes, as I do, that it will be necessary literally to re-invent democracy if it is to be practised successfully and legitimately in such a large-scale and diverse polity, then ICT should be seriously considered in any eventual effort at reinvention.

Notes

1   For the purposes of this essay, e-democracy should be clearly distinguished from e-government. The latter refers to efforts by public authorities and agencies to

provide information about their services and to allow citizens to use ICT to make transactions with governments that they previously had to do in person or by post. e-democracy refers to the use of these same technologies by citizens in an attempt to select their rulers, to hold them accountable or to advocate changes in their behaviour or policies. Note that e-democracy is by no means confined to the act of voting, but could be extended to the full range of petitioning, protesting, pressuring and proscribing. Therefore, in the text, I refer occasionally to 'e-politicking' rather than 'e-voting' in an effort to capture that wider range of citizen activity.

2 I am reminded of the *boutade* about an economist is a person who resolves the problem of opening a tin on a deserted island by imagining that he has a can-opener. In this case, I am asking the reader to imagine that both the ICT industry and the EU have managed to resolve a series of existing and quite difficult problems before using ICT as a democratic can-opener.

3 My suggestion is that, prior to actually using it, the EU should experiment on a small scale with several 'simulated' electronic voting arrangements and announce a prize to be awarded to the hacker or hackers who can disrupt any or all of them.

4 During an interim period in order to accommodate those on the other side of the 'digital divide', it would be desirable to sustain a dual system in which, by choice, citizens could vote, communicate, join and support through an alternative means, for example, gratis via the postal service. Studies have shown (see e.g. Kies, R. and Trechsel, A.H. (2001) 'Le contexte socio-politique', in A. Auer and A.H. Trechsel (eds) *Voter par internet? Le projet e-voting du canton de Genève dans une perspective socio-politique et juridique*, Geneva, Basle, Munich: Helbing & Lichtenhahn, p. 47f.) that where traditional poll voting and mail-in voting exist side by side, the latter rather quickly tends to drive out use of the former – with, however, a perpetual residual. It is these (presumably older and less educated) citizens who would have to be enticed to participate by providing public kiosks and making introductory ICT courses easily available to them so that, in the longer run, the low cost advantages of e-politiking can be fully realised.

5 The present draft elaborated by the Convention definitely does not satisfy this assumption. It pays far more attention to efficiency and effectiveness concerns than to democratic ones and, when it comes to ratification, will not be perceived by mass publics as constituting a serious commitment to democracy. For this to happen, the much discussed but never present 'democracy gap' has to become much more salient and closely linked to the legitimacy of EU directives. This, in turn, is linked to the negative impact that EU institutions are having upon the democratic legitimacy of national institutions ('domestic democracy' as I have called it elsewhere) and to the increasing embarrassment caused by the disparity between the results of elections to the European and national parliaments. Awareness of these two, interconnected processes should be sufficient to induce national politicians to act – even if there is little mass-based protest against EU institutions or policies.

6 That would mean, for example, holding EP elections under a single procedure for registration (preferably, lowering the age limit to 16 and making it permanent with a Euro-ID card utilisable no matter where one resides within the EU) during the same time-period (perhaps, over an entire week to encourage higher turn-out and continuous discussion) with the same definition of eligible citizens (hopefully, to include denizens not just from other EU countries) with the same restrictions on revealing the results (ideally, only during a single evening at the end of the voting period) and upon revealing and distributing the identity of the voter (ideally, under strict assurances of anonymity) and, finally, with the

same arrangements for campaign financing and even candidate nomination (presumably, using EU funds and nomination procedures set by Euro-level party secretariats).

7 It would be utterly utopian to assume that all of the multi-levels of European government (and governance) would switch to e-politicking within the same time-frame. As mentioned above, there is already considerable experimentation going on, mostly at the local and provincial levels and this will, hopefully, give some citizens greater confidence in its reliability and confidentiality. Evaluating these experiments thoroughly and publicising their results before trying them out at the EU-level is an important task to be accomplished. The longer-term objective should be to try to co-ordinate the national and sub-national electoral cycles with that of the EU as much as possible. By holding elections electronically and setting aside a sufficient period of time, say, a week, there should be enough time for citizens to make their choices for offices at various levels. Moreover, doing so might reduce the 'distribution gap' whereby the 'second level' EP elections that usually fall in the middle of the regular parliamentary cycle provide voters with a 'costless' opportunity to send more extreme messages to their rulers at the primary national level. Also, co-ordinating electoral levels might be an instrument for improving the turn-out for EP elections – or, at least, harmonising the social and political characteristics of those who do turn out.

8 See, for example, Moravscik, A (2002) 'If it Ain't Broke, Don't Fix it!', *Newsweek*, 4 March 2002; Moravscik, A. (2003) 'Europe Comes of Age', *Newsweek*, 23 June 2003.

9 For my doubts on why 'orthodox' federalism may not be enough, see my unpublished paper, Schmitter, P. 'Is federalism for Europe a solution or a problem: Tocqueville inverted, perverted or subverted?', paper presented at the ECPR Joint Sessions of Workshops, Edinburgh, March 2003.

10 For example, never has there been more of a European public sphere than during the period leading up to the American-led invasion of Iraq. The virtually instantaneous development of common symbols and continent-wide co-ordination of protests was unprecedented and much of it was conducted 'in the name of Europe'. Despite efforts to divide the 'New' from the 'Old' Europeans, the popular mobilisation easily bridged the divide between governments and those supporting the American action were all disavowed by the majority of their public opinion. Unfortunately for the development of deliberative democracy (and fortunately for the evolution of world politics), this was a 'one off' event – although if the US were to repeat the experience, say in Iran or Syria, the Europe-wide reaction would probably be even greater.

11 See the chapter by Norris in this volume.

12 Actually, Slovenia has pioneered a system of representation for its Second Chamber based on professions and sectors of production. Unfortunately, these have been fixed in a corporatist fashion and cannot be changed by the voters themselves.

13 I stress the word 'potential'. Despite all the 'hype', ICT has not revolutionalised the practice of democracy at the national or sub-national level and its application has generated a good deal of normative controversy. For a balanced discussion of the pros and cons, I have found very useful: Bentivegna, S. (1999) *La Politica in Rete*, Rome: Meltemi. Her conclusion that 'the web ... can contribute to the evolution of democratic processes in a society but, certainly, it cannot be the driving element of such processes' (p. 14) strikes me as sensible. It will take an explicit willingness on the part of rulers to experiment via public policy, a shift in public attitudes and confidence – and the fulfilment of what I have called above some rather hefty 'assumptions' before such a revolution

takes place. But, as I stressed initially, this is a 'thought piece' not a piece of empirical research.

14 For details see Bentivegna, op. cit., p. 15.

15 For my initial advocacy of this, see Schmitter, P. (2000) *How to Democratize the European Union ... and Why Bother?*, Boulder, CO: Rowman & Littlefield, pp. 36–7.

16 The possibility of doing this to secure popular approval of the draft 'constitutional treaty' was raised at the end of the Convention and quickly rejected. Several countries (not least, Germany) have no national constitutional provisions for holding referendums and there would undoubtedly have been 'scheduling conflicts' in others. Obviously, applying ICT to this on a European scale would have to be a long-term project and involve prior and unanimous agreement on a treaty.

17 See Schmitter (2000), op. cit., pp. 36–7.

18 It is important to note that such a source of EU funding would not preclude their also receiving funds from national governments, private organisations or individual persons. In other words, it would not completely 'level the playing field', but it would contribute significantly to improving its surface.

19 The reason for this should be obvious from survey research, namely, the markedly greater hostility of citizens to political parties. If they were forced into competition with associations and movements, I suspect that they would receive little or no support. I would also favour allowing Euro-citizens to assign their party or association-movement vouchers to 'none of the above' to indicate that they supported no existing European-level intermediary organisation to protect or further their interests or passions. Money accruing to this account could be made available on an experimental basis to newly founded parties, associations or movements to enable them to compete for vouchers in the future.

20 And, not incidentally, they would generate a fabulous new source of data on preferences for social scientists to analyse – much cheaper and much better in quality than what they have been collecting via survey research.

10 e-Voting: a new political institution for the network society?

New life for an old democratic procedure

Karl-Heinz Ladeur

e-Voting – just a technological issue?

As contributors throughout this volume argue, there is more to e-voting than its hypothetically positive effect on the efficiency of the voting process.[1] This chapter will try to complement the list of potential features that e-voting could – or should – trigger within the EU. It will do so by assessing novel forms of electoral techniques that could lead to profound changes of our democratic institutions. The societal changes induced by the 'cyberrevolution', essentially caused by the development of new forms of communication, represent challenges for the functioning of contemporary democracies. It is the aim of this chapter to present these societal changes, their impact on the traditional idea of representative democracy and the way in which e-voting could refine, adapt and even improve the latter.

It goes without saying that e-voting, should it be implemented for local, national or European elections, would meet similar criticism as other recent electoral innovations. For example, techniques such as postal voting never were beyond doubt. While voters in some countries, such as in Finland or Switzerland, extensively make use of postal voting, its introduction in the UK still is the subject of open controversy.[2] Above all, as with postal voting, e-voting raises procedural problems concerning the secrecy of the voting process.[3] Comparing e-voting and postal voting is not interesting just because of their relative newness. A closer look at the contexts in which postal voting was implemented will allow us to gain insights for discussing the implementation of e-voting. For example, with the ever growing mobility of citizens, many arguments in favour of postal voting became more and more compelling. Today, a voter being absent from home on the day of the elections is no longer an exception to the rule. On the contrary, the physical absence of a major part of voters on election day has become a new rule.

It could be argued that e-voting could be attractive only for younger generations as the latter are much more used to new technologies. For younger voters, it could be simply 'cool' to vote via the internet. Of course, such an argument would not constitute a sufficiently adequate basis for constitutional reform. However, this example shows that the internet is not just a new medium for the transportation of content (including a ballot) such as the 'online' newspaper, etc. The same goes for the rise of e-commerce within the economic realm. Each medium generates its own usage pattern, its own formats, even if this process takes its time. Similar effects could be measured with the introduction of television. In its first stage, television was considered to be 'radio plus pictures' or a means of transportation for movies (produced for movie theatres) or for plays (produced for traditional theatres). Later on, however, television developed its own formats for news, TV series, shows, etc., within new aesthetics, radically different from the ones used by radio or in movies. In the long run, the same could happen with e-voting, despite the fact that at first sight, internet voting does not seem to bring upon radical change.

In the following section of this chapter we will address the overall transformation of the communication system caused by the rise of the internet. Could this transformation not only trigger e-voting but, in addition, lead to new forms of electoral engineering? The third, fourth and fifth sections will go even further. To what extent are we witnessing a transformation of liberal democracy, the rise of the network society and its implication for modern political institutions. Before concluding, the sixth section will attempt to tie these developments and the potential of e-voting together.

The internet and the transformation of the communication system – consequences for e-voting

'Hybrids' – crossing the line between individual and mass communication

The internet offers some particular features and has some singular consequences on modern communication. In our context, the most relevant one is the fact that the internet allows for 'hybrid' forms of communication, linking hitherto separate formats of communication, mass media and, in particular, individual communication.[4] A communicator no longer has to choose between addressing a message to a large anonymous public ('point-to-multi-point', e.g. through newspapers, broadcasting) or to individual addressees ('point-to-point', e.g. by telephone, letter). The internet – much more than any alternative means of communication – now allows for sending 'content' to a very large number of persons, selected on the basis of personalised criteria.

This evolution expands the formerly exclusive set of 'point-to-multi-point' and 'point-to-point' forms of communication. Thanks to the internet, these two alternatives are now, simply, two different forms of communication within a whole range of possible communication forms, embedded in a 'network'. Moreover, this evolution not only allows for different formats of communication but also for different combinations of these formats. It can be taken as granted that the greater variety of forms of communication will not yet annul pre-existing differences between more and less powerful communicators. However, on the internet, individuals can each communicate with a very large number of persons by making use of a whole range of different communication formats. We will return to this crucial point later.

e-Voting leads to a greater flexibility of voting procedures

With the appearance of e-voting procedures, the 'hybridisation' of communication on the internet ('personalised mass communication' and 'anonymous personal communication') could lead to the transformation of traditional voting procedures. For example, while the latter usually consist of relatively rigid procedures, e-voting could be conducive to implementing various forms of vote-swapping. Such forms of vote-swapping could be arranged between different constituencies, between political parties within the same constituency and between candidates' positions on individual party lists. This latter possibility actually exists already in the European context. Mostly, however, the possibility for voters to alter party lists is only provided at the local level. Luxembourg and Switzerland are exceptions to this general trend as, in both countries, the so-called 'panachage' of candidates is offered in national elections. In both cases, voters can remove individual candidates from the proposed party list, double their vote for individual candidates ('cumulating') and even compose a personalised party list by voting for candidates belonging to different parties ('panachage'). It is not surprising that these two small countries provide such opportunities to their voters given that the procedure of 'panachage' places a heavy burden on the vote-counting procedure. Therefore, one could assume that the larger the constituency, the greater the technical and administrative complications in PR systems with 'panachage'. The vote-counting overload of such procedures could be avoided if one were to make use of the huge informational resources of the internet (computers). Of course, such vote-swapping techniques are still rather conventional in as much as they already are in use in various contexts. With the exceptions of Luxembourg and Switzerland, they would remain innovative on the national level. By gradually implementing vote-swapping techniques, the relationship between voters and political parties would be considerably transformed, departing from the traditional standardised model of ordering candidates on party lists. Voters clearly would have more possibilities of influencing the decisions of political parties, particularly candidate selection which has always been one of the most important functions of political parties. Illustrating such a shift one can think of women, for whom it would be possible to check whether enough women have been placed in favourable positions on the ballot and, if necessary, change the order and weight of the candidates on the list. Candidates who stand for certain political values, as opposed to mainstream priorities, might get the support of more voters than the party would normally attract. Their positions could be changed as a result of public campaigns.

A different and even more far-reaching version of voting flexibility induced by e-voting procedures might be introduced in majoritarian electoral systems: political parties and voters might set up agreements about vote swaps between constituencies. In cases where, for example, party A expects a 'safe' victory over party B in a given constituency it could agree on shifting a part of its vote surplus to a party C in another constituency where a narrow decision between party B and C is probable. A kind of 'stock exchange' for votes could be developed which would introduce a certain collective element into the voting procedure. The result would be some kind of collectively agreed upon 'virtual gerrymandering'. The question of whether and how such a swap might, or even should, have a binding character is difficult to answer. The 2000 Presidential elections in the US have shown that, even under current conditions, there is a growing interest in vote swapping. In the 2000 Presidential race, such attempts were based on the willingness of 'green voters' to vote for the Democratic Party candidate Al Gore in constituencies that were at risk of being won by the Republican Party, whereas supporters of Al Gore should, in return, have voted for Ralph Nader in constituencies which were either safe for the Democrats or lost from the outset. This process, which had been organised in a private way, was regarded as being illegal by public authorities and was hindered by administrative and judicial means wherever possible.[5] From a technical perspective, it would be feasible to force voters to respect such agreements through administrative means. However problematic such 'binding' solutions might be, informal vote-swapping procedures that are solely based on mutual trust would be possible. One might even think about a possible mediator in such procedures, who could function as an intermediary, collecting votes to be swapped and voting in the name of groups of citizens. This would imply a new collective element in the voting procedure. However, certain risks, e.g. of making votes the object of sales to political parties, may not be excluded but could, at least, be mitigated by the participation of a trusted mediator. Nonetheless, such a formalised procedure is not essential or required for implementing the idea of vote swapping.

'Virtual constituencies'

Let us briefly reflect on a less far-reaching innovation that would be equally well adapted to 'cyberspace' and the virtual relationships between individuals and groups introduced by the latter. Instead of swapping *votes*, one could think of ways of swapping *constituencies*. In other words, constituencies could become 'virtual'. Let us imagine a 'stock exchange' where instead of votes one could exchange constituencies on the basis of reciprocity. Such a procedure would remain legitimate as, at the end of the day, it would not misrepresent the overall will of the voters. Quite to the contrary, this system would contribute to a more balanced electoral outcome. Constituency swapping, whether binding or non-binding in form, would introduce more flexibility into an e-enabled election procedure. Moreover, it should be mentioned that first experiences – spontaneously organised over the internet – have occurred during the 2000 US Presidential elections. 'Pairs' of voters, willing to exchange their respective votes, could be identified thanks to the internet. We believe that such processes should not be regarded as illegitimate, for the simple reason that the territorial basis of voting has lost much of its credibility. Introducing such 'virtual' elements into the election procedure can be seen as a consequence of the general trend towards a devaluation of citizens' territorial attachment.[6] Particularly in majoritarian electoral systems,[7] the major aim of the procedure consists of the constraint imposed on citizens to opt for pre-structured alternatives in order to bring about a stable majority in parliament.[8] However, this aim could remain valid and would not be affected by the aforementioned vote-swapping procedures.

Conditional voting

Rendering voting more strategic – and therefore potentially raising the voters' interest in participating at the polls – could take place in electoral systems that contain certain quorums for parties to gain seats (e.g. in Sweden which has a 4 per cent threshold, or Germany with a 5 per cent threshold). Such quorums produce a certain risk for the voter of 'wasting' their votes on parties that cannot attain the threshold required for gaining seats in Parliament.[9] For example, the strong partner in a coalition might want to give votes to the smaller one should the latter be at risk of failing to meet the quorum requirement.[10] In such a case, forms of 'conditional voting' could be introduced into the electoral system, where votes for a party that fails to attain the threshold would instead go to another, more successful party. Using the same logic, conditional voting could be based on a variety of criteria – not just the criterion of obtaining a certain quorum – such as the winning of an absolute majority. Such conditional voting would give more influence to those voters whose choice would otherwise be subject to the high risk of 'throwing away' their vote. On the other hand, it would allow voters to assign a more complex message to their ballot, enabling a more differentiated communication flow between political parties and voters. Political parties would, in such a system, get the information that a part of their voters would have preferred another party.

Such a conditional vote might also help implement the procedure of swapping votes described above: adding a condition (concerning the number of votes going to a certain candidate) might create the trust that is necessary for this procedure, as long as the latter is not binding for the partners of a vote-swapping agreement.

Finally, one might even think of allowing for a conditional vote in order to enable voters to influence, for example, the formation of a coalition government after an election has taken place. The legitimacy of such a procedure could, of course, be questioned with regard to the principles of the representative mandate given that the formation of a coalition government might turn out to be extremely complicated if all kinds of conditions are tied to a vote.

More participation by flexible voting

As we have seen, e-voting techniques may enhance voting flexibility thanks to the computational power of new communication technologies. The effects of e-voting may therefore encompass much more than simply making voting more convenient for the voter and the voting process more efficient for the electoral administration. By imagining new e-enabled forms of voting the quality of the latter can be considerably increased. Our propositions fall in line with the general tendency that can be observed in the field of new communication technologies: such technologies do not simply accelerate traditional forms of communication but have a truly transformative character, creating new regimes of communication. The same turns out to be the case for voting, which can also qualify as some kind of communication, for example between citizens and political parties. The new flexibility that we have described might allow for experiments with different types of ballots, the use of which might bring new life to democratic voting. Agreements about vote swapping, for example, might even take place in public – at least partially – and bring new ideas and solutions into political deliberation. It would enable citizens to add more 'content' to their vote and to learn from others how to use this new potential. One might be sceptical concerning the impact of the rather far-reaching proposition of conditional voting – especially if coalition formation is part of the initial set of conditions. We would argue, however, that conditional voting as such, including vote swapping, would not be incompatible with representative democracy. Quite to the contrary, its impact on democracy could be truly positive. In the current context, where citizens' trust in liberal democracy and its institutions has decreased in most European countries (with the exception of the Netherlands),[11] such innovative forms of voting may be conducive to higher levels of trust and political participation. In addition, we doubt that erratic shifts of votes from one constituency to the other constitute a realistic risk. Also, by not just proposing voting via the internet but by adding such flexible voting procedures to the set of electoral institutions, one could avoid stimulating the participation of voters who are disinterested in politics and who simply vote over the internet because it is convenient and cheap. It goes without saying that if e-voting would simply stimulate this latter type of political participation, the legitimacy of democratic decision-making may be devalued.[12]

e-Referendums?

Before looking more deeply into the contemporary challenges that party systems are facing, we would like to propose yet another idea: the introduction of more elements of direct democracy into the electoral procedure. Institutions of direct democracy and, most prominently, the referendum process, exist in various EU Member States. None, however, can look back to such a long tradition of holding regular referendums and popular initiatives as Switzerland. While internet-based voting procedures could not only make direct democratic decision-making procedures more easily available, 'internet referendums' could provoke transformations of the political process that go beyond the known effects of 'off-line' referendums. The internet might not only make the organisation of referendums easier, it might also allow for a qualitatively enhanced pre-voting stage[13] and introduce novel ways of publicly deciding on what the electorate should vote. Similar to the novel procedures in the electoral realm, it might also be possible to add conditions and to considerably differentiate the voter's choice in the referendary realm.[14]

The legitimacy of 'virtual elections'

The evolution of the classical liberal system towards the party system

When considering holding e-enabled parliamentary elections, or, in a more precise way, when asking ourselves whether a 'virtualisation' of the electoral procedure is compatible with our democratic institutions, one first of all has to bear in mind the fundamentally local character of early models of representation. In particular, this was the case in England and, subsequently, on the continent and in the US.[15] Members of Parliament were above all regarded as the representatives of their constituencies. This stood in contrast with the overarching idea that parliaments were chambers in which the people were primarily represented (consider the American formula 'We the people . . .'). However, with the rise of both the welfare state and political parties, parliamentary elections have changed their function. In 'group-based' welfare states, the electoral process became increasingly mediated by political parties. Furthermore, as mentioned in a decision by the German Federal Constitutional Court, parties pre-structure political alternatives, which are then decided by both parliament and government within the institutionalised sphere of the state.[16] Staying within the German context, the Federal Constitution even makes explicit reference to political parties as participating in the process of public opinion formation. In many democracies, nowadays, it is difficult to imagine a candidate becoming a Member of Parliament without the support of a political party. This evolution towards an increased 'party-dependency' has created tensions within many political systems: on the one hand, there is the principle of the free mandate for Members of Parliament – again, in the German context, this principle has even been consecrated by the Federal Constitution – while, on the other, due to the ever more important role of political parties, the role and political stances of party leaders has increased at the expense of individual candidates and Members of Parliament. Not only does this tension have a political character, it also comes to the fore when, for example, parties set out the time schedule for parliamentary debate and allocate time for discussion which does not permit each Member of Parliament to speak.[17] At the end of the day, a Member of Parliament no longer represents the constituency that has voted for him but is, instead, part of a political machine that is brought to power through elections. Rather than individual Members of Parliament, it is party factions that have gained much more importance and influence.

The classical liberal model of politics was closely linked to the idea of local representation and, as a consequence, to the importance of the locally elected Members of Parliament. The 'society of individuals' found its political form in an assembly of 'representative' individuals elected in each constituency – a procedure that gave them a high level of political independence and legitimacy. This constitutional construction has been transformed by the welfare state: increasingly, organisations take on a 'representative' function based on the co-ordination and accommodation of interests within 'encompassing' groups (such as employers' associations, trade unions, churches, etc.) and a corresponding increase in the importance of political parties that organise themselves on the basis of group interests.[18] At the same time the position of the individual Member of Parliament is weakened in this 'society of organisations'. Although this evolution does not lead to a complete reversal of liberal political institutions – as Carl Schmitt thought[19] – it may trigger the emergence of a parallel system of co-existence of liberal and group-based institutions.

The erosion of the party system

The model of 'concentric circles' with which one may describe the institutional organisation of the welfare state ('representative groups', such as political parties, collect the opinions and views of group members, translate them into pre-structured policy options and introduce the latter into the formal institutional framework) is increasingly challenged by a new process of self-transformation of society. The integrative power of political parties and representative groups is weakening, therefore calling the model of 'concentric circles' into question. Symptoms of this development are the rise of single purpose movements, the questioning of the hitherto established separation of private and public ('the private is political'), as well as the rise of direct co-operation between private and public actors ('contracting government')[20] which passes over the mediator role of representative organisations. Furthermore, one could argue that identity formation of individuals is getting more fragmented and no longer follows the traditional tracks of socialisation: individuals are no longer solely defined by their affiliation with stable groups, milieus, churches, etc., therefore making their political orientations more volatile.

The rise of the network society

The network economy and its impact on the institutions of the 'society of organisation'

The repercussions of this evolution are felt within society and through the transformation of the established hierarchical forms of organisations – e.g. firms working for standardised mass-production that increasingly reproduce elements of the market within the enterprise, or joint-ventures between competing companies that generate new knowledge which can also be used in different ways by competitors. This somehow blurs the difference between inside and outside:[21] relational contracts interfere with the 'internal affairs' of the partners in ways that in the past would only have been conceivable after a take-over, etc. Network structures increasingly replace hierarchical ones.[22] Societal knowledge changes as well: experience is being devalued and experimentation, design and modelling take the lead. These trends weaken both the private and public institutions that have emerged in liberal societies. As a consequence, the role of the media changes as well. In the past, the conception of the public realm was closely linked to the idea discussed above of 'concentric circles'[23] whose disruption also has serious consequences for the media. Increasingly 'private' issues penetrate the borders of the 'public sphere' whose criteria of relevance is dominated by the 'economy of attention'[24] rather than stable separations and priorities. This development has its upshot in the transformation of public broadcasting as well, which, in a sense, was an institution of the former 'society of organisations'. This leads to a growing interest in procedural forms of self-design and self-control of public broadcasting no longer based on a stable setting of pluralist groups. The stable basis of a common knowledge upon which both public and private actors used to rely when taking decisions is now replaced by new auditing[25] and evaluation methods.[26] As a consequence of this evolution, the question has to be asked whether e-voting might fit into a strategy of democratic reform following the aforementioned line of 'hybridisation'.

The evolution of new, 'hybrid' forms of communication on the internet

It might be a fruitful exercise to address the new forms of communication developing on the internet[27] that could be tied to liberal institutions in general, and to voting procedures in particular. Against this background a new perspective on e-voting might emerge. First, one might take a closer look at the chat-rooms and discussion forums that have spread on the internet. In the past they have *primarily* been used for private purposes. These platforms for interactivity can be either moderated or non-moderated. Supervision of these platforms varies greatly. The same variance can be found with regard to the participants' behaviour, attitudes and interactions: sometimes close relationships among them emerge, while in other cases more or less anonymous public forms of communication dominate the discussion forums. The great variety of communication structures in chat-rooms, discussion forums and the like corresponds to the heterarchical nature of many post-modern, network-like societal institutions whose single common denominator is the absence of stable hierarchies and of stable functions that are characteristic of traditional mass[28] and individual communication. While most participants do not know each other, there is as yet no 'point-to-multi-point' communication. The ambivalence of this form of communication is reflected in the complex issue of responsibility:[29] to what extent is the provider responsible for content put on the website, and to what extent is he legitimated to remove content from chat-rooms, censor speech in discussion forums, etc.?[30]

The example of 'epinions': creation of a non-individual common knowledge 'bottom-up'

A different and quite fascinating new form of communication emerges in moderated exchanges, which are meant to produce something like a non-individual 'common knowledge' and are generated from 'bottom-up' process of individual contributions. As an example, one might cite 'epinions', a website that collects opinions on goods, services, etc., which consumers, users, etc., place on the website and which are consecutively evaluated and reflected in the opinions of other customers so that an accumulated 'common knowledge' is produced. This is a new form of opinion formation, functioning neither in a strictly collective nor in a private-individual way: it is an anonymous process that has an emergent character and which cannot be reduced to a simple exchange of opinions. The incentive to participate and to place an evaluation of a produce on the website is, in this case, created by the expectation of receiving a financial compensation which corresponds to the number of concurring opinions. This form of communication, of which available space does not allow us to go into details, somehow replaces professional test procedures. Also, the broad collection of opinions of users may even be more reliable than a professional test. This method generates a kind of 'common knowledge' in an explicit form, whereas, in the past, such knowledge usually remained implicit. Generating such 'common knowledge' can take various forms, such as more active moderation that tries to get information on specific questions or the inclusion of competing opinions. Through such innovative methods new, hybrid forms of 'common knowledge' may be spontaneously generated from this 'bottom-up' process.

The specific interest of this new form of communication resides in the fact that it is neither exclusively organising a discussion nor preparing a decision, but accumulating dispersed knowledge by involving a great number of persons. The involvement of as many persons as possible becomes feasible only because the cost of participation for online users is very low. In an offline context the incentive to participate is too weak for generating feedback from a great number of persons. Our example can be linked to the above mentioned ideas concerning the transformation of private production processes: they confirm that a fundamental transformation takes place in both the private and public institutions of liberal societies. The common characteristic of both trends lies in the 'network-like' relational structure of a tentative search for emergent, self-organised patterns of new knowledge creation, generated in a 'bottom-up' mode by linking basic elements and testing for the tenability of a stable frame for further communication.

Epinions is a new type of non-individual opinion formation that does not follow the traditional 'top-down' logic of mass media communication. In a way, it corresponds to the 'flat hierarchies' of spreading economic organisations which are also drawing on the assumption that there no longer exists a clear separation between general and individual knowledge. Such new forms of communication are also possible offline, but the transaction costs on the internet are so low that it is much easier to generate this open process of non-individual communication on the internet than in the offline world.

Transformation of communication between governments and citizens

Why have we described at length these internet-induced transformations of communicative exchange? We did so because we believe that similar types of exchange will emerge between the state and the citizens.[31] Governments are putting an increasing volume of information on the internet that is freely accessible, downloadable and storable by any citizen who goes online. This evolution is far from being unproblematic as on the one hand, governments can, at least partially, take over the role of the media or news agencies, while, on the other hand, the management of newsgroups, chat-rooms, discussion forums, etc. by governments raises the fundamental question as to what the role of public authorities in such hybrid forms of communication could and should be.[32] It may be desirable and productive for the democratic process to get citizens involved in discussions with government; however, the government's role as a moderator should be carefully considered. Should the government be allowed to remove content from newsgroups? Can it intervene in public discussions and structure the latter against the will of participants? This rather complex problem, which is again linked to the hybrid character of communication processes that do not allow for a clear separation of roles, can only be managed by procedural rules that impose certain transparency requirements on the government, and, perhaps, by using the organisational elements of institutionalised pluralism which have been applied to public broadcasting. This conception again demonstrates the ubiquity of new, hybrid organisational forms. Private providers of new forms of communication have to accept legal requirements for their role as moderators. Such rules have to be transparent, even if private autonomy should not be further restricted by substantive standards. Even in this respect, the limits are no longer clear. Nonetheless, independently of whether a private or a public actor opens a discussion forum the rules of free speech have to be respected.

'Hybrid' forms of commercial communication

If one has a look at the new forms of commercial speech – a domain between public opinion and commercial organisation – one again faces the same phenomenon of hybridisation: past forms of advertising tried to attract a broad public, whereas, on the internet, new forms of personalised advertising are spreading. Content is combined with small sets of different advertisements addressed to members of focus groups whose personal profiles have been derived from the informational footprints that they have left on the internet.[33] A similar phenomenon can be observed with respect to data protection: more and more data can be accumulated, interpreted, and used in various ways. A new method of using artificial 'personae' by both users and firms emerges. One can structure one's stream of communication by making use of these 'masks' as frames of reference for actively gathered or passively received information collected and interpreted by businesses. New forms of unstable 'collectives' form and dissolve in this way.

Combining the new logic of communication in networks and e-voting

New intermediaries for internet communication

The common denominator of these new versions of hybrid communication is the fact that stable communities of taste, of political identification, etc., break down and are replaced by unstable networks of common interest which are generated in a 'bottom-up' and self-organised way. The new forms of 'bottom-up' aggregation of information in patterns and personae also require new intermediaries which replace the formerly stable intermediaries – such as representative organisations, political parties, etc., whose roles are weakened. With regard to data-protection, information brokers[34] and intermediaries who observe the use of data by private enterprises emerge; and it is they who might help to establish more balanced agreements between firms and individual users of the internet.

A new type of institution that plays an important role in the structuring of the vast amount of information processed over the internet is the search-engine. The latter replace old-fashioned information resources such as directories, dictionaries, encyclopaedias, etc. by more flexible, tailor-made resources that are adapted to individual needs and are capable of learning. Search-strategies may be developed strategically and then linked to all kinds of goals defined by both users and providers of search-engines. The evolution towards more sophisticated methods for searching the internet has to be observed very closely,[35] and may well demand public intervention, if only with a view to imposing a strategy of self-regulation that ensures transparency of methods and procedures. It may well be that pluralist institutions which have imposed procedural and organisational requirements on public broadcasting have to be reconfigured and transferred to this new meta-level of communication.

These reflections on the transformation of internet communication should have shown that it is not only communication which is at stake: the whole institutional architecture of post-modern societies undergoes a fundamental process of change. The established integrative functions of public institutions are losing power, while, simultaneously, new intermediaries emerge reflecting the new, hybrid forms of communication that go beyond the classical lines of the separation of private and public, individual and mass phenomena, market and organisation, etc.

'Relational democracy' – an emerging paradigm for political institutions of the network society

When we now look again at the role of political opinion formation in the stricter sense, the question arises whether the crisis of the political intermediaries (political parties and stable representative groups which pre-structure public decision-making in parliament and government) and the self-transformation of economic organisations could also lead to new forms of collective public communication and discussion that might change the link between voting and public deliberation. This could be considered as a useful question to pose because – as shown above – even the transformation of the liberal state towards the welfare state was the result of a transformation of society at large, leading to a fundamental change of both electoral procedures and institutional infrastructures. Could there be a link between the emerging 'network society' and a new set of political institutions which parallel the transformation of the group-based corporatist society and the political institutions of the corporatist state? In other words, is there a possibility of conceiving a 'relational democracy' that would be more adapted to the 'society of networks' that emerges beyond the crisis of the welfare state?

Traditional political institutions, both of the classical liberal variety and of the corporatist type within the welfare state, were based on rather strong and stable affiliations to groups, religions, and so forth. It should be possible to find ways of remodelling liberal institutions, including elections, which are more finely tuned to the emerging pattern of the loosely coupled society of networks.[36] In a liberal society, this correspondence appears to be quite obvious because of the absence of a substantive set of public interests and a focus on procedural approaches that are dependent on a pre-structuring of private interests by society. This does not exclude the possibility that the institutions of both the liberal society and the welfare state will also play an important role in the future. However, new institutional elements that are better adapted to the new network paradigm of social organisation might be put in their place.

e-Voting as a hybrid form of participation

The internet and virtual political movements

One might imagine that the hybrid forms of communication that go beyond the clear-cut separation of individual and mass communication – in particular the interactive 'bottom-up' mode – could also be used for a reinvigoration of electoral systems. The interactive mode of combining elements of individual and universal public communication might be used for the adaptation of the political system. Once public opinion formation based on stable orientations of political parties (social-democratic, liberal, conservative, etc.) no longer corresponds to the self-conception of individuals who are constrained by permanent 'self-management' in a changing society, it might be useful to link interactive 'bottom-up' procedures of discussion to political processes of opinion formation and of voting.

It is possible, although not certain, that the transformation of society described above could be reflected in the emergence of new forms of political participation. The political 'single-purpose'-movements of the 1980s might be regarded as an 'offline-version' of a more individualised direct participation beyond clear party lines. Indeed, single-purpose-movements may even have deterred many citizens because of the extremely inefficient and time-consuming way of political organisation that they have brought about. However, the internet may lead to the organisation of more sophisticated 'online' single-purpose-movements. The possibility of self-organisation in a political forum without observing fixed dates and times and without being subject to extremely uninteresting fights among 'alternative bureaucrats' could be quite attractive, all the more so because there may be different ways of combining one's expertise, or one's specific interest, as well as spontaneously emerging overlapping with other political groups, etc. 'Bottom-up' networks of communication can be set up and can produce some collective effects in the public sphere and, in particular, in the electoral realm.

As mentioned above, it is far from sure that this will happen but at least there is a possibility that this might lead to a new form of correspondence of *living* in networks and *politically interacting* in networks. How can such new forms of opinion formation be institutionalised? Following the line of argumentation that has been put forward, one could consider offering subsidies to newspapers in order for them to establish political chat-rooms, discussion groups, forums and so forth, which would build a bridge between articles and opinions of the readers. There should be incentives to experiment with new methods and procedures of interactive discussion, which might be linked, before elections, to the strategies of vote swapping and other flexibility-enhancing methods described above. These new forms of flexible voting might be put into practice only through discussion groups and new types of political brokers, able to develop strategic designs for collective and public interactive preparation for the elections. Such new intermediaries might be used for fulfilling the function of some kind of 'relational' democratic 'bottom-up' procedures, producing collective effects, such as common opinions, thanks to the multiplicity of participants.

Institutionalising political discussion groups and collective e-voting on the internet

It could be important to avoid simple alternatives of 'yes' or 'no' which still dominate the existing websites simulating e-voting today. The specificity of the internet in the political realm is to be seen in the fact that it can combine individual and collective effects which are different from stable political party affiliations. One could think about experimental forms of moderation that would structure e-voting and public opinion in a more flexible way. Such a procedure could be linked to 'regulated forms of self-regulation' which, in the end, produce self-binding rules of discussion and of moderation. There could be new approaches to structuring alternatives, which should not create a bias towards certain opinions but could, instead, generate more interest in elections.

Most e-voting procedures that exist today (e.g. vote.com) are based on a rather reductionist approach to e-voting that tries to make use of the simplification and the efficiency of internet voting but neglects the potential for interactive, hybrid forms of internet communication. One cannot exclude, however, that the potential combination of internet voting and newspaper-based e-forums could be detrimental to the fulfilment of the function of both the press and broadcasting because of a temptation to explicitly use such e-forums as an instrument of power for favouring either a 'pro' or 'con' position. As long as political discussion forums are set up by individuals or private organisations, some basic requirements of transparency for patterns of communication and openness for counter-arguments should be implemented. Nevertheless, e-voting could, in fact, help to identify individual preferences and introduce the latter into decision-making procedures, especially the act of voting. The public discussion in its online version could contribute to a more network-like structure of will-formation in overlapping forums.

This evolution would also correspond to the decreasing importance of local values. On the other hand, different forms of interactive combination of interests, expertise and values might be brought together in order to generate discussion processes that could be arranged by a moderator, with the aim of producing a deliberate overlap of networks which, in turn, would provide and provoke new lines of argumentation.

Avoiding tendencies towards a 'me democracy'

In the literature on political information and the internet, one can read about worries concerning the potential one-sidedness of opinion formation on the internet. This may be realistic, but some countermeasures are at hand for fighting against this risk: through self-regulation, discussion forums might oblige themselves to confront different arguments. Against this fear, one might also invoke the fact that internet communication has low transaction costs which allows for easy access to all kinds of forums.[37] In the recent literature, one finds the symptomatic reference to the political function of the internet as guaranteeing an 'eGora': on the 'eGora', it is neither individuals nor groups that meet but overlapping networks of communication that create their own collective effect by means of a 'bottom-up', common knowledge: in this vein, one might assume that 'democracy in networks is formed in a multi-lateral mode'.[38] It could also be possible for governments and/or experts to be invited to contribute to such discussions. Finally, networks of discussion might be set up to overlap or to integrate for a short period in order to join for the voting procedure and promulgate a common strategy. This shows that there should be room for moderation by third persons.

Because of the high rate of uncertainty with respect to the question of whether all this will work, there is only one answer: we should try and see.

e-Voting and the elections of the European Parliament: towards a more European process of voting?

As a consequence of the above-mentioned strategic possibilities, one might think of whether this means, for the EU, that network-like discussion groups might also be a perspective for voting in a supranational setting that does not have a public sphere of its own. In the light of the ideas ventured about the nature of the public sphere and its transformation in this chapter, new light might be shed on the problems of a European public: the specificity of the EU might reside in the fact that most of the 'concentric circles' which, in the past, contained the public realm at the level of the Member States are focused on the state level and not on the EU. This will only change gradually. In the past, the main contributors to this processing of information over the 'concentric circles' were, again, groups whose role could not, and cannot, simply be transferred to the EU. These groups have created a whole body of conventions, rules, roles, expectations, etc., that create their own inertia. The often bemoaned lack of a European public sphere is not due to the narrow-mindedness of citizens. The whole infra-structures of 'common knowledge', experience, conventions, expectations etc., have to be integrated gradually.

It could be conceivable to set up specifically European focuses, in order to bring together discussion groups from different Member States with the aid of translation for some crucial contributors whose knowledge might help us understand what is going on in different Member States. It might be possible to create at least a core element of a European public on the internet. At this point, it might be particularly helpful to design a link between discussion groups and more flexible forms of e-voting at the European level. One could think about giving people more than one vote and also allow them to vote for candidates in another country and to cumulate votes in European Parliamentary elections.[39] Citizens could be given the possibility of voting in their own constituency and have two or more votes in a different country. The possibility of manipulation by political parties or of creating erratic shifts of votes could be reduced by an election system that is finely tuned to the different systems in the Member States. In fact, one has to realise that much more erratic results can be produced by the high rates of abstention of average people, which enable radical parties or outsiders to get into the European Parliament. A bonus could be granted to candidates who receive votes not only from their home country but also from other constituencies. Swapping procedures could also be established at European level – again, perhaps, with a bonus for transnational votes.

Conclusion

This sketchy design of a link between internet voting and European public discussion cannot claim to be exhaustive in its approach. But to be able to acknowledge the limits of European public opinion formation is a precondition for the design of solutions that might be found using the internet. This chapter took the view that there is a necessary correspondence between the overall transformation of society towards a network-like structure and the possibility of using the internet and its hybrid forms of communication for a new link between interactive political discussions and e-voting. In this vein, e-voting would not just be yet another technical form of voting. Instead, it would give more strategic decision-making power to citizens, an approach that corresponds to the multiplication of alternatives in economic life and the necessity of developing more open and flexible decision-making structures for individuals who have to adopt flexible structures of 'self-management' in the economy, too.

This is the background against which a comprehensive strategy of e-voting might develop, which would be combined with innovative approaches of discussing political issues in internet forums. A new approach to the 'bottom-up' procedures both of generating knowledge and of the creation of strategic decisional designs might be a common framework for private and public ways of decision-making and discussing. The internet might be helpful in opening up the whole procedure of voting by introducing many more possibilities which may help build a bridge between the institutions of the liberal state and of the welfare state, and it may simultaneously stimulate a discussion process on the internet with a view to the collective use of a more flexible vote on the internet. It is, perhaps, interesting to notice that, in this way of flexibilising e-voting and stimulating interactive discussion processes on the internet, the collective element of voting is no longer concentrated in the hands of political parties but is partly given to citizens, who might then set up their own strategies of vote swapping etc.

Notes

1 See also Buchstein, B. and Neymanns, H. (eds) (2001) *Online-Wahlen*, Opladen: Leske & Budrich; CalTech and MIT, *Voting – What is, what could be? Report of the CalTech/MIT Voting Technology Project*, www.vote.caltech.edu/reports; Alvarez, M.R. and Nagler, J. (2000) 'The likely consequences of internet voting for political representation', *Loyola University Law Review* 34(3): 1115–53; for Germany see Otten, D. (2000) *Zwischenbericht des Projekts 'Strategische Initiative: Wahlen im Internet'*, Bundesminister für Wirtschaft und Technologie, www.internetwahlen.de; Tauss, J. (1999) 'E-Vote. Die "elektronische Briefwahl" als ein Beitrag zur Verbesserung der Partizipationsmöglichkeiten', *Jahrbuch Telekommunikation und Gesellschaft*, 7: 285–311; Tauss, J. (2001) 'e-Recht und e-Demokratie', *Zeitschrift für Gesetzgebung*, 16(4): 231–45; Rüss, O. (2001) 'E-democracy, Demokratie und Wahlen im Internet', *Zeitschrift für Rechtspolitik*, 34(11): 518–20; Leggewie, C. and Maar, Ch. (eds) (1998) *Internet & Politik. Von der Zuschauer- zur Beteiligungsdemokratie*, Cologne: Bollmann.

2 For further insights on postal voting see the chapter by Norris in this volume.

3 For Germany see Bundesverfassungsgericht Reports 21, pp. 2004–7; 59, pp. 119–28; Buchstein, H. (2000) 'Präsenzwahl, Briefwahl, Online-Wahl und der Grundsatz der geheimen Stimmabgabe', *Zeitschrift für Parlamentsfragen*, 31(4): 886–902.

4 For Gemany see only Hoffmann-Riem, W. (2000) *Regulierung der dualen Rundfunkordnung*, Baden-Baden: Nomos, p. 241 ff.

5 See Randazza, M.J. (2001) 'The forgotten electoral controversy', *intermedia*, 29(2): 33–7; Bieber, Ch. (2000) 'Ein Hauch von Napster: Vote-Swapping im US-amerikanischen Präsidentschaftswahlkampf', in R. Meier-Walser and Th. Harth (eds) *Politikwelt Internet. Neue demokratische Chancen im Internet?*, Munich: Olzog, pp. 198–222; Norris, P. (2002) 'What revolution? The internet and US elections 1992–2000', in E.C. Kamarck and J.S. Nye Jr (eds) *governance.com*, Washington, DC: Brookings Institution Press, pp. 59–80.

6 In the same vein, let us mention that Members of Parliament cannot be regarded as primarily representing their local constituency. For a discussion of German electoral principles see Bundesverfassungsgericht Reports 2, pp. 1–79, 72; 5, pp. 85–393, 392; Meyer, H. (1987) 'Wahlgrundsätze und Wahlverfahren', in J. Isensee and P. Kirchhof (eds) *Handbuch des Staatsrechts der Bundesrepublik Deutschland, Vol. 2*, Munich: Beck, pp. 269–311.

7 For the risk of manipulations in Germany see Bundesverfassungsgericht Reports 13, pp. 127–9, 128; 79, pp. 169–72, 171.

8 For the question of legitimacy and the functioning of different electoral systems see Bundesverfassungsgericht Reports 1, pp. 208–66, 244.

9 For the constitutionality of such clauses see Bundesverfassungsgericht Reports 1, pp. 208–61; Linck, J. (1986) 'Sperrklauseln im Wahlrecht', *Jura*, 8(6): 460–5.

10 See, already, Ladeur, K.-H. (1980) 'Ein systemimmanenter Vorschlag zur Änderung der 5% – Klausel', *Demokratie und Recht*, 8(1): 81–4.

11 See Alesina, A. and Wacziarg, R. (2000) 'The Economics of Public Trust', in S.J. Pharr and R.D. Putnam (eds) *Disaffected Democracies. What's Troubling the Trilateral Countries?*, Princeton: Princeton University Press, pp. 149–68; Nye, J.S. Jr., Zelikow, P.D. and King, D.C. (eds) (1997) *Why People Don't Trust Government*, Cambridge: Harvard University Press; Norris, P. (ed.) (1999) *Critical citizens: Global Support for Democracy*, Oxford: Oxford University Press.

12 See Lange, N. (2001) Click 'n' vote – Erste Erfahrungen mit Online-Wahlen', in Buchstein and Neymanns, op. cit., footnote 1, pp. 127–44.

13 See in particular the propositions put forward in the chapter by Kies and Kriesi in this volume.

14 See Holznagel, B., Grünwald, A. and Haußmann, A. (eds) (2001) *Elektronische Demokratie. Bürgerbeteiligung per Internet zwischen Wissenschaft und Praxis*, Munich: Beck.

15 See generally Mill, J.S. (1995) *Utilitarianism, on Liberty: Considerations on representative government: Remarks on Bentham's philosophy*, edited by Williams, G., Everyman Paperback Classics.

16 See Bundesverfassungsgericht Reports 5, pp. 85–393, 392; 20, pp. 56–119, 113; 44, 125–97, 140; Preuss, U.K. (2001) 'Art. 21', in *Alternativkommentar zum Grundgesetz*, Neuwied: Luchterhand, 3rd edn, no. 34 ff.

17 See Bundesverfassungsgericht Reports 2, pp. 1–79, 72; 5, pp. 85–393, 392.

18 See Ladeur, K.H. (2000) 'Rechtliche Möglichkeiten der Qualitätssicherung im Journalismus', *Publizistik*, 45(4): 442–61.

19 Schmitt, C. (1926) *Die geistesgeschichtliche Lage des heutigen Parlamentarismus*, Leipzig: Duncker & Humblot, 2nd edn.

20 See Freeman, J. (2000) 'The private role of public governance', *New York University Law Review*, 75(3): 543–645.

21 Kahin, B. and Varian, H.R. (eds) (2000) *Internet Publishing and Beyond*, Cambridge, MA: MIT Press.

22 See Rohe, M. (1997) *Netzverträge*, Tübingen: Mohr.

23 See Ladeur (2000), op. cit.

24 See Franck, G. (1998) *Ökonomie der Aufmerksamkeit*, Munich and Vienna: Hanser; Wolff, M.J. (1999) *Entertainment Economy*, New York: Times Books.

25 See Power, M. (1998) *The Audit Society*, Oxford: Oxford University Press.

26 See Freeman, op. cit.

27 See Flichy, P. (2001) *L'imaginaire d'internet*, Paris: La Découverte.

28 This was the presupposition of the role attributed to the public media by the German Constitutional Court; see Ladeur (2000), op. cit.

29 See Freytag, A. (1999) *Haftung im Netz*, Munich: Beck.

30 See Ladeur, K.-H. (2001) 'Ausschluss von Teilnehmern aus Diskussionsforen im Internet', *Multimedia und Recht*, 4(12): 787–92.

31 See Jansen, S. and Priddat, B. (2001) *Electronic Government*, Stuttgart: Klett-Cotta; Kleinsteuber, H. (1999) 'Elektronische Demokratie. Visionen einer technischen Erneuerung des politischen Systems?', in O. Drossou (ed.) *Machtfragen der Industriegesellschaft*, Marburg: Bund Demokratischer Wissenschaftler, pp. 29–45; for the transformation of state bureaucracies in the future see Fountain, J.E. (2001) *Building the Virtual State: Information Technology and Institutional Transformation*, Washington, DC: The Brookings Institution.

32 See Ladeur, K.-H. (2001) 'Verfassungsrechtliche Fragen der regierungsamtlichen Öffentlichkeitsarbeit und öffentlicher Wirtschaftstätigkeit im Internet', *Die öffentliche Verwaltung*, 55(1): 1–9.

33 See Schaar, P. (2002) *Datenschutz im Internet*, Munich: Beck, no. 135 ff.; Gounalakis, G. and Rhode, L. (2002) *Persönlichkeitsschutz im Internet*, Munich: Beck, pp. 195, 228, 274.

34 This evolution might end up in shifting data-protection from the domain of personal rights to property rights, Basho, K. (2000) 'The licensing of our personal information', *California Law Review* 88(6): 1507–46.

35 For a perspective on an 'intelligent' network, see Berners-Lee, T., Hendler, J. and Lassila, O. (2001) 'The Semantic Web', *Scientific American*, 286(5): 28–34; Staab, S. and Maedche, A. (2001) 'Knowledge portals – ontologies at work', *Artificial Intelligence Magazine*, 22(3): 63–75.

36 See Galston, W.A. (2002) 'The impact of the internet on civic life: An early assessment', in Kamarck and Nye, op. cit., pp. 40–58.

37 See Sunstein, C.R. (2001) *Republic.com*, Princeton, NJ: Princeton University Press.

38 See Leggewie and Maar, op. cit., pp. 3–25.

39 See also the chapter by Schmitter in this volume.

Epilogue

Internet voting and democratic politics in an age of crisis and risk

Stephen Coleman

The contemporary interest in e-voting is about more than the realisation of technological potential. Rather, it is based upon the claim that the internet can help to address a range of contemporary anxieties about the state of representative democracy. These are seemingly inescapable anxieties, suggesting nothing less than a crisis of democratic politics. The terms of this crisis are well known. In most liberal democracies, including newly established ones, turnout in elections is falling, as are trust in government and political institutions, participation in parties and traditional political activities, and levels of public efficacy. As Figure E.1 shows, national parliaments, governments and parties across the EU member states are distrusted by most people.

The ambitious rhetorical claims made for the internet as a force for modernisation have been well-rehearsed: the internet is a domesticated technology that can be used in the safety of the home; it is popular with young people, who are traditionally the least likely to vote; it is associated with hypermodernity, flexibility and fun; it is the quintessential communication medium of globalisation. But, beyond the cyber-sloganising and e-posturing of astute politicians who want to be associated with images of the future, the internet is implicated in profound structural configurations in democratic politics. Four key aspects of these transformative tendencies are considered here: changes in the function, locus, speed and symbolic content of democratic politics.

The function of democratic politics

Twentieth-century liberal democracies adopted parsimonious theories of public participation, expecting citizens to do little more than vote for members of the political elite in periodic elections. As Schumpeter put it:

> Democracy does not mean and cannot mean that the people actually rule in any obvious sense of the terms 'people' and 'rule.' Democracy means only that the people have the opportunity of accepting or refusing the men who are to rule them. But since they might decide

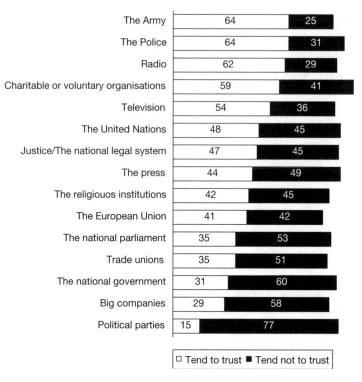

Figure E1 Trust in institutions in the EU member states
Source: Eurobarometer 60.

this also in entirely undemocratic ways, we have had to narrow our definition by adding a further criterion identifying the democratic method, viz., free competition among would-be leaders for the vote of the electorate.[1]

In such a minimalist democracy, the function of elections is essentially one of contracting out power to trusted leaders. Two factors constrain electoral participation under such conditions. First, gathering information, upon which trust can be established, is not cost-free: it takes time, energy and sometimes money. As Downs famously argued: 'In general, it is irrational to be politically well informed because the low returns from data simply do not justify their cost in time and other scarce resources.'[2] Second, even if voters do know what they want, the nature of preference scheduling and aggregation usually leads to outcomes that do not reflect the wishes of most voters. This is especially so in non-marginal elections or where competing parties share common values. As one member of a focus group of non-voters in the 2001 UK general election explained,

If it made a difference, then yes I would vote. If I knew that by me doing that I would make a difference, then yes. But right now I don't think if I did vote, or didn't vote, it would make a difference. Because irrespective of what I say, or what I think, whoever goes into power is just going to do the same old thing.

And as the British MP, Tony Wright, astutely observed in a House of Commons debate on the problem of declining public participation,

If people feel that politicians are not making their lives better, and that they can do nothing about their circumstances, the act of voting becomes a legitimising act that they are not prepared to bestow on the system. They were prepared to do that, perhaps, when they were motivated by civic duty and thought that they simply had to vote. However, such people are disappearing. We must put the argument to new kinds of people who will vote and legitimise the system only if they think that it is doing enough for them.

Against these motives for disengagement, there are three countervailing factors that might mitigate against these trends. First, information is becoming less scarce and easier to acquire. In an age of multi-channel TV and almost ubiquitous access to online material, it is both easier for smaller groups and individuals to distribute messages and for citizens with limited time or money to find out what they need to know. As online communication becomes ubiquitous and information abundant, the threshold of access to the arena of collective action is lowered, potential mobilisers of public opinion find it easier to disseminate their messages and it becomes less costly for citizens to engage in civic and political activities.[3]

Second, a trend from contractual to permanent representation has been taking place in recent times. Whereas contractual representatives entered into a relationship with voters based upon offers and obligations, permanent representatives tend to be reactive and reflexive, dependent upon monitoring and adapting to public opinion. Stated another way, Mansbridge argues that 'representation by promising' is giving way to 'anticipatory democracy' in which 'the voter's power works backward and the representative's attention forward'. In such circumstances, the electorate becomes more like a standing jury, reviewing the ongoing performance of government; and representatives become more like advocates, seeking to connect with citizens via a range of tools, including polls, focus groups media management and interest-group networking.

Third, at the level of democratic theory, there has been a recent turn away from the minimalist, Schumpeterian conception of democracy, which is, itself, regarded as being a principal cause of democracy's current discontents, and towards a more deliberative form of democracy in which public discussion is regarded as being as important as mass voting. Deliberative democrats see the public's preferences as being open to rational adaptation rather than the fixed, self-serving motives for political behaviour that dominated former liberal and rational choice analyses. Experiments with citizens' juries, deliberative polls, policy consultations and people's panels have sought to involve citizens in the formation of social opinion as reflexive and morally autonomous agents. While some arguments for deliberative democracy have assumed too much, seeking to take politics out of discussion and interests out of politics, more pragmatic supporters of public deliberation argue that experientially informed public discourse can contribute to a more mature and inclusive approach to policy-formation and decision-making.

As information becomes more abundant and freer, political legitimacy becomes more anticipatory and less contractual, and preference ordering becomes more deliberative and less aggregatory, political institutions come under pressure to pursue old activities in new ways. As Schmitter and Ladeur argue in this volume, and I have argued elsewhere,[4] e-voting technologies could be utilised to contribute to a broader democratisation of politics, facilitating new opportunities for disseminating electoral information, consulting on policy issues and promoting active participation in civic and political life. By making the link between voting, broader participation and outcomes there is scope to redress popular feelings of inefficacy and the futility of political engagement.

The locus of democratic politics

As globalisation shrinks the planet, traditional spaces of democratic politics are becoming decentred and dislocated. Historically, power has been organised geographically and hierarchies tended to be vertical and linear. From the nation state to the political constituency, power had its place and its boundaries. As global flows of information have come to play a central role in social dynamics, so networks which are unbounded by territoriality, have come to characterise social organisations, including some of those concerned with the exercise of political power. According to Castells:[5]

> Networks dissolve centres, they disorganize hierarchy, and make materially impossible the exercise of hierarchical power without processing instructions in the network, according to the network's morphological rules. Thus, contemporary information networks of capital, production, trade, science, communication, human rights, and crime, bypass the nation-state, which, by and large, has stopped being a sovereign entity . . .

The institutional response to the network is not to collapse or implode, but to adapt. Castells argues that: 'The state reacts to its bypassing by information networks, by transforming itself into a network state. So doing, its former centres fade away as centres becoming nodes of power-sharing, and forming institutional networks.'

Decentred and dislocated democracies face major problems of legitimacy (sovereignty) and accountability. Citizens become unsure about which institution of governance has real power; which vote counts for most; which body to complain to when things go wrong. A consequence of this is a civic movement away from constitutionally rooted politics towards local neighbourhood, single issue and global campaigning. Traditional mobilisation into parties, with their umbilical connections to governance, gives way to networks of activism, often of a form that does not resemble formal politics and does not seek outcomes in terms of electoral voting. As Ladeur argues in this volume the dispersal and decentring of democratic politics serves to destabilise the territorially constructed state, requiring the state to respond with opportunities for participation that are more mobile and flexible.

The movement away from the polling station towards remote, online voting offers one, but not the only, alternative to the geographical rootedness of political representation. Another policy that could facilitate greater voter mobility without the risk and expense of remote voting would be to digitise the electoral register, thus enabling anyone to vote at any polling station and have their votes checked against a single national database. The UK Office of the Deputy Prime Minister has established the CORE (Co-ordinated Online Register of Electors) project designed to standardise local electronic electoral registers across the UK and make them fully interoperable regardless of the local system in use.

The speed of democratic politics

The world has become faster. Life has become busier. Political decisions tend to be made quickly, under the pressures of the global clock of commerce and diplomacy, the twenty-four-hour news cycle and the incessant flow of information networks. In the terms of Virilio's dromological analysis, cyberspace introduces 'a new form of perspective . . . to reach at a distance, to feel at a distance, that amounts to . . . contact-at-a-distance: tele-contact'.[6]

For citizens, the decision to pursue acts of civic duty or political commitment is temporally competitive. In the face of increasing pressures to make time for work, travel and socialising, many people regard the walk to a polling station where they are required to tick a box as a time-consuming inconvenience. As former Leader of the UK House of Commons, Robin Cook, put it in a newspaper interview:

> I suspect for anybody under 40, polling day is the only point in the year when they actually see a pencil stub, and that's probably why it's tied to a piece of string, because it's so rare and they might pocket it as a souvenir.[7]

After the precipitous fall in turnout in the UK 2001 general election, the Electoral Commission commissioned a survey of voters and abstainers. When asked their reasons for non-voting, a fifth of all abstainers (21 per cent) claimed that they 'couldn't get to the polling station because it was too inconvenient'. One in six non-voters (16 per cent) said that they 'were away on election day'. One in ten (11 per cent) said that they 'did not receive a polling card/postal vote' and 10 per cent said they were just 'not interested in politics'. These figures gave considerable impetus to the argument that more convenient voting would result in higher turnouts. After the electoral pilots in May 2002 more polling was conducted, this time of voters and abstainers in the e-voting pilot areas. In this poll abstainers were first asked to give their own reasons for not casting a vote. Despite the availability of new voting methods, one in ten (10 per cent) said that they were 'busy working/couldn't get time off'; and 7 per cent said that they were 'busy'. These were the two main reasons given for non-voting. But when prompted by interviewers with a range of scripted reasons for non-voting, abstainers' reasons changed dramatically: almost a third (32 per cent) of abstainers stated that 'voting makes no difference' and 28 per cent said that they did not 'know what the issues are'. 32 per cent still insisted that 'I didn't have time to get to a polling station', but this position was far less clear-cut once non-voters were offered responses which they had perhaps been embarrassed to raise themselves in the unprompted interviews.[8] These findings suggest that inconvenience might be an overstated account of why people do not vote: more a convenient answer than a candid explanation of reasons for non-voting. Similarly, Norris' contribution focuses on electoral choices (e.g. the range of parties, candidates and issues listed on the ballot paper) and electoral decisiveness rather than the convenience of voting, as one of the explanations for the decline in participation.

Nonetheless, governments are under pressure to find ways of making democratic politics simpler and faster to access. The idea that one can vote from one's bed at home, one's desk at work or one's mobile phone while doing the shopping, accords with the contemporary trend towards multitasking and flexible living.

The symbolism of democratic politics

Policy-makers and political scientists have sometimes undervalued or ignored the affective and symbolic elements of political behaviour, as if they were marginal or incidental. But, as Kertzer has suggested:

> The widespread complaint by political analysts that elections . . . have become too preoccupied with melodrama and hoopla, with villains and heroes, is misplaced . . . The often-heard claim that things were

different back in the good old days should itself be seen as part of the mystification of our election rituals.[9]

Elections are, indeed, a good example of the kind of political ritual that mainstream political science tends to neglect. For many people, the act of going to cast a vote is an expression of duty, belonging and moral disclosure. Elections may exist instrumentally so that majorities may express themselves and governments can be mandated, but we know that in practice authorisation is not a reflection of majoritarian will and governance is rarely a reflection of public mandates. In reality, as Edelman observes in his magisterial study of *The Symbolic Uses of Politics*, voting gives:

> people a chance to express discontents and enthusiasms, to enjoy a sense of involvement. This is participation in a ritual act . . . Like all ritual, whether in primitive or in modern societies, elections draw attention to common social ties and to the importance and apparent reasonableness of accepting the public policies that are adopted.[10]

The atomised experience of sitting at home, in an unregulated, possibly overlooked domestic space, and pressing a button on a computer keyboard, is less likely to generate a sense of civic coadunation than the act of going to a polling station to participate in a sacred democratic ceremony.

Attempts to technologise culture are doomed to failure: administrative procedures can be replicated online, but the nuances of custom, ritual and rites cannot be coded into software. As I have argued elsewhere, the symbolic repertoire of contemporary politics is failing to resonate with 'ordinary' people. Politicians are seen not only as distant and aloof, but eccentric and incomprehensible. The institutions and processes that the politically active take for granted, the majority of citizens regard as somewhat irrelevant and other-worldly. Symbolically, there has never in the history of democracy been such a gap between the political class and the politically represented.[11]

The contemporary politics of mediated spectacle[12] raises important questions about the nature of political obligation. In the past it was assumed that the duty to vote should be inculcated in citizens, but, as other forms of symbolic spectacle, such as shopping, listening to music and watching reality TV, become more remotely interactive, the passive task of casting a one-off vote becomes harder to sell as a symbolically enriching activity. Simple voting, whether by marking a ballot paper, pulling a lever or pressing a keyboard, lacks either emotive or deliberative depth, begging the question of whether democratic participation could amount to more than such a transient and disjointed moment of self-disclosure. As argued in the chapter by Kies and Kriesi, rather than isolating the ritual of voting, there is the prospect of integrating e-voting within broader democratic practices, such as virtual communities, online deliberative fora and electronic voter guides.

The problematics of risk

Having addressed the underlying context for the policy debate about internet voting, there remain two factors that must be addressed in an evaluation of a new method of voting: cost, which is an accountant's category and need not be considered here, and risk, which is a highly problematic factor in any proposed process of complex change.

The Enlightenment view of risk as a calculable and measurable equation becomes unsustainable as society becomes more technologically and globally complex and culturally reflexive. According to Beck:

> In contrast to all earlier epochs (including industrial society), the risk society is characterised essentially by a lack: the impossibility of an external attribution of hazards. In other words, risks depend on decisions, they are industrially produced and in this sense reflexive.[13]

Whereas earlier notions of risk were embedded in ideologies of nature or science, there is now a more dialectic apprehension of risk as something that results from contested decisions in response to potential or existing dilemmas, threats or catastrophes. But it is a mistake to apply a unidimensional conception of risk; what is a risk under certain circumstances might not be under another; what is high risk for one person might be a relatively risk-free opportunity for another.

In the context of e-voting, risk should be conceptualised in terms of multiple contexts and a plurality of actors. This set of risk relationships is represented by the taxonomy in Figure E.2.

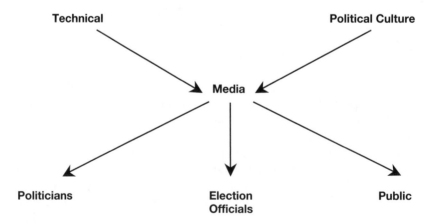

Figure E2 Taxonomy of risk relationships

Risk – from actors' perspectives

Politicians

The final judgement about risk must be made by politicians, but they generally lack the kind of technical knowledge that informs the security debate. Politicians' main concern is the legitimacy of political authorisation. They want the relationship between voting and political legitimacy to be transparent and trusted. Politicians should be concerned about the following risks:

- The danger of internet voters being unrepresentative of the general electorate, thus skewing the vote in favour of certain socio-demographic groups. In the (UK) Swindon pilot in 2002, where internet voting was an available option, half (50.3 per cent) of internet voters were from professional or managerial/technical occupations, compared with 20.7 per cent of phone voters and 32.2 per cent of voters at polling stations. This accords with findings from public opinion research conducted as part of a Government-sponsored study which concluded that:

  > Among those who have access to the technology, middle-aged and older people are more likely to use internet voting than younger people, and social grades AB are, similarly, more likely to do so than grades C2DE. This finding suggests that even if access to the internet was universal, fewer people from lower socio-economic grades would use the technology for voting than older, more middle-class people. Such a finding has important implications for the implementation strategy for e-voting and especially the criteria by which implementation might be evaluated. Turnout through electronic means is likely to mirror conventional voting patterns rather than greatly alter them.[14]

- Little research has been conducted so far on the effect of e-voting upon political campaigning, especially when the period allowed for remote voting is longer than the usual one-day period for voting in a polling station, as has been the case in the UK pilots. Election campaigns are highly ordered and rhythmic processes, culminating in a single vote on a single day. What might happen to voters' decision-making when voting is spread over several days?
- The danger of organised vote rigging cannot be ignored. Unlikely as it may be for such attempts to occur or succeed, within a centralised system of e-voting such manipulation could have an impact upon millions of votes, rather than one ballot box, polling station or local count.
- The right of candidates to demand a recount in the case of highly marginal results is a key symbolic guarantor of trust in the electoral

system. In the case of an e-election, if a candidate or his agent demands a recount, the only recourse available to them will be to press the buttons on the computer. If this produces the same result (as it should), they will be dissatisfied, but will have no way of proving the inaccuracy of the count; if the result is different, they will quite reasonably question the validity of the computer program.

Election officials

On the ground, it is the officials who administer the electoral process who must have full confidence in internet voting if it is to function effectively. A limited UK survey of electoral administrators in 2001 suggested that there was a surprisingly high level of support for e-voting.[15] But election officials must address a number of highly technical, legalistic and procedural risk issues:

- Election officials are not necessarily technicians or software specialists. This could result in them losing control or scrutiny over key areas of the electoral process, and possible dependence upon e-voting vendors who have an interest in protecting their systems from public criticism.
- Related to the above risk, there is the problem of vote audits. The paradoxical legal requirement, which exists in the electoral law of some countries, that votes must be both secret and traceable, has not caused much public unease, but implementing both secrecy and audit of the vote electronically is a far more complicated process. Can election officials be sure that they would be able to satisfy a Judge that Voter A voted online for Candidate X?
- How would election officials deal with the risk of duplicate voting? If a voter arrived at a polling station claiming not to have voted online, even though the marked register indicates that she has, would she be refused a vote (in which case she will be disenfranchised if she had tried to vote online, but failed) or allowed to vote (with the obvious possibility that she has voted twice)? There would only need to be a few examples of this happening to undermine public trust in the fairness of the election.

Public

Members of the public, as eligible voters, are the trusting users of the electoral process, not particularly interested in its detailed operation, but very concerned about perceptions of fairness. The public want elections not only to be fair, secure and accurate, but to be seen to be so. The symbolic significance of rituals of voting secrecy and counting transparency are crucial to this sense of public trust. For the public, key risks to be considered include:

- Citizens will want to be sure that their votes remain secret and protected with as great or greater force than any other personal data. The common fear that all online activity leaves tracks and that anyone who is clever enough can find out how one has behaved online must be allayed before e-voting could win public trust.
- e-Voting – and all remote voting – occurs in unregulated space and is potentially open to interference. Some family units are authoritarian, with one member (usually the father) insisting upon the right to influence or control many important decisions. In some workplaces employees could be under excessive influence from superiors. How can we be sure that remote e-voting will remain a private act?
- Citizens who do not have – or want – internet access could come to regard e-voting as an act of discrimination, especially if there is a policy of cutting the number of polling stations as more people vote at home.

Risk – in different contexts

Technical

Most discussion of the risks involved in internet voting have concerned technical questions of system security. Although it would be a mistake to see these as the only risks to assess, they are undoubtedly central to any risk assessment. Unfortunately, the terms of this debate tend to be opaque and exclusive, precisely because they are concerned with criteria that are not easily comprehended by non-experts. This has resulted in the policy debate being surrounded by mystique, as huge political trust has come to depend upon the discourse of experts. Analysing this discourse, the following risks seem to be paramount:

- The possibility of system attack or breakdown. Computer scientists have expressed deep anxieties about the security of internet-based voting. In California the State Secretary, Bill Jones, established an Internet Voting Taskforce to consider whether voting via the internet could be made sufficiently safe for public elections. The report found that:

    The implementation of internet voting would allow increased access to the voting process for millions of potential voters who do not regularly participate in our elections. However, technological threats to the security, integrity and secrecy of internet ballots are significant. The possibility of 'Virus' and 'Trojan Horse' software attacks on home and office computers used for voting is very real and, although they are preventable, could result in a number of problems ranging from a denial of service to the submission of electronically altered ballots. Despite these challenges, it is technologically possible to utilize the internet to develop an additional method of voting that would be at least as secure from vote-tampering as the current absentee ballot process in California. At this time, it would not be legally, practically or fiscally feasible to develop a comprehensive remote internet voting system that would completely replace the current paper process for voter regis-tration, voting, and the collection of initiative, referendum and recall petition signatures.

- Democratic elections in mass societies require means of ensuring that voters are who they say they are. Without ubiquitous electronic signa-tures and/or biometric identification, it is very difficult to authenticate the identity of a disembodied, remote voter.
- As Lessig and others have argued, all software programming reflects certain relationships of power. The only way to ensure the trans-parency of these underlying relations is to have open code or open source e-voting software.[16] Alexander argues that 'One way to build public confidence in computerized voting is to require voting software code be made public' and that 'there is consensus in the security industry that public source code leads to more secure computer systems than closed source'.[17]

Political culture

Although there has been an understandable emphasis upon questions of technical security, even e-elections are not purely technical events. Voting is a culturally situated event; one that is changed radically when it moves from a regulated place to ubiquitous public spaces of domesticity, employ-ment and leisure. It could turn out that this change in the environment for physically casting votes raises more risks – in the sense of unpredictable circumstances – than the relatively controllable environment of an online system for collecting and counting votes. There are two main political-cultural risks:

- The unregulated nature of the voting environment and the legal and symbolic losses in moving elections from official to unofficial spaces;
- The nature of information reaching voters shortly before or even while they are voting. This could be received online, via links to partisan websites, or offline, via radio or television transmissions being broad-cast immediately before or during the act of voting.

Europe as laboratory for new politics?

As I have argued elsewhere, the European Union needs new ways of connecting with its citizens, perhaps more than any other democratic polity.[18] Other democratic governments seek to *re*connect with those they represent, at least harbouring the illusion that they were once connected. The EU can make no such claim. Most European citizens feel not only removed, but disassociated from the institutions and processes of EU governance. As several authors in this volume have suggested, the second-order nature of EU elections could rule them out as satisfactory testbeds for e-voting. By contrast, is it too idealistic to suggest that the EU could, if its political imagination were enlarged as much as its borders, become a laboratory for a new kind of e-politics?

For this to happen, the EU would need to address both sets of problems outlined in this chapter: those relating to the changing nature of democratic politics and those relating to the multi-dimensional assessment of risk. Such an evaluation would be difficult to conduct well and could lead to painful conclusions about the weakness of the European polity and the limits of technology as a panacea. But, given that the EU constitutes the second largest democratic bloc in the world, the potential gains from invigorating the representative process, both at the level of electoral legitimacy and inter-electoral participation, could be enormous. It is within that historic context that the adoption of internet voting should be debated.

Notes

1 Schumpeter, J.A. (1976). *Capitalism, Socialism, and Democracy*. London: Allen & Unwin. pp. 284–5.
2 Downs, A. (1957). *An Economic Theory of Democracy*. New York: Harper.
3 Bimber, B.A. (2002). *Information and American Democracy: Technology in the Evolution of Political Power*. Cambridge: Cambridge University Press.
4 Coleman, S. forthcoming. e-Voting and Something More: Can Voting Technologies Enhance Democratic Representation?
5 The following is taken from: Castells, M. (2000). Materials for an exploratory theory of the network society. *British Journal of Sociology*. 51(1): 5–24.
6 Virilio, P. (1986). *Speed and Politics: An Essay on Dromology*. New York: Columbia University.
7 Cook, R. (2002). Intent on change, radical Robin returns to the fray, *The Guardian* (Monday, January 7, 2002). London.
8 Electoral Commission. (2003). Attitudes to voting and the political process 2003. London.
9 Kertzer, D.I. (1988). *Ritual, Politics, and Power*. New Haven, CT: Yale University Press.
10 Edelman, M.J. (1985). *The Symbolic Uses of Politics*. Urbana, IL: University of Illinois Press.
11 Coleman, S. (2003). A Tale of Two Houses: the House of Commons, the Big Brother house and the people at home. London: Channel 4/Hansard Society.
12 Debord, G. (1973). *Society of the Spectacle*. Detroit: Black & Red; Kellner, D. (2003). *Media Spectacle*. London, New York: Routledge; Mount, F. (1972). *The Theatre of Politics*. London: Weidenfeld and Nicolson.
13 Beck, U. (1992). *Risk Society: Towards a New Modernity*. London: Sage Publications, p. 183.
14 Pratchett, L., Birch, S., Candy, S., Rogerson, S., Stone, B. and Wingfield, M. (2002). The implementation of electronic voting in the UK: LGA.

15 Independent Commission on Alternative Voting Methods. (2002). Elections in the 21st Century: from paper ballot to e-voting, Electoral Reform Society, London.
16 Lessig, L. (1999). *Code and Other Laws of Cyberspace.* New York: Basic Books.
17 Alexander, K. (2001). Ten Things I Want People To Know About Voting Technology. Paper presented at *The Democracy Online Project's National Task Force* in Washington, DC, 18 January 2001.
18 Coleman, Stephen (2002). Hearing Voices: The Experience of Online Public Consultations and Discussions in UK Governance. London: Hansard Society; Coleman, S. and Nathanson, B. (2003). e-Coverage of Europe. In M. Bond (ed.) *Europe, Parliament and the Media.* London: Federal Trust.

Index